The Moon's Dominion

The Moon's Dominion

Narrative Dichotomy
and Female Dominance
in Lawrence's Earlier Novels

Gavriel Ben-Ephraim

Rutherford • Madison • Teaneck
Fairleigh Dickinson University Press
London and Toronto: Associated University Presses

© 1981 by Associated University Presses, Inc.

Associated University Presses, Inc.
4 Cornwall Drive
East Brunswick, New Jersey 08816

Associated University Presses
69 Fleet Street
London EC4Y 1EU, England

Associated University Presses
Toronto M5E 1A7, Canada

Library of Congress Cataloging in Publication Data

Ben-Ephraim, Gavriel, 1946-
  The Moon's dominion.

  Originally presented as the author's thesis,
Hebrew University.
  Bibliography: p.
  Includes index.
  1. Lawrence, David Herbert, 1885-1930—Criticism
and interpretation. 2. Lawrence, David Herbert,
1885-1930—Characters—Women. 3. Sex role in literature.
I. Title.
PR6023.A93Z5668   1980   823'.912   78-75172
ISBN 0-8386-2266-6

98990

Printed in the United States of America

For Reena
who charmed magic casements

Contents

Acknowledgments

Doctoral dissertations are usually unloved documents, enjoyed by neither their writers nor their readers. This book, I confess, began its career in that unhappy category. Yet the writing of it became a rich intellectual experience, because I was fortunate in my dedicated and sympathetic thesis advisor, Prof. H. M. Daleski. With a true instinct for the insight that leads onward, Bill showed by example and suggestion how to separate the valuable from the facile or merely clever. Any failures in the present work to see things steadily and see them whole are my fault, not his.

In the course of my writing *The Moon's Dominion* various people looked at all or part of the manuscript with helpful interest. Accordingly, thanks are due to Harold U. Ribalow, Eugene Goodheart, Mark Spilka, Mark Kowitt, Paul Gabriner, Steven J. Reisner, Moshe Ron, and especially Baruch Hochman for a brilliant critique of an early version.

I feel a profound gratitude toward the late novelist and man of letters Charles Angoff, who demonstrated, in one of his last professional gestures, a faith in me I only hope I deserve.

My deepest obligation is to my wife, who, over a period of years, sacrificed precious time for this book from her own talents. And I owe no less to my parents, Felix and Esther Reisner, who provided me, in so many ways, with the possibilities.

I wish to express my appreciation to the Humanities Faculty Committee for Grants to Research Students of the Hebrew University, which made available a series of grants allowing me to lessen my teaching duties and get the job of writing done.

My publisher, Julien Yoseloff, and editors, Barbara Tieger and

Peggy Roeske, have been admirably patient; and my typists, Sylvia Farhi and Nomi Landau, were unfailingly cooperative.

Acknowledgments are due to Laurence Pollinger Ltd. and the estate of the late Mrs. Frieda Lawrence Ravagli, and to the Viking Press, for permission to reproduce material from D. H. Lawrence's published works. I am grateful to the editors of *The Literary Review* for their consent to my reprinting of the chapter on *The White Peacock*, which first appeared in their journal in very different form. The cover illustration is reproduced courtesy of the City of Manchester Art Galleries.

"Beware of it—this mother-incest idea can become an obsession. But it seems to me there is much truth in it: that at certain periods the man has a desire and tendency to return to the woman, make her his goal and end, find his justification in her. In this way he casts himself as it were into her womb, and she, the Magna Mater, receives him with gratification. This is a kind of incest. . . . I have done it, and now struggle all my might to get out. In a way, Frieda is the devouring mother. It is awfully hard, once the sex relation has gone this way, to recover. If we don't recover, we die."

D. H. Lawrence, letter to Katherine Mansfield,
November 1918.

"Ay! The moon looks like a woman with child."

The White Peacock

Introduction: On Tales, Tellers, and the Dominating Woman in the Fiction of D. H. Lawrence

The artist usually sets out—or used to—to point a moral and adorn a tale. The tale, however, points the other way, as a rule. Two blankly opposing morals, the artist's and the tale's. Never trust the artist. Trust the tale. The proper function of a critic is to save the tale from the artist who created it.[1]

1

These words of Lawrence the critic are a key to the work of Lawrence the artist, yet the key resists turning for the words are mysterious. "Never trust the artist. Trust the tale." Lawrence's aphorism is provocative, but puzzling. Absolutist statements of such daring breadth, which bring forward fundamental changes in our way of reading literature, are the province of artist-critics of genius: writers (like Johnson, Coleridge, and T. S. Eliot, as well as Lawrence) for whom criticism is not altogether separated from poetry. Hence, Lawrence's insight has a far-reaching inclusiveness elusive precisely as it is illuminating: the wisdom threatens persistently to escape.

Partly as a result of Lawrence's pronouncement, awareness of a potential gap between the narrator and his narrative is widespread in contemporary criticism. Critics are quick to accuse writers of simplifying, or avoiding, or reversing the true implications of their work.[2] The accusation is usually compelling because the wide expanse of the novel rarely evades incompleteness and imperfection. There are special problems of coherence and belief peculiar to an awkward genre that blends poetry and drama by combining the feelings of the storyteller with the events of his story. Charging that there is discord between tale and teller, the critic employs a formula with a built-in complexity, a duality of perception both plausible and subtle. Yet the method's virtue is its danger.

Lawrence's claim that the novel contains conflict between the creator and his creation provides a prospect from which to begin. But, indifferent to the critical procedures bridging categorical principles and evaluations of particular texts, Lawrence fails to develop his distinction; after reading his critical apothegm we know little about the difference between the teller and the tale, though we do know, emphatically, which of them to prefer. Lawrence, indeed, rarely supports his idiosyncratic responses to books, an omission obscured by the fierce skill of his intuitions and perhaps a prerogative of artist-critics on his level. In relation to the conflict between the artist and his art, however, the logical gap undermines the significance of the perception. The problem is intensified since neither Lawrence's specific applications of his idea[3] nor the somewhat arbitrary uses of the concept by subsequent critics thoroughly examine the division they invoke. Both take for granted a dichotomy whose precise nature is far from self-evident; neither explains just what in the fictional work constitutes the tale or novel, what specifically expresses the artist or teller.[4] Yet the lacunae in Lawrence's utterance must be filled before its potential usefulness for literary analysis can be realized.

2

First, the terms teller and tale are preferable to the terms artist and novel. The artist creates everything in his work, story and storyteller, and the novel includes the entire fictional construct. Lawrence's idea becomes practicable if we focus on the authorial voice in the novel, the teller-in-the-tale not the artist-behind-the-tale.[5] These two figures cannot be identified, but neither can they be entirely separated; it is as aesthetically clumsy to believe that teller and author are interchangeable as it is psychologically naive to assume that the two are unrelated.[6] To insist that persona and actual author are unconnected is to fail to understand the true function of the mask, which is not so much disguise as alternative expression. But if it is illegitimate to ignore the biographical author, he must remain a very minor figure in a study of tale/teller conflict. Examining the difference between the narrator and his narrative is a technique for understanding novels, not writers. When the division is analyzed in a specific novel, it is reasonable to discuss the author as he exists in that novel.

The initial point about the teller of the tale is that he invariably exists, *that all narrative comes to us through the medium of a narrating personality*. (Whether the teller is a medium for the tale or the tale a medium for the teller bears on our assessment of the work.) Wayne Booth is the critic to whom we are all indebted for increased consciousness of this fact; arguing against the possibility of the objective narration that Jamesian critics claimed for the style of their master, Booth makes a comprehensive case for the necessary presence of the storyteller in his story.[7] His arguments are nearly definitive and I should add that the teller inescapably figures in the tale because statements characterize their speakers as they describe their objects, pointing in at least two directions simultaneously. Moreover, while a description must be unusually skillful and fortunate to apprehend its object, it *unfailingly* apprehends the describer. When friend A tells us his opinion of friend B, we only sometimes accept the analysis of B but are always attentive to A's unintentional self-revelation. In drama the dual exposure of subject and object occurs in characters' speeches. In fiction the author makes himself as he makes his novel, attitudes, opinions, and interpretations accompany events, characters, and images. In the end tales create tellers as tellers create tales.

Tale and teller depend on one another, but there is no symbiosis and the two are detachable. The teller is the subjective element in fiction where the tale is objective. The teller is to the tale as the self is to the world and the teller is to the reader as the self is to the other. The self communicates with the other through the medium of the world, his language referring to that which is perceptible and actual to the other; he cannot communicate the self-within-the-self which is opaque and refers the other only to *his* private self. Similarly the teller communicates with his reader through a fiction apprehending that which is real and significant to both. The establishment of an authentic relation in life or in art—the only protection our metaphysically uncertain world offers against an isolating relativism—requires transcending the enclosed ego with its hermetic concerns.

But the teller brings with him the full subjectivity of a human personality (think of the novels of Dickens or Jane Austen) so that the novel contains the true sense of a *self*, that assortment of needs, desires, and reactions whose ultimate source remains a mystery to the outside observer. Though an aesthetic creation, the novel is unavoidably accompanied by the fictional equivalent of the human ego. The success a novel has with us depends mightily on the pleasure we take in the particular self it contains (some readers prefer the benevolent Charles to the acerb Jane, some have the contrary view). But beyond the question of the nature of the teller, he will be meaningless to us if he fails to bridge his interiority and ours through exterior form. Statements that express only the self are of impenetrable irrelevance to the listener. More than this, the unmediated, or perhaps the word is untranslated, contents of the ego disturb and repel other men. Freud has written about the "feeling of repulsion" that creates barriers between the inner selves of people.[8] (Psychoanalysts themselves overcome this problem by seeing their patients' monologues as coded statements with ascertainable meanings.) The narrator involves the reader through the coherent and applicable content of his narrative, clarifying his responses by exposing their causes.

The tale is the teller's connection to the reader; it takes as its source the known world which it makes more intelligible. Novels consist of a series of created events: these imaginary facts need to refer to experiential facts if they are to move the reader. The reader judges literature by his experience (his fantasies are part of what he knows) and when literature loses its relation to common experience its author imprisons his audience in a will that masquerades as imagination. Literature is an empirical art, basing its imagined worlds on aspects of shared human existence. We respond to literature according to how skillfully it both reflects and transmutes our previous knowledge. It may add to our knowledge by reconstructing (or deconstructing) life in original ways, but if it divorces itself from experience it divorces itself from communion. At this late point in history no one will suggest that art is a simple imitation of existence; literature interprets experience by means of the immense resources of language. But mimesis does precede poiesis because poiesis develops from mimesis. The tale in the novel, then, is the fictional recreation of universally, or at least culturally, shared experience; it is the created connection which develops from the actual connections between men.

The tale's imaginary facts exist independently of the teller's attitudes (just as the self's approach to reality may or may not be appropriate and effective). Created facts fall into two fundamental categories: the dramatic and the symbolic. Dramatic facts imitate man's activity, his being-in-the-world, symbolic facts reflect the hidden meanings in man's experience. Through drama the imagination confers *existence*, through symbolism the imagination confers *significance*. The combination of the two in *symbolic action* is the technique underlying the tale in most novels.[9] Yet there is a clash between symbol and action since action is kinetic and temporal where the symbol is spatial and timeless. Part of the novelist's art consists in bringing the symbol into time, the context of his story. This is sometimes accomplished by showing the interaction of the temporal and the timeless and finding the meaning of events at the point of the encounter. Actions have a separate integrity because they reflect the perceived world, symbols have a separate integrity because they accrue implications within a culture and a language; these are discrete and universal systems that cannot be subordinated to a personal conception. The teller is free to be original in his symbolic actions but he cannot impose borders on their meaning for they go beyond his conscious intentions. This takes us back to the question of persona, for the teller is the author's conscious mask, prone to the flattery of self-conception. Yet no contemporary account of art can ignore the part played in creation by the unconscious. For these reasons we may say that the work's intention is inseparable from the teller while its achievement is almost certain to escape him.

The teller is obligated to the tale as the tale is obligated to experience. His subjective responses to his fiction are incidental to the structure of events and characters that connects him to the reader. The first responsibility of the teller is to the facts of the empirical imagination. (The novelistic imagination may be termed empirical because it begins in the observation of experience and ends in a fiction the reader tests against his own knowledge.) The novel begins in empiricism, rising with the mind's disinheritance from received wisdom.[10] But if free to analyze the world apprehended by his sense-impressions, the narrator in the novel has never been free *from* that world. In persuasive fiction the made has its analogy in the known as the claimed is based on the demonstrated. The teller is on the surface of a tri-level structure, and his role, central as it surely is, remains subsidiary to the mediate fiction of the tale itself.

3

Whatever objections may be raised to an inclusive theory that the novel's tale is in its figurative drama (there is always *hubris* in such general suggestions), it is demonstrable that D. H. Lawrence's own novels have their life and power in *the cumulative series of symbolic scenes they present*. The dramatized scene is the structural unit of his fiction, and the series of scenes, with its gradual accumulation of realized meaning, provides the work's organizing principle. The scene itself is composed of action. Lawrencian action is always symbolic action because Lawrencian drama is peculiarly figurative and dual. This dualism is created by the use of exterior events to project the inner states of characters.

Lawrence's novels include the highly ambitious endeavor to bring the hidden interior of the self into the light of perceivable images and acts. His final concern is the nature of the self; an artist whose themes are ontological, his writings taken as a whole constitute a vast poem of being.[11] He manages to overcome the paradox inherent in his believing that the invisible self is more significant than the visible at the same time as his art demands manifestation. His success is that makes us so aware of the hidden while he presents us with the revealed. Lawrence gradually loses interest in the personal ego, which he comes to see as an unimportant link between the larger world of nature and the deeper area of instinctive being. The social self with its predictable and repetitive forms is overshadowed by its dark counterpart, the Lawrencian unconscious. Distinct from the Freudian sanctuary for repressed desires, the Lawrencian unconscious is our too-frequently obscured vital source of being.

Through figurative events Lawrence analyzes his characters' concealed identities. His typical procedure is to employ an image with inherited meaning in the context of an original scene which broadens the symbol's range of reference. Like the Romantic he is, Lawrence brings universal symbols into the life of man to find meaning in psychic analogies. (Unlike most Romantics, Lawrence finds no tragic incongruity in the comparison; he is sure man and nature are finally one.) The method is notable in the Lawrencian use of cosmic or natural symbols like sun, fire, and water. Preeminent among these symbols is the moon, the luminous image that comes to signify the dominating character in Lawrence's fiction. Natural images play a role in scenes composed of human actions whose suggestive intensity implies hidden meaning.[12] Through these techniques Lawrence works toward the revelation of unknown parts of the self.

Lawrence's symbolic actions develop dramas of identity, stories of ontological[13] struggle. The drama has a particular style for its subject is the ego *in extremis*, the self under the threat of disintegration. At the plot's climactic moments, the novels' protagonists undergo a crisis of being that endangers their sanity or their very lives. The cycle of outward events culminates in the achievement or dissolution of the character's inner self and there is always the implicit question of whether salvation or catastrophe will claim him.

The characters' ultimate fates—and all of Lawrence's work is overshadowed by an eschatological concern with ultimacies—cannot be viewed in isolation. For Lawrence, the greater part of being is being-in-relationship. On the level of plot his fictions describe passionate relationships between men and women and on the hidden psychic level as well the self is involved in the processes of connection. Even the withdrawal into singleness so often depicted is correctly understood as one of the stages in the dialectic of relationship. Contest and conflict are integral to liasons in which the sexes are often opposed, sometimes creating the feeling that the death of one partner is the birth of the other.

The final victor in the struggle between man and woman is a foregone conclusion. A careful examination of the way symbolic scenes give form to inmost conflicts reveals something remarkable in the fiction of D. H. Lawrence: the consistent demonstration that *on the deepest level of self, women are stronger and wholer than men*. Lawrence's female characters are independent while his male characters lack self-sufficiency. This is shown as women maintain themselves in isolation where men establish a stable sense of self only through the other sex. Beyond the ability to be separate, Lawrence's female characters have life capacity and survive; more than being emotionally dependent, his males are death directed. Alone, the men suffer from the sense of being incomplete. Yet when with a woman the Lawrencian male is threatened by engulfment. The imbalance is destructive, but a fact of being, beyond the will and consciousness of the characters. The women are not deliberately domineering for their lives are sterile and unfulfilled when they divide themselves from men. The men, however, are hollow and disintegrative without women, hardly able to live at all. The tale tells of this inequality and its consequences.

The focus of this study is the work not the man, yet it would be evasive to ignore that something in Lawrence's own mind perceived women as having greater integrity of self than men. A reading of *Sons and Lovers* suggests the imbalanced perception may be traced to Oedipal feelings that were never fully dissolved. But this is not to imply that Lawrence shared the incomplete identity of his male characters. It is more convincing to see his fiction writing as a way to equilibrate his personality, as the giving of artistic form to tendencies Lawrence rightly intuited as threatening.[14] In any case, anyone who thinks the author of Lawrence's complete works had a weak identity has a mystifying notion of strength.

Another issue worth dealing with at the outset is the question of whether Lawrence's unbalanced view of the sexes is not an artistic flaw. For Lawrence's apprehension of the psyches of women as more integrated than those of men (assuming I can show this was his apprehension) would seem to distort reality. One relevant point is that universal experience may be inner as well as outer, that the work of art may refer to images from the unconscious as well as sensory images from the external world. It remains debatable whether our primary pictorial visions are external (following the Freudian view of inner visualization as introjection) or internal (following the Jungian view of outer images as projection). Freud sees visual memories beginning outside, Jung finds their source within, but both see a unity between the images of the actual world and the language of the unconscious. (Against his will, Lawrence finds his context as thinker and writer among the pioneers of psychoanalysis.)[15] The artist may go deep within himself to get out

of himself. Hence the uncanny perfervid quality of some of
Lawrence's symbolic action may denote the simultaneous presentation of external and unconscious experience. The voice of the
teller, in Lawrence or other writers, would thus articulate the
evasion of *two* powerful objective forces. Using Lawrencian terms
to understand an element in his own work, we may speak of the
teller as the fictional equivalent of the personal, self-conscious ego,
an entity consisting largely of defenses against inner reality and its
external parallels.

The constellation in Lawrence's work uniting a disintegrative
man and a woman of greater, sometimes absorptive, ego-strength,
recalls the figure of the *magna mater*, the Great Mother or Triple
Goddess.[16] A primary image of myth, art, and according to
psychoanalytical hypotheses, man's unconscious mind, the *magna
mater* is an archetype who either precedes (in the Jungian scheme)
or succeeds (in the Freudian) man's experience of woman as
enveloping, overwhelming, and essential for life. The sequence
which enforces her significance comprises the enclosure of the
womb, the sustenance of the omnipotent nursing mother, the
beauty of the mother who is the first love object, the centrality of
the woman to whom man turns for sex and love. Hence the corollary
of the *magna mater* is the male in a series of subsidiary functions:
foetus, infant, child, and sexual seeker afraid of rejection. In
relation to the last of these roles it is true that women equally need
men, but the relationship between man and woman completes a
group of situations which contribute to man's sense of dependency.
Possibly the need to achieve erection also causes men to approach
sex with the unconscious knowledge of potential incompleteness.
(Frigidity is the biological parallel in women to impotence, but
again the point is not what women are but how they are transformed
in the psyches of men.)

The *magna mater* plays a central role in Lawrence's work and
Jungian concepts, like the theories of Freud, fit naturally into a
critique of Lawrence. Yet just as I intend no formal psychoanalysis
of Lawrence, so there is no attempt at a systematic examination of
his contribution to the literature of the collective unconscious.
Such a study would make a serious addition to our knowledge of
Lawrence—it is no coincidence that Quetzalcoatl and Huit-
zilopochtli, the dark Gods of *The Plumed Serpent*, are celebrated in

Aztec mythology as the vanquishers of the Great Mother.[17] But in the present work the importance of the archtypal imagery is that it is intrinsic to the Lawrencian tale—discovering such imagery *per se* is not my purpose. Moreover, it is possible to distinguish novels from myths by observing that novels reflect particular environments while myths present archetypes in dramatic form. Lawrence's accomplishment is as a novelist, and at the same time as his work points to archetypal material it demonstrates the social and psychological verisimilitude traditional in the novel. The unbalanced relationships between men and women take their own distinct forms in every Lawrence novel and can be appreciated only through extended analyses of the specific texts. Thus in Lawrence's first two novels, *The White Peacock and the Trespasser*, there is no true *magna mater* figure, although her shadow darkens the novels, explaining the unnamed malaise which affects their central male characters and the unjustified hostility the narrator aims at the female protagonists. The image of a domineering and maternal woman is not directly confronted until *Sons and Lovers*. In *The Rainbow* and *Women in Love* all of the women have elements of the *magna mater* and the narrator grows increasingly conscious of her as a threat to male integration. Yet Lawrence's three greatest novels are individual complex creations each of which must be examined according to its particular patterning of symbol and action. I have employed lengthy and frequent quotations to isolate this pattern as I see it and to share my experience of the tale with the reader.

Against the tale there is a counter-tale "pointing the other way." Taking the Freudian notion of reaction-formation as a model, the contra-force has a certain inevitability since any comprehension deep enough to touch upon unconscious material will impel a conscious resistance. This countertale consists of elements in the novel contradicting the evidences realized by the structure of scenes; it is largely imposed by the authorial voice. I have argued that the symbolic drama of the tale is created by the successful fusion of unconscious and external images. The teller could thus be seen as a narrational defense mechanism, distorting the actualities of the outer world and avoiding the configurations of the inner by operating in a middle range of will and wish fulfillment. The teller works primarily through intrusive commentary but may also use figurative elements—including myth, image, and symbol—that oppose the inherent integrity of the structure of scenes. The disharmony thereby created reveals the untrustworthy teller; but he is also exposed by a failure of execution, a diminishment of conviction and convincingness, a substitution of ideology for art.

The careful examination of narrative dichotomy in Lawrence reveals that the function of the teller is to subvert the integrated identity of woman and evade the failed autonomy of man. The narrator's counter-tale works almost invariably to reduce the strength of women and reverse the weakness of men. The teller's intention in the end is to distort the inequality at the heart of D. H. Lawrence's fiction.

The limitation of this study to Lawrence's first five novels should be explained. The simple matter of length is the larger part of my answer: neither my subject nor my method lends itself to brevity. Without space to do all the novels I chose the first five over the other logical choice, the "major" five of *Sons and Lovers*, *The Rainbow*, *Women in Love*, *The Plumed Serpent* and *Lady Chatterley's Lover*, because I could thus deal with a sequence of development while still covering Lawrence's three richest works. The earlier novels also suffice to show a revealing aesthetic pattern—using tale/teller agreement as the criterion—of tension, harmony, and the reappearance of discord. The first two novels show tale/teller division as the narrator simplifies the nature of womanly force while averting his gaze from the self-destructiveness of men. The interfering teller plays a smaller role in *Sons and Lovers* as Lawrence apprehends the underlying reason for the disparity in his perceptions of men and women. In *The Rainbow* the imbalance between the sexes is accepted and explored, leading to the disappearance of conflict between narrator and narrative and creating a unified work of art. In *Women in Love* the relationship between Gerald and Gudrun acknowledges the demoniacal underside of inequality, but in presenting the involvement of Ursula and Birkin the teller reverses the man's dependency on the woman. This marks the beginning of a new phase in Lawrence's novel writing, characterized by a teller who plays an increasing role as apologist for male superiority. The subtle *Women in Love* introduces a problem which grows more glaring in the later novels: it is notable in the strategies of the teller against the female protagonists of *The Lost Girl* and *Kangaroo;* becomes striking in the subordination of woman to man in *The Plumed Serpent,* and perhaps culminates in the ritual murder of the *magna mater* herself in the short story "The Woman Who Rode Away." Tracing the encroachment of teller on tale in those works is a task that remains to be done. Yet a complete account of the cycle would have to take account of the miraculous final resolution of *Lady Chatterley's Lover*. Lawrence's last novel is in a separate category from the others, showing little evidence of the inequalities, genuine and forced, which fill the earlier works with tension. In an amazing spiritual effort Lawrence escaped himself in his dying years, finally seeing men and women in proportionate dignity and delicate equality: *Lady Chatterley's Lover* is a tale of balance in which an artist of torment finds at last his vision of peace.

Notes to Introduction

1. D. H. Lawrence, *Studies in Classic American Literature* (1924; reprint ed., Harmondsworth, Middlesex: Penguin Books, 1971), p. 8.

2. Leslie Fiedler provides one striking example when he assumes, in writing about contrivance and evasion in *The Blithedale Romance*, that Hawthorne's fear of female sexuality subverts the work: "Zenobia . . . in whom feminism is real, contemporary, and unrepented . . . is visited with a final fate more vindictively stage-managed than any other doom in Hawthorne. Described as 'Woman, bruising herself against the narrow limitations of her sex, Zenobia is actually bruised against the ambivalent hostility of Miles Coverdale, the narrator . . . and of Hawthorne, who speaks almost directly through the mask of Cloverdale [sic]." *Love and Death in the American Novel*, rev. ed. (New York: Stein and Day, 1966), p. 223. The point is arresting, testifying, it would seem, that as the teller rejects his tale, so the reader rejects the teller; but we badly lack information about *how* Fiedler arrives at the conclusions presented by his persuasive rhetoric.

3. When Lawrence uses the tale/teller gap as a tool of practical criticism, the results can be brilliant, as in his analyses of American literature, but also reductive and domineering, as in the remarks on Tolstoy. The *American Studies* penetratingly examine a "split in . . . American art" and in the American psyche. In the essays Lawrence vividly formulates this bifurcation, arguing that the innocence of American life covers a hidden violence, and, relatedly, that the saccharine "goody-goody" surface of American literature contrasts with an inner meaning of the blackest "diabolism" (*SCAL*, p. 89). Through this dichotomy Lawrence legitimately establishes his claim that, in the American novel, there is conflict between the

artist's conscious intention and his unconscious performance. But his critique of *Anna Karenina* reveals the glaring subjectivity behind his decisions about what is true and what false in the novel; Lawrence's choices, it becomes apparent, are made according to *a priori* notions about the value of beliefs. Accordingly, Lawrence finds that Tolstoy's "didactic" ideals mar the novel by forcing the Russian writer to artificially condemn Vronsky and Anna. For, Lawrence insists, Tolstoy actually admired the "phallic splendour" of the relationship and disapproved of the societal "monster" that ostracized the couple. And yet this reading is based on the remarkable notion, both arrogant and naive, that in the end Tolstoy must be understood in Lawrencian terms. Still more to the point, the disintegration of Vronsky and Anna's relationship is consummately dramatized, demonstrating through novelistic art that a sexual relationship deprived of its social context loses its viability—a perception Lawrence resisted because of his biases, not Tolstoy's. See "The Novel," in *Phoenix II: Uncollected, Unpublished and Other Prose Works by D. H. Lawrence*, ed. Warren Roberts and Harry T. Moore (London: William Heinemann, 1968), pp. 416–17.

4. Theorists of narrative, moreover, have generally ignored the issue. One exception is Wayne Booth who, while paying only incidental attention to the tale/teller problem, nevertheless makes a passing comment of considerable relevance: "some works are marred by an impression that the author has weighed his characters on dishonest scales. But this impression depends not on whether the author explicitly passes judgment but on whether the judgment he passes seems defensible in the light of the dramatized facts." Booth notes, as well, that whatever the assertions of the narrator, the deepest commitments of an author are "expressed by the total form" of his work. Hence, if "a narrator who by every trustworthy sign is presented to us as a reliable spokesman for the author professes to believe in values which are never realized in the structure as a whole, we can then talk of an insincere work." *The Rhetoric of Fiction* (Chicago & London: The University of Chicago Press, 1961), pp. 79, 75.

5. The existence of the teller in the tale is not substantially affected by whether the story is told in the first or third person. In either case the image of an author is formed, and in neither is the connection between authorial voice and biographical author simple. There is a complication when an ironic first-person narrator is employed, because then we have an explicit teller being manipulated by an implicit teller. In such a case, we are intended to quarrel with the narrator so there is a division between tale and teller only if we reject the stance of the implied author.

6. A striking example of the identification of writer and persona is found in the criticism of Louis D. Rubin, Jr. Writing about the ending of *Huckleberry Finn*, with its regressive lapse into the style of *Tom Sawyer*, Rubin makes a peculiar defense: "Narrative consistency and the unity of plot notwithstanding, we will go along with Mark Twain wherever he chooses to take us, sentimentalities, inconsistencies, lapses of taste, and all. This is all a part of the novel, which in turn is the embodiment of the man." *The Teller in the Tale* (Seattle, Wash.: University of Washington Press, 1967), pp. 82–83. Aside from confusing author and narrator, Rubin is rather sentimental himself, insisting on a wholesale acceptance of the "Mark Twain" who subverts the intrinsic logic of his story. Contrarily, formalist commentators, whether New Critical or structuralist, disregard the man behind the mask as they concentrate on analyzing the functions of the persona.

7. Booth notes various terms for this figure: "the official scribe," "the author's 'second self' " and the "implied author." He further observes that "the reader will inevitably construct a picture" of the author connected to the voice. *The Rhetoric of Fiction*, pp. 71, 73.

8. Freud, Sigmund, "Creative Writers and Day-Dreaming," reprinted in David Lodge, ed., *20th Century Literary Criticism: A Reader* (London: Longman, 1972), p. 42.

9. Kenneth Burke argues that language itself is a kind of symbolic action, the tool that the symbol-making animal, man, uses to influence his environment. Burke also stresses that language alters the phenomena it describes. *Language as Symbolic Action: Essays on Life, Literature, and Method* (Berkeley: University of California Press, 1966), pp. 3–9, 44–47. Burke makes his case with fluent dexterity and is generally persuasive. My qualification would be to note that descriptive language (like the perceiving ego) influences the reality apprehended without determining it; language is, in its overall sense, referential. For Burke language is symbolic action in essence, in my use of the term language is symbolic action when it refers to the symbolism—cultural, social, psychological, moral—of events.

10. In an important study, Ian Watt makes the generally accepted point that "literary traditionalism was first and most fully challenged by the novel, whose primary criterion was truth to individual experience." *The Rise of the Novel: Studies in Defoe, Richardson, and Fielding* (Harmondsworth, Middlesex: Penguin Books, 1963), p. 13.

11. Criticism of Lawrence has only begun to switch its emphasis from the theme of sex to the theme of identity. The change is indicative of contemporary concerns. As Western intellectuals worry less about the orgasm and more about the self, they change their approaches to a twentieth-century writer with a chameleon-like ability to remain relevant. Two recent works which focus on the subject are: Marguerite Beede Howe, *The Art of the Self in D. H. Lawrence* (Athens, Ohio: Ohio University Press, 1977) and the chapters on Lawrence in Robert Langbaum, *The Mysteries of Identity* (New York: Oxford University Press, 1977). Howe's book is mistitled for it is less about Lawrence's art than about his theories of the self. This is just as well since her strength is her understanding of Lawrence the theorist, not Lawrence the artist. Langbaum's is a more balanced study, and his introductory points are likely to have prophetic importance for work on Lawrence in the near future: "We oversimplify Lawrence when we think of him only as the apostle of sex. . . . Lawrence might just as appropriately be called the great writer on identity, since he never writes about sex without writing about identity." p. 251.

12. Peter K. Garrett notes that "what distinguishes Lawrence's method is that he . . . creates powerful symbolic scenes where hidden unconscious states are revealed in the form of dramatic presentation." *Scene and Symbol from George Eliot to James Joyce: Studies in Changing Fictional Mode* (New Haven, Conn.: Yale University Press, 1969), p. 183.

13. My use of the word "ontological" is similar to that of R. D. Laing. Laing points out that he uses "the term in [an] . . . empirical sense because it appears to be the best adverbial or adjectival derivative of 'being'." *The Divided Self: An Existential Study in Sanity and Madness* (Harmondsworth, Middlesex: Penguin Books, 1965), p. 39.

14. Simon O. Lesser observes that we master an experience when we successfully describe it, thus removing its threat to us. *Fiction and the Unconscious* (New York: Vintage Books, 1957), p. 164.

15. Lawrence was impelled by his fierce disagreements with Freud's ideas to construct his own psychoanalysis. See D. H. Lawrence, *"Psychoanalysis and the Unconscious" and "Fantasia of the Unconscious,"* introduction by Philip Rieff (New York: The Viking Press, 1960).

16. A comprehensive and masterly examination of the *magna mater* as she appears in Western art and culture is performed by Erich Neumann in *The Great Mother: An Analysis of the Archetype* (London: Routledge & Kegan Paul, 1955). Freud refers to the transformations

of the maternal image in an essay on *King Lear*, giving her three primary roles: "They [Lear's three daughters] are the three forms taken by the figure of the mother in the course of a man's life—the mother herself, the beloved one who is chosen after her pattern, and lastly the Mother Earth who receives him once more." "The Theme of the Three Caskets," in *The Standard Edition of the Complete Psychological Works of Sigmund Freud*, ed. and trans. James Strachey (London: The Hogarth Press, 1958), 12:301.

17. Neumann, *The Great Mother*, pp. 186, 203.

The Moon's Dominion

1
The Pastoral Fallacy:
The White Peacock

Separating the tale from the teller is comparatively uncomplicated in *The White Peacock*. The novel's *commentary* is expressed by a *commentator:* Cyril, its first-person narrator. Nor is Cyril the only commentator. Annable, a minor but vivid character, controls the narrative at certain points and also utters statements that contradict its inherent conclusions. Annable and Cyril make representations that defy the novel's intrinsically rendered presentations.

Cyril's narration is problematic throughout (in his subsequent novels Lawrence dispensed with the first person form). Neither a reliable narrator, whose opinions we implicitly accept, nor an unreliable narrator, whom we view with consistent irony, Cyril is situated disconcertingly between the two.[1] Some of the events we see through his eyes compel and move us, but his interpretations of what he sees often seem forced. His narrative uncertainty makes our experience of *The White Peacock* correspondingly uncertain. The best way to regard Cyril, perhaps, is as a fairly trustworthy witness, but a prejudiced judge. He is our intermediary to the fully dramatized story, shown coherently through symbolic action. But his evaluations of this story may often be disregarded. We gradually begin to feel that the removal of Cyril would improve the novel.[2]

Lawrence's control over his first person narrator, moreover, is sometimes careless. Early in their relationship, Cyril leaves the novel's two protagonists, George Saxton and Lettie Beardsall, alone, to play out the subsequent scene without the benefit of his presence.[3] Cyril's withdrawal, as Lawrence apparently did not realize, leaves the two characters in a narrational vacuum. Yet the scene in question, which begins with George and Lettie arguing the merits of various English painters, and ends with the dramatic exposure of their hidden feelings about one another, is of central importance. It seems hardly coincidental that it is precisely when George and Lettie are freed from Cyril's self-conscious commentary that they reveal themselves with a memorable intensity. Lawrence's technical oversight hints, therefore, that Cyril's commentary is a stricture on *The White Peacock*, not an enhancement of it.

Cyril's subjectivity derives from emotional needs whose source and manifestations emerge steadily in the course of the novel. The subjectivity expresses itself in a keen sympathy for George and Annable, and ultimately gives a decidedly favorable slant to Cyril's depiction of the two men. Conversely, Cyril takes a harsh view of Lettie, who is presented with unearned disfavor.

Himself an effeminate character (frequently called "Sybil"), Cyril admires strong male figures like George and Annable, both of whom are described positively as earthy, vital, and close to nature. Yet he views the two men as victims in an unequal struggle between the sexes. The novel's women gradually emerge as its dominant, not to say dominating, figures. Lettie, in particular, becomes the villain of the piece. A superimposed layer of imagery that fails to develop naturally from the presented character identifies Lettie with various traditional images of feminine perfidy. The figure of Eve attains a central position because Lettie-Eve appears in a novel whose lush and abundant pastoral landscapes have Edenic overtones.[4] Cyril's commentary ultimately creates, within the larger tale of *The White Peacock*, a version of the ancient myth of a pastoral Eden where men live in perfect harmony with nature. Cyril perceives this natural unity as a state disrupted by women. In his version of the Biblical Fall, original sin is equated only with Eve's pride as Adam is an intrinsic part of the peaceful innocence she destroys.

As Cyril subverts the tale with a superimposed myth, so Annable contradicts the tale with a reductively elucidated symbol. Annable's autobiography parallels Cyril's myth: he describes how his

own natural energy had been undermined by a woman, a pretentious lady who perpetrated her vitality-sapping culture and abstract ideas on an unwitting and innocent man. The stimulus for Annable's narrative is the sight of a peacock that befouls a statue of an angel. Annable quickly turns the peacock into a metaphor for "the soul of a woman"—a bit of symbol-interpretation too pejorative and biased to be valuable in itself, or to contribute seriously to our understanding of the novel. (The ensuing story makes clear that the angel is identified with Annable himself.)

The myth and symbol through which the commentators operate form a didactic, ideological underlayer in the novel: the ideology, a misogynistic vitalism, upholds intimacy with nature as an ultimate value, considers men capable of the desirable union, and views women as not only removed from nature but as an interference with the connection enjoyed by men. Most critics of *The White Peacock* have interpreted the novel in the light of its ideology, thereby taking commentary more seriously than incident, believing the myth at the expense of the story.[5] But this is to fail to observe the narrative dichotomy that develops when the teller employs an assuaging ideology for the purpose of creating an alternative fiction. By means of this strategy he attempts to evade a reality at the heart of his story. Yet if we look to *The White Peacock* as "living novel," as separate, realized work of art, we will be told a different tale.

The White Peacock presents a fundamental (perhaps *the* fundamental) Lawrencian story: the struggle for fulfillment experienced by a woman with a strong, integrated sense of self. Lettie has a complexity of personality and wholeness of being lacking in the novel's male characters. (The function of the teller is to simplify this destructive and self-destructive ontological superiority into mere malice: *to turn the true dominance of self into the false dominance of will*.) The confrontation of a woman with a formed, clear identity, and a man who possesses a less developed self, has a rare clarity in *The White Peacock*. Lettie is caught between George and Leslie Tempest, the son of a wealthy mineowner. Both men exhibit severe limitations, and are prototypical of the two kinds of unrealized men found throughout Lawrence's fiction. George, the man of the soil, is an early but unmistakable version of the passionate, "dark" male. George's handsome body communi-

cates an intense sexual vitality, but suggestions of brutality and
blindness are mixed with his power and Lettie fears the threat that
accompanies his promise. Contrarily, Leslie is socially polished
and apparently sensitive. But on a deeper level he manifests
sexual weakness and a countervailing will-to-domination of a
cowardly type. Yet Lettie's unimpressive suitors cannot be blamed
for all the failure and misery that overtakes the three characters.
Lettie's willful passivity (qualities that can combine when the will
is exerted to maintain an untroubled state) is also at fault. Lettie's
strength-of-being, moreover, culminates in her isolation (this bitter
consequence of feminine strength becomes increasingly important
in Lawrence's fiction). The tale tells of a woman frustrated by both
the flawed men around her and her own errors; *The White Peacock*
is a novel in which *all* the central characters fail.

   Cyril opens his story with a description of the valley and lake of
Nethermere, scene of most of *The White Peacock*. The once vital
Nethermere (its name is a pun meaning both "under the sea" and
"under the mother" thereby suggesting a connection between the
two concepts) is now in a state of decay: "I stood watching the
shadowy fish slide through the gloom of the millpond. They were
grey, descendants of the silvery things that had darted away from
the monks, in the young days when the valley was lusty. The whole
place was gathered in the musing of old age" (p. 13). Fittingly, the
stagnant valley has a sleepy occupant; George, the young farmer, is
firmly linked to his environment. He is "stoutly built" but "lazy,"
and enjoys the dull place because it is "all right for a doss [nap]."
"Your whole life," says his friend, Cyril, "is nothing but a doss. I
shall laugh when somebody jerks you awake." Cyril's comment
ironically foreshadows the miseries that will date from George's
partial awakening. At this point, however, George and the valley
are both distant from realization: the place is senescent, the person
is torpid: there is a general devitalization of man and nature.

   The paradox is that later in the novel Nethermere and George
will become ideals for Cyril. During his frequent bouts of adolescent angst he turns to nature for solace. This leads to a sentimen
talization of Cyril's rustic past and of George, with whom he share
earthy experiences in the valley. At these times Cyril works
cross-purposes: he elevates George to a kind of Rousseaui

innocent though the character's own actions present him as highly flawed. But this is the novel speaking one way, the myth another.

The nature of George's flaws are soon made apparent. Sitting at the lakeside he insists on examining some bees whose wings do not function.

> 'Leave them alone,' said I [Cyril]. 'Let them run in the sun. They're only just out of the shells. Don't torment them into flight.'
>
> He persisted, however, and broke the wing of the next.
>
> 'Oh, dear—pity!' said he, and crushed the little thing between his fingers. Then he examined the eggs, and pulled out some silk from round the dead larva, and investigated it all in a desultory manner, asking me all I knew about the insects. When he had finished he flung the clustered eggs into the water and rose. (P. 14)

For a man of rural background, George is surprisingly indelicate. His brutality is caused by ignorance, and he cannot explore without damaging. After his "desultory" examination he heedlessly casts aside the eggs, destroying the bees' world altogether.[6] The faults George displays in this minor incident bear on Lettie's hesitations with him. His clumsiness is intrinsic; he probes, but lacks the patience to discover without harming. After satisfying his half-hearted interest, he becomes lethally indifferent. It is a complex of qualities that could hardly reassure a woman.

The second chapter begins the interaction between Lettie and George. (Its arch title, "Dangling the Apple," develops the Adam and Eve subtheme.) One of the Saxtons' cats is caught in a trap and badly mangled. Cyril, Lettie, and Emily stand helpless in the face of the animal's suffering. George shows an ability to do the cruelly necessary thing and drowns the cat. During this minor but genuine confrontation with death, his behavior is two-sided. He shows a courageous decisiveness, but takes a smug pleasure in his competent brutality. "The quickest way [to kill the cat] . . . is to swing her round and knock her head against the wall," he points out with more accuracy than sensitivity. When Lettie objects he happily provides an alternative method: " 'I'll drown her, then,' he said with a smile." Yet George also communicates a hint of self-mockery, and a suggestion of crudity deliberately exaggerated to distress hypocritical moralists: "If . . . the poor old cat had made a prettier corpse, you'd have thrown violets on her" (p. 26). Emily, indeed, accuses him of "callousness and brutality," but Lettie understands that the incident finally betokens strength: "He's only healthy, he's never been sick . . ." Lettie is reminded of her own corporeality, and feels she must adjust: "If we move the blood rises in our heel-prints." She admires George for being in touch with their surrounding world of flesh and death.

If Lettie feels she must make some accommodation to George's values, to his acceptance of natural life-processes, she also fears a relationship with him will diminish her fine sensibility. Perhaps for this reason, she attempts to draw George out and add sensitivity to his robustness. The endeavor to provide George with culture occurs over Lettie's piano. So genteel an artifact provides an insight into her aspirations; further, her piano playing is analogous to George's self-involvement: "She flattered herself scandalously through the piano." But the clash over the musical instrument challenges their mutual isolation.

> . . . she gave him, "Drink to me only with thine eyes." At the end she turned and asked him if he liked the words. He replied that he thought them rather daft. But he looked at her with glowing brown eyes, as if in hesitating challenge.
>
> "That's because you have no wine in your eyes to pledge with," she replied, answering his challenge with a blue blaze of her eyes. Then her eyelashes drooped on to her cheek. He laughed with a faint ring of consciousness, and asked her how could she know.
>
> "Because," she said slowly, looking up at him with pretended scorn, "because there's no change in your eyes when I look at you. I always think people who are worth much talk with their eyes. That's why you are forced to respect many quite uneducated people. Their eyes are so eloquent, and full of knowledge."
>
> . . . .
>
> "[You] keep your senses asleep—half alive."
>
> "Do I?" he asked.
>
> "Of course you do;—'bos—bovis; an ox.' You are like a stalled ox, food and comfort, no more." (Pp. 27–28)

Telling use of detail turns this into a figurative encounter. The song sets the tone; through their eyes they watch one another and reveal themselves. Its title, "Drink to me only with thine eyes," invokes the gap between them, the struggle of body and soul. Lettie extolls delicately Platonic communication while George fails to grasp the use of such insubstantial intimacy. (The misogynistic interpretation of *The White Peacock* would see this as the attempt of a sexually attenuated female to emasculate a healthy male. Such would hardly be the point since Lettie often shows her appreciation of George's physicality.) But far from wanting to reduce George, Lettie is using the human eye as a microcosm of consciousness. Concerned about his apparent benightedness, she attempts to expand his awareness. The range of his responses is dismayingly narrow.

> ". . . how did the music make you feel?"
>
> "I don't know—whether—it made me feel anything," he replied deliberately, pondering over his answer, as usual.
>
> "I tell you," she declared, "you're either asleep or stupid. Did you really see nothing in the music? But what did you think about?"
>
> . . . "Why!" he admitted, laughing, and trying to tell the exact truth, "I thought how pretty your hands are—and what they are like to touch—and I thought it was a new experience to feel somebody's hair tickling my cheek." (P. 29)

George is honest in this interchange, while Lettie is supercilious and self-protective. But she is trying to challenge him into being something more than an exclusively sensual creature. He returns the challenge by covertly asking, with barely-hidden male conceit, whether she is really all that artily abstract. Nor is she, but she is wary of the compromises a strong, brutish male might demand of her. That is why she finds the well-mannered but comparatively weak Leslie "more agreeable on the whole than—than my Taurus."

In the next chapter, "A Vendor of Visions," painting replaces music as the vehicle for intensifying George's awareness. Painting presents new approaches to visual experience, and Lettie tries to stimulate George's passive imagination through art. George and Lettie disagree about the rustic landscapes of George Clausen; the young farmer fails to see the beauty in the labor he himself does daily as Lettie insists on its grandeur. His skepticism contains the force of experience, while her enthusiasm is dilettantish: "[Clausen] sees the mystery and magnificence that envelops us even when we work menially, I *do* know and I *can* speak." Still, it is true that George's imperviousness extends to nature. Finally,

provoked by George's stolid incomprehension and her own exacer-
bated nerves, Lettie enters upon a tirade that is perceptive about
George and self-revealing.

> "You are blind, you are only half-born; you are gross with good living
> and heavy sleeping. You are a piano which will only play a dozen
> common notes. Sunset is nothing to you—it merely happens anywhere.
> Oh, but you make me feel as if I'd like to make you suffer. If you'd ever
> been sick; if you'd ever been born into a home where there was
> something oppressed you, and you couldn't understand; if ever you'd
> believed, or even doubted, you might have been a man by now. You
> never grow up, like bulbs which spend all summer getting fat and
> fleshy, but never wakening the germ of a flower. As for me, the flower is
> born in me, but it wants bringing forth. Things don't flower if they're
> overfed. You have to suffer before you blossom in this life. When death
> is just touching a plant, it forces it into a passion of flowering. You
> wonder how I have touched death. You don't know. There's always a
> sense of death in this home. I believe my mother hated my father before
> I was born. There was death in her veins for me before I was born. It
> makes a difference—"
>
> As he sat listening, his eyes grew wide and his lips were parted, like
> a child who feels the tale but does not understand the words. (Pp. 42)

The spleen in this passage is explained (if not entirely justified)
by Lettie's painful memories and profound hesitations. Her longing
for fulfillment is stated in nearly sexual terms: "the flower . . .
wants bringing forth," but where, her bitterness implies, is the man
able to arouse it. The flower-image refers not only to sexuality, but
to the question of identify and being-formation. Flowering is
frequently associated with being in Lawrence,[7] and when Lettie
speaks of being "born" she is metaphorically referring to her own
independence of self. The same imagery of birth and flowering
indicates that George has failed to achieve being.

Nor is Lettie's complexity of being advanced only through
imagery. The personality revealed by her words is intricate; she is
passionate as well as intelligent, the one moderating but by no
means cancelling the other. Her personality, indeed, is strong
enough to invigorate the novel in which it appears. *The White
Peacock* improves when Lettie becomes its focus.[8] Her furious
statement develops an energetic and concentrated level of figurative language far superior to the artificial diction the novel generally employs. The life and poignancy Lettie demonstrates here

pervade the entire scene and result in an intensity exceptional in *The White Peacock*. The suggestion intrudes itself that the character in *The White Peacock* to whom Lawrence felt most intimately connected was Lettie, and that Cyril's later rejection of her was an attempt to forcibly reverse this natural empathy. (We remember that Cyril has no role in the paintings-scene.) Lettie's subtle linkage between suffering and the achievement of self is significant because it describes her own consciousness, in comparison to which George's healthy oblivion seems rudimentary. But the connection also recalls Lawrence himself, whose genius grew strangely from disease, its flame burning with a sickly brilliance.

Another important subject Lettie raises in her speech is her feelings about her father. Her fury toward George comes from the combination of physical attraction and fear of repeating her mother's experience. Lettie has already been betrayed by a weak man; later in the novel we learn that Mr. Beardsall was a sensual, irresponsible man who abandoned his family. Like Cyril, Lettie has grown up bereaved and is acutely, nearly morbidly, sensitive as a result. But (unlike Cyril) Lettie will not glorify a man who seems to recapitulate her father. She will rather be wary of him, poised and ready to reject. (As in the cases of Gertrude Morel and Ursula Brangwen, we can trace the roots of a brittle isolation in the female character to a problematical relationship with her father.) Yet to speak of rejection here is premature; the point to note is that Lettie is normally passionate, only seeking a man with stability and self-possession that she can trust. Critics who view Lettie as a frigid underminer of healthy instincts ignore the nearly unbearable sexual tension that pervades this chapter.

This tension reaches its climax as the two characters view a print of Maurice Greiffenhagen's painting, "Idyll." The superiority Lettie achieves through her cleverness dissipates before the work; here the power-roles she works to establish are figuratively reversed so that the male's sexual force dominates.

> "Wouldn't it be fine?" he exclaimed. . . .
> "What?" she asked, dropping her head in confusion.
> "That—a girl like that—half afraid—and passion!" He lit up curiously.
> "She may well be half afraid, when the barbarian comes out in his glory, skins and all."

"But don't you like it?" he asked.

She shrugged her shoulders, saying, "Make love to the next girl you meet, and by the time the poppies redden the field, she'll hang in your arms. She'll have need to be more than half afraid, won't she."

She played with the leaves of the book, and did not look at him. (Pp. 42–43)

Though feigning indifference, she recognizes the strength of George's masculinity and her characteristic banter lacks conviction. The painting has aroused both of them; the sensual promise in George, always compelling, threatens to overwhelm her defensive cleverness. She returns to her verbal challenges with a new vulnerability, a tacit acknowledgement of what exists between them.

"Didn't you know the picture before?" she said, in a low toneless voice.

He shut his eyes and shrank with shame.

"No, I've never seen it before," he said.

"I'm surprised," she said. "It is a very common one."

"Is it?" he answered, and this make-belief conversation fell. She looked up, and found his eyes. They gazed at each other for a moment before they hid their faces again. It was a torture to each of them to look thus nakedly at the other, a dazzled, shrinking pain they forced themselves to undergo for a moment, that they might the moment after tremble with a fierce sensation that filled their veins with fluid, fiery electricity . . . They felt the blood beating madly in their necks. (Pp. 43–44).

Both epiphany and call to action, this passage affirms passion as the animating principle between them. Afterward, Lettie tries her familiar strategies to reassert dominion over her "barbarian." She rails, in French, "at men in general, and at love in particular." But it is all hollow; George has reached her, and through the flesh. When she sees a gash on his thumb she is suddenly chastened and tender, troubled by this wound on the body that moves her. At the end of the chapter, Lettie is not only a seller of visions but a buyer. Sexuality has passed from her imagination to her blood.

Yet George and Lettie never act on their moment of revelation; their relationship remains unconsummated. The problem, for George especially, is largely passivity. A "fat and fleshy" flower bulb, a "blind" and "half-born" man, he is always disastrously inert where Lettie is concerned. Leslie Tempest succeeds where George fails, ultimately marrying Lettie, partly because he is actively demanding and desirous where George is paralyzed. George's will is as undeveloped as his consciousness.

Similarly Lettie suffers from passivity. Like many of Lawrence's heroines, her abilities seem incipient, dependent for deliverance on an energizing force, a male who can free her through the gift of Eros. Lettie does not act, she waits. But more than being unable, she is unwilling to act in favor of her suitor. The question arises whether Lettie's subsequent suffering stems from the denial of her momentary blood-feeling. And while the factors leading to her later unhappiness are complex, her hollow and desiccated marriage to Leslie suggests that George might have provided a preferable alternative. The process by which she rejects the impecunious farmer and accepts the wealthy manufacturer is, therefore, of importance.

Lawrence's typical patterns of symbolic action, in their spontaneous germination, are found throughout *The White Peacock*. Lettie asserts her independence in such a passage. (She thereby moves closer to Leslie; he never threatens her independence because he never deeply touches her.) The relevant scene, filled with implicative action, opens with George, Leslie, and Cyril chasing after a rabbit. Each of the men is revealed by his performance. George acts swiftly, directly, untroubled by the hesitations that hamper the other, more self-conscious, men. "The little wretch was hard pressed; George rushed upon it. It darted into some fallen corn, but he had seen it, and had fallen on it. In an instant he was up again, and the little creature was dangling from his hand" (p. 65). We observe that George can throw himself into a violent physical experience, even when it contains an element of killing. Lawrence always admired this untrammeled capacity for purely physical activity with its suggestion of unity between mind and body. Such a capacity becomes a prerequisite to the sexual redemption Lawrence formulates in his later work. George serves here, as in many other places, as a harbinger of the later "dark men." Contrarily, Lawrence's autobiographical figures are divided from their own instinctive impulses.[9] Cyril fails with the rabbit because his inhibitions interrupt a total involvement with the experience. "If I could have let myself fall on it I could have caught it, but this was impossible to me, and I merely prevented its dashing to the hole into safety" (p. 65). Leslie, too, is placed by his handling of the rabbit. The young industrialist catches the animal only after George's father gives it a blow on the head. "It was all lame. Leslie was upon it in a moment, and he almost pulled its head off in his excitement to kill it" (p. 66). Leslie's unnecessary brutality derives from weakness, and connects him to a later character who shares many of his qualities: Gerald Crich of *Women In Love*. Leslie is a type similar to Cyril, but with the serious difference that he compensates for his instinctual shortcomings with violence and the gratuitous exercising of the will.

Lawrence's specific hierarchy of values, therefore, and the technique of symbolic action that breathes life into his value-scale, were already fairly well conceived by the time he wrote *The White Peacock*. This is one of the reasons that *The White Peacock*, for all its immature unevenness, is a much better novel than is generally recognized.[10]

As after the related cat-drowning incident, Lettie is disturbed by the rabbit scene; she recoils from a show of male destructive power: "Don't you think it's brutal . . . isn't it degrading and mean to run the poor little thing down?" she asks George. She is doubly nonplussed because, earlier, she had been unable to conceal her admiration for him. "Firmly planted, he swung with a beautiful rhythm from the waist. On the hip of his belted breeches hung the scythe-stone; his shirt, faded almost white, was torn just above the belt, and showed the muscles of his back playing like lights upon the white sand of a brook. There was something exceedingly attractive in the rhythmic body. . . . 'You are picturesque,' she said, a trifle awkwardly. 'Quite fit for an Idyll' " (p. 63). George, as captured in Lawrence's verbal landscape painting, reminds her of the Greiffenhagen print, and, undoubtedly, of the intense, heady attraction they shared over it.

Lettie's dilemma is based on the painfully contradictory nature of her feelings for George: she desires his vitality as she fears its disintegrative potential. (To her discredit, she fails to recognize the more contemptible brutality in Leslie.) It is the ambiguity about George's physical force that troubles her. The same power that promises sexual fulfillment threatens dense insensitivity and something approaching physical brutality. George's force suggests satisfaction and obliteration at once, and to Lettie's mind the one cannot be had without the other.

Lettie's solution is to assert herself against George—to best his vitality, not to benefit from it. This assertion occurs under the rising of the moon.[11] Moon is the most central and significant of the various cosmic or natural symbols Lawrence uses consistently as analogues for inner states of being. The moon is associated—and Lawrence makes creative use of tradition here—with independent, inviolable feminine being. Thus, in *Sons and Lovers*, the moon restores Gertrude Morel to peaceful self-possession after she suffers from a particularly violent bout of her husband's drunkenness. In the "Moony" chapter of *Women In Love* Birkin shatters the reflection of the moon in a pond, emblematically destroying the dimension of Ursula—part virginal Diana, part uncontrollable Cybele—that is inaccessible to his maleness. Accordingly, the appearance of the moon in *The White Peacock* coincides with a depiction of strong, self-sufficient femininity; the moon engenders a feeling of defiance and excitement in Lettie: "Where the sky was pale in the east over the rim of the wood came the forehead of the yellow moon. We stood and watched in silence. Then, as the great disc, nearly full, lifted and looked straight upon us, we were washed off our feet in a vague sea of moonlight. We stood with the light like water on our faces. Lettie was glad, a little bit exalted" (p. 70). Lettie's ensuing actions demonstrate more than a "little" exaltation. Breaking "free" of Leslie, who had been about to propose marriage and "bind" her, she gives herself over to independence and impulse. She expresses her mood in wild dancing, in the course of which she wears out the easily fatigued Cyril, and dismays the elegant Leslie by her unabandoned actions. Only George can match her energy, and the two now meet in an encounter whose sexual connotations are obvious: "It was a tremendous, irresistible dancing. . . . At the end, he looked big, erect, nerved with triumph, and she was exhilarated like a Bacchante" (p. 72).

Yet this moment of contact causes no rapprochement between Lettie and George. On the contrary, subsequent to this scene her alliance with Leslie becomes more of an accepted fact. Her abandon under the moon thus appears as purely self-assertive, containing no promise of intimacy or warmth for the men who pursue her. The female force Lettie feels during the moonlit evening leads to no union with a man, but rather expresses superiority and separateness. She shows herself able to subsume George's energy and verve into her own moods and then returns to a less demanding relationship. In the end she is unapprehended and untouched.

Women in Lawrence's fiction are frequently depicted in this mood of cruel independence—a mood often accompanied by the appearance of the moon. This moon-state is associated with a kind of femininity that men can never approach, that never gives reassurance or satisfaction. The mood is oppressive to the men who suffer from it but also victimizes the women who experience it. Thus the Lawrence women often endure a strength-in-isolation nearly as painful as the weakness-in-disintegration undergone by Lawrence's men.

It begins to be clear that there are negative forces in Lettie precluding her from a challenging sexual relationship. Her strength is paradoxially passive, for she is only forceful enough to achieve isolation and unable to go beyond herself to a fruitful connection. This corresponds to a paradox in George's character, for despite his heavy power he is unable to act effectively to obtain an object he strongly desires. In a third paradox, the weak Leslie courts Lettie with an aggressive persistence that succeeds in winning her. The interrelationship of weakness and strength in the three characters is organic and inseparable, and we feel that the unhappiness they incur is based on the deeply flawed beings all of them show.

Yet after she rejects George the teller attempts to place all of the blame on Lettie and she appears in a progressively negative light. She decides to marry Leslie but seems uncertain about her decision and maddens him with her willful moodiness; she continues to play ambiguously with her rejected suitor. When Lettie offers George an apple, that richly emblematic fruit, he is wary of its ancient symbolism. " 'Mother,' he said, comically, as if jesting. 'She is offering me the apple like Eve.' Like a flash, she snatched the apple from him, hid it in her skirts a moment, looking at him with dilated eyes, and then she flung it at the fire" (p. 114).

This is one of many references (some of them found in chapter-titles) connecting Lettie to Eve. In light of this imagery, the knowledge Lettie offers George is disruptive and disunifying: a suggestion strongly reinforced by George's gradual ruination that corresponds to his dislocation from his pastoral environment. In this view, Lettie's enlightening influence is apportioned destructively: she gives George enough awareness to disorient him, but not enough to stabilize him. George himself implies this when he claims that, having "awakened" him, Lettie is now under an obligation: "you start me off—then leave me at a loose end. What am I going to do?" The assumption is that Lettie is now responsible for his life.

The difficulty with references identifying Lettie and Eve is that they radically simplify Lettie's character. Certainly Lettie is painfully elusive; but there is an enormous difference between a woman who wounds men because, being integral and inviolate, she remains frustratingly apart and a woman who deliberately tempts men out of innocence and leads them to ruin. In *The White Peacock* (as in *The Trespasser*) the teller *confuses* the two kinds of feminine destructiveness; the one is profound and irrevocable, occurring beneath the conscious mind and deliberate will, the other is a comparatively superficial conscious malevolence.

Also omitted from the Lettie-as-Eve equation are the major revelations of the interaction between Lettie and George: that her self-assertion is at least partially a form of self-protection, and that, finally, *he* is the potentially destructive one. Lettie, in sum, is no Eve, and figurative language describing her as such is not only unilluminating—it is misleading.

Leslie's very emotional weaknesses attract her. He is childish and selfish, a "Narcissus"; he is also mechanically oriented, "rattling" his noisy automobile between the trees of Nethermere valley. (Leslie, like Gerald Crich, uses the machine to compensate for inner devitalization.) Lettie chooses the unformidable Leslie because she assumes he will leave her free. Their relationship, in fact, often seems more like that of a mother and child than that of a man and a woman. Lettie eventually prefers the dominating sentimentality of the maternal role to the accommodating emotions required of a mutual relationship between two adults. But her preference is destructive, as Lawrence shows in an oblique, delicate passage. At the end of a well-constructed chapter, "The Irony of Inspired Moments" (during which George, Leslie and Lettie all have some of their dearest expectations smashed), circumstances allow the engaged couple to spend a night together. Both are excited at the prospect: "They looked at each other with wide, smiling eyes—like children on the brink of a stolen pleasure." But, without a direct word, Lawrence demonstrates that the first sexual experience of Lettie and Leslie is a disaster. The reader is not allowed a glimpse of the couple until the morning after, and then Lettie is in a dark mood though Leslie is oblivious of any deeper problem. He returns unexpectedly after an unhappy leave-taking.

> "I don't see why—why it should make trouble between us, Lettie," he faltered. She made a swift gesture of repulsion, whereupon, catching sight of her hand, she hid it swiftly against her skirt again.
> "You make my hands—my very hands disclaim me," she struggled to say.
> He looked at her clenched fist pressed against the folds of her dress.
> "But—," he began, much troubled.
> "I tell you, I can't bear the sight of my own hands," she said, in low, passionate tones. (Pp. 204–5)

Lettie's hands are an emblem of the flesh that has betrayed her (partly because she has betrayed it). The life of the hands, of touch, of tactile pleasures, is now a source of pain to her. Not that the failure was foredoomed by any sexual incapacity in Lettie. Both the intense anticipation of the previous evening and the passionate moments with George make that explanation doubtful. More likely that the problem is Lettie's choice of a man who is sexually repugnant to her. She has made secondary matters primary, and now looks ahead to a life that is empty and frustrating at its hidden core.

In the final third of *The White Peacock*, Lettie becomes an entirely negative character. In general, the novel grows steadily more amorphous and its literary quality gradually deteriorates. In the last section painfully awkward time-shifts combine with maladroit narrational technique to make the always episodic novel nearly disjointed. As Lawrence's writing gets weaker, he seems to forget his earlier painstakingly complex portrait of Lettie. Her transformation into an arrogant, castrating woman is jarring—and unconvincing. She flirts with George, domesticates Leslie and emasculates them both. In one striking passage Cyril describes her as the picture of pride and triumph, while Leslie humbles himself before her.

> Leslie knelt down at her feet. She shook the hood back from her head, and her ornaments sparkled in the moonlight. Her face with its whiteness and its shadows was full of fascination, and in their dark recesses her eyes thrilled George with hidden magic. She smiled at him along her cheeks while her husband crouched before her. . . . As she turned laughing to the two men, she let her cloak slide over her white shoulder and fall with silk spendour of a peacock's gorgeous blue over the arm of the large settee. There she stood, with her white hand upon the peacock of her cloak, where it tumbled against her dull orange dress. She knew her own splendour, and she drew up her throat laughing and brilliant with triumph. . . .
> "Won't you take off my shoes, darling?" she said, sinking among the cushions of the settee. Leslie kneeled again before her. (Pp. 292–93)

The excerpt, marred by the forced tone that infuses it, portrays Lettie as a dangerous temptress unattractive in the garish stylization of her seductiveness. Furthermore, the use of the word "peacock" specifically links her to the novel's central image: the white peacock. The image is worth examining because most critics have taken it as the repository of the book's meaning and because Lawrence is careful to give the symbol centrality.

The white peacock image is introduced and developed by Annable. Annable's experiences, and the code he derives from them, provide a theoretical framework for the events of *The White Peacock*, a simplifying rationale, complete with victim and villain, for the misfortunes of the novel's male characters. The gamekeeper himself is an early version of a certain type of Lawrencian character: the deliberate primitive who chooses the life of the instincts and repudiates the surrounding culture. He shares many of George's qualities, but what is instinctive in George is brought to articulate understanding in Annable; he can thus live according to his principles and avoid George's confused self-division. Deliberate primitiveness is only one of many characteristics Annable shares with Oliver Mellors, the equally philosophical gamekeeper in *Lady Chatterley's Lover*.

Annable is both a vitalist, who believes in the fundamental healthiness of man's natural being, and a nihilist, who entirely rejects the culture man superimposes on his environment. His credo is "be a good animal," (one explanation for his peculiar name is that it rhymes with "animal") and, accordingly, he ignores his docilely enduring wife and lets his children run wild. At the same time he feels the civilization he disowns is "the painted fungus of rottenness. He hated any sign of culture. . . . When he thought, he reflected on the decay of mankind—the decline of the human race into folly, and weakness and rottenness." The gamekeeper himself represents a kind of antidote to the "rottenness."

Critics have generally admired Annable, either because of his intrinsic vividness: "Annable . . . reduces all the other characters to shadows,"[12] or because of his importance as a theoretical forerunner: "[Annable] is the first bearer of the Laurentian philosophy."[13] Whatever the truth of these judgments, and the first is patently untrue, while the second badly requires elucidation, Annable's worldview does little justice to the complexities of *The White Peacock*. He, and not Lawrence, really is a ranting misogynist, but to accept his theories as the whole meaning of the novel is to fall into the fallacy that has trapped some of its critics.

Cyril's attitude toward the woodland anarchist is admiring, but the portrait presented to the reader is considerably more equivocal. In his function as gamepreserver for the impoverished but landowning squire whose rabbits ravage the local farms, Annable takes the side of privilege in the classwar. Moreover, in the important scene where the arch-symbol of the novel is introduced, Annable is too hostile in his attitude to be compelling in his judgment. The bird makes its foreboding appearance in a gloomy abandoned churchyard on a spring evening.

> A peacock, startled from the back premises of the Hall, came flapping up the terraces to the churchyard. Then a heavy footstep crossed the flags. It was the keeper. . . . The peacock flapped beyond me, on to the neck of an old bowed angel, rough and dark, an angel which had long ceased sorrowing for the lost Lucy and had died also. The bird bent its voluptuous neck and peered about. Then it lifted up its head and yelled. The sound tore the dark sanctuary of twilight. The old grey grass seemed to stir, and I could fancy the smothered primroses and violets beneath it waking and gasping for fear.
>
> ....
>
> Again the bird lifted its crested head and gave a cry, at the same time turning awkwardly on its ugly legs, so that it showed us the full

wealth of its tail glimmering like a stream of coloured stars over the
sunken face of the angel.

"The proud fool!—look at it! Perched on an angel, too, as if it were a
pedestal for vanity. That's the soul of a woman—or it's the devil."

[Annable] was silent for a time, and we watched the great bird
moving uneasily before us in the twilight.

"That's the very soul of a lady," he said, "the very, very soul. Damn
the thing, to perch on that old angel. I should like to wring its neck."

Again the bird screamed, and shifted awkwardly on its legs; it
seemed to stretch its beak at us in derision. Annable picked up a
piece of sod and flunt it at the bird, saying:

"Get out, you screeching devil! God!" he laughed. "There must be
plenty of hearts twisting under here,"—and he stamped on a grave,
"when they hear that row."

He kicked another sod from a grave and threw it at the big bird. The
peacock flapped away, over the tombs, down the terraces.

"Just look!" he said, "the miserable brute has dirtied that angel. A
woman to the end, I tell you, all vanity and screech and defilement."
(Pp. 174–75)

Shortly thereafter Annable clearly connects this image to the
details of his own life; in his youth he had been a suffering angel,
maltreated by his own peacock. He, a proud, physical creature
("You don't know what it is to have the pride of a body like mine,"
he says to the duly impressed Cyril) becomes involved with a
woman who lives according to her imagination instead of her
instincts. She sleeps with him because she was taught to do so in a
"sloppy French novel" (she is a fictional descendent of Madame
Bovary). Then she tires of him, begins to get "souly," and, in a
clear parallel with Lettie's mocking of George, refers to him as "her
animal—*son animal—son boeuf*." Unlike George Annable refuses
to accept his humiliation. He realizes that the society his wife
represents is corrupt, and he withdraws into the sanctuary of the
natural world. Thus Annable verbalizes what the increasingly
negative portrait of women in *The White Peacock* suggests: that
women direct de-energizing forces at the vitality in men. At the end
of the conversation Annable mitigates his antagonism somewhat:
" 'I suppose,' he said, 'it wasn't all her fault.' 'A white peacock, we
will say,' I suggested." But his basic attitude remains.

The peacock-sequence reduces the character of Lettie as it
contains a dual amplification of Annable: he is both an aggressive
recusant and a tragic victim of his manipulating "Lady Crystabel."

Hence, while Cyril considers him powerful, Annable describes himself as a man in a state of deterioration. Yet, as in George's case, we cannot blame this deterioration primarily on the woman who resists him. To do so is to entirely deny self-responsibility. And short of reversing our ideas about the influence one human being legitimately has over another, we must accept that *the disintegrative tendency is in the destroyed men themselves*. The tellers of *The White Peacock* avoid this male inner friability, compensating for the disintegrative quality with exaggerated, Romantic inflations of George and Annable. (In Annable's case, this constitutes a self-inflation.) The pastoral fallacy is committed when the tellers of the tale turn evasion and regression into natural, vital innocence.

But if the novel's commentators see Annable as a martyr, the tale places his sufferings in a different light. Annable's self-ironic comments may be meant to evidence the degree to which he has been abused, but they also articulate his inability to endure and maintain himself: "I'm like a good house, built and finished, and left to tumble down again with nobody to live in it" (p. 175). Placed against his story, this suggests that without Lady Crystabel there is no one to uphold him, and that apart from her he is "nobody." Again, the bleak view he takes of his present existence implies that his "good animal" existence, far from being an ideal, is something for which he had to settle; and extending the implication further we realize that for a fuller life he was dependent on Lady Crystabel. Annable's death—he is caught in a rock-slide—thereby becomes the final evidence of his inability to establish and sustain a viable life for himself. For he is a man of gloom and recklessness who almost invites death from the nature in which he is figuratively, and then literally, immersed.

Annable is self-pitying, as well as self-congratulating—both these emotions make the degree of his objective understanding suspect. Because of his self-serving bias, his interpretation of the bird's defecating on the angel's head is so grossly, not to say humorously, obvious and prejudiced, so unequivocal in the relative moral positions it ascribes to males and females, that the image is virtually stripped of any suggestive implications.

This is not to say that the peacock-symbol fails in and of itself. It is not legitimate to make a value judgment of a symbol *per se*. The symbol has a potentially infinite range of reference, but its meaning is shaped and formed by context. The success of the contextual setting an artist creates for his symbolic image can be estimated. If the context narrows the area of influence, the symbol will have an impoverished quality as well.[14] Hence a successful symbol must make tangible a substantial range of abstractions: the realized literary symbol has a setting that establishes adequate moral and thematic complexity. This is especially so with a key emblem, one at the core of a work's meaning. Lawrence gives the peacock contextual centrality, like that of the insect in "The Metamorphosis" or the white whale in *Moby-Dick*, by taking his title from it (he was originally planning to call the novel *Nethermere*), and surrounding the image with portent. But while the symbols of Kafka and Melville have multiple reverberations that give their works both greater unity and greater complexity, Lawrence's peacock image reduced his novel to its simplest level. Because of Annable's slanted elucidation, the figure is unworthy of the narrative.

The richness of *The White Peacock*, much of which resides in Lawrence's subtle depiction of the conflicts within Lettie, is denied in the Annable passages. Annable adds to the reworkings of the myth-of-Eden elements in this novel. In his version, Adam finds his way back to the Garden (Nethermere) after he realizes that Eve is a paradise-destroyer. Lettie, like Lady Crystabel, is in the line of destructive females represented by the peacock—an image borrowed from the iconography of the Beardsleyan nineties.[15]

To understand the marked division between what is told and what is shown in *The White Peacock* it is necessary to examine Cyril's psychology: his radically subjective way of perceiving the world. Cyril is engaged throughout on a quest—a quest vague and amorphous in its manifestations, but specific and precise in its source. Since he tells the story, this search pervasively colors the narrative.

Cyril grows up without a father, his youth having been dominated by his mother and sister. Early in the novel Cyril and his mother are called to the bedside of the dying father. (He had not been seen since Cyril's early childhood.) They arrive to find the man dead,[16] and, confronting his fatherlessness, Cyril receives a grievous shock: "I felt the great wild pity, and a sense of terror, and a sense of horror, and a sense of awful littleness and loneliness among a great empty space. I felt beyond myself as if I were a mere fleck drifting unconsciously through the dark" (p. 52). The experience has a shattering effect on his ontological integrity (the death of a parent has similar effects on Paul Morel and Gerald Crich), and this feeling of disconnection, of being adrift among nothingness, is what Cyril tries to assuage when he searches for substitutes for paternal stability and reassurance.

It is a comparatively simple psychological step from the vacuum left by the absence of a father to an exaggerated admiration for those two dark men of *The White Peacock:* Annable and George. The glorification takes several forms. First, the overmothered Cyril reveres strong masculinity in a way that is not so much homosexual as compensatory. "He held out his arm to me and bade me try the muscle," says Cyril, describing Annable: "I was startled. The hard flesh almost filled the sleeve." Second, Cyril is directly in search of a surrogate father:[17] "He treated me as an affectionate father treats a delicate son"; this, again, describes Annable. Thirdly, never having dealt with the reality of his father, Cyril overvalues the "masculine" qualities—sensuality, irresponsibility, living outside the confines of the female-dominated culture— associated with the elder Beardsall.

As he idealizes natural men, so he idealizes nature itself. Cyril's frequent recourse to the pathetic fallacy is a species of emotional legerdemain whereby an indifferent cosmos is converted into a benevolent nature. This self-deception occurs when the need for some kind of solace dominates Cyril's reason and objectivity. At such times he sentimentalizes the pastoral tranquillity of Nethermere—scene of his early, assuaging experiences—and makes nature itself into a paternal force. "The hills of Nethermere had been my walls, and the sky of Nethermere my roof overhead. It seemed almost as if, at home, I might lift my hand to the ceiling of the valley, and touch my own beloved sky, whose familiar clouds came again and again to visit me, whose stars were constant to me, born when I was born, whose sun had been all my father to me" (p. 298).

Males, specifically George and Annable, are the human component of the idyll, while women, bearers of enlightenment and culture, represent the disillusioning forces of reality. For Cyril, closeness to George is closeness to nature; the dual intimacy fills him with a sense of pleasure and peace. When, after swimming, Cyril and George have a homoerotic encounter, they briefly enjoy natural innocence.

> We stood and looked at each other as we rubbed ourselves dry. He was well proportioned, and naturally of handsome physique, heavily limbed. He laughed at me, telling me I was like one of Aubrey Beardsley's long, lean ugly fellows. I referred him to many classic examples of slenderness, declaring myself more exquisite than his grossness, which amused him.
>
> But I had to give in, and bow to him, and he took on an indulgent, gentle manner. I laughed and submitted. For he knew not I admired the noble, white fruitfulness of his form. As I watched him, he stood in white relief against the mass of green. He polished his arm, holding it out straight and solid; he rubbed his hair into curls, while I watched the deep muscles of his shoulders, and the bands stand out in his neck as he held it firm; I remembered the story of Annable.
>
> He saw I had forgotten to continue my rubbing, and laughing he took hold of me and began to rub me briskly, as if I were a child, or rather, a woman he loved and did not fear. I left myself quite limply in his hands, and to get a better grip of me, he put his arm round me and pressed me against him, and the sweetness of the touch of our naked bodies one against the other was superb. It satisfied in some measure the vague, indecipherable yearning of my soul; and it was the same with him. When he had rubbed me all warm, he let me go, and we looked at each other with eyes of still laughter, and our love was perfect for a moment, more perfect than any love I have known since, either for man or woman.
>
> We went together down to the fields. . . . The cool, moist fragrance of the morning, the intentional stillness of everything, of the tall bluish trees, of the wet, frank flowers, of the trustful moths folded and unfolded in the fallen swaths, was a perfect medium of sympathy. The horses moved with a still dignity, obeying his commands. (Pp. 257–58)

The satisfaction of a strong homoerotic impulse simultaneously satisfies Cyril's "vague, indecipherable yearnings." This connection perhaps makes his feelings less mystifying, for union with a male figure compensates for a lost father. Both men are relieved to escape the "fear" associated with women, and the harmony emanating from the scene thus depends in no small degree on the fact that women are absent from it. (Emily briefly appears, but is, significantly, chased away before the men's intimacy properly begins.) Not only are women banished from the scene, but all consciousness of the troubling world is closed out of this unifying experience. As Cyril indicates, his encounter with George not only provides a less disturbing alternative to the man-woman relationship but offers a replacement for the father-child connection. Putting himself into George's authoritative hands, Cyril finds relief and escape for his divided spirit.

Nature plays a parallel role in the passage. United with George Cyril also moves toward a pastoral unity, a "sympathy" between inner and outer worlds that leads to contentment of mind and soul. George and nature are inextricably interconnected in Cyril's perceptions: the two assuage Cyril's sufferings by lessening the pain of consciousness and memory, and creating a healing sense of enfoldment and merger. Annable is recalled in this affirmative scene; we remember that he, too, assuages and compensates Cyril, and that an intimate, mutually responsive connection to nature is also attributed to him. Hence Annable's funeral, described with lush pervasive pathos, betrays many of the features of the pastoral elegy.[18] During the procession, Cyril finds his grief transfused into the surrounding world as nature mourns the loss of one of its own: "The bearers lift up the [coffin] again, and the elm-boughs rattle along the hollow white wood, and the pitiful red clusters of elm-flowers sweep along it as if they whispered in sympathy—'We are so sorry, so sorry—'; always the compassionate buds in their fullness of life bend down to comfort the dark man shut up there" (p. 184).

The state of oneness Cyril searches for in nature and the men he associates with it, despite fleeting gratifications, must finally be viewed as a species of wish-fulfillment. All the characters in *The White Peacock* have been affected by education and industrialism, and have accordingly lost their Eden; once out of the state of innocence their longing for pastoral unity can only lead to nostalgia and self-deceiving fantasy. George, Annable, and Cyril have all come too far to return.

Jessie Chambers suggests another, final, reason for the narrator's bias in *The White Peacock*. Cyril, she claims, is not the only Lawrence-persona in the novel: "Cyril and Lettie are each aspects of Lawrence."[19] This helps explain the disappointingly pallid characterization of Cyril—remarkable considering that he is an autobiographical persona in a first novel—and implies that at this point in his career Lawrence could fictionally project himself more convincingly as a woman than as a man. In the light of Chambers' speculation, the parts of *The White Peacock* that elevate George and Annable at the expense of Lettie appear to express Lawrence's rejection of his own femininity.

Though the tellers of the tale, Cyril and Annable, slant *The White Peacock* in various ways, the integrity of the narrative reasserts itself even in the inferior closing chapters. Whatever Cyril's personal feelings, he sees that George's marriage to a local bar-girl, Meg, is a failure. George decides on the match because the simple girl admires him, and there is physical passion between them. He now believes that "the best part of love is being made much of," and he turns from Lettie's harshly critical appraisals with relief. The earthy George has a suitable partner at last and all should go well for him; but the marriage ends in a shambles.

We do, indeed, hear Cyril's characteristically misogynist tone in some of his later descriptions of Meg. She begins as a confused and ignorant girl but abruptly turns into a church-going matron, full of deracinating Christian ideals, and becomes an oppressive presence to her now-degenerating husband. Cyril labors to place Meg in the category of destructive females. He describes her as domineering in a passage employing the ornithological imagery that, for some obscure reason, he associates with female tyranny. In Meg's case, presumably because it would be incongruous to link the lower-class girl with the most gorgeous of birds, the white peacock is replaced, rather absurdly, by a green ostrich: "Meg had grown stouter, and there was a certain immovable confidence in her. She was authoritative, amiable, calm. She wore a hardsome dress of dark green, and a toque with opulent ostrich feathers. As she moved about the room she seemed to dominate everything, particularly her husband, who sat ruffled and dejected, his waistcoast hanging loose over his shirt" (p. 353). Yet the most that can fairly be said against Meg, who within the action of the novel is neither prudish nor emasculating, is that she grasps for middle-class respectability in a stifling way.

But George begins the marriage by genuinely undermining Meg. The blind greediness Lettie always feared infuses George's treatment of his bride-to-be. He unexpectedly thrusts a marriage license upon her and insists on having the ceremony on the same day. It is only Meg's grandmother, an old crone whose rural dialect intensifies the Hardyesque melodrama of the scene, who calls him to order: "Well, tha'rt a nice'st un, I must say! What's want goin' in this pig-in-a-poke fashion for? This is a nice shabby trick to serve on a body! What does ta mean by it?" (p. 277). The old woman will not allow Meg to cover this crude treatment with a flimsy veneer of dignity. Reaching up from her sickbed, she knocks Meg's sadly respectable "hat with its large silk roses" askew. (Because of George's insistent haste, wearing the hat is one of the few gestures Meg is able to make in preparation for her own wedding.) The scene shows George beginning the marriage badly—and nothing indicates that he later changes his fundamental disregard for Meg. Symbolic action therefore demonstrates that Lettie's hesitations with George were finally justified. The insensitivity with which he hurries Meg, and the blind selfishness he displays throughout the incident, recall the qualities he manifested in the introductory bees-scene.

At the novel's conclusion George becomes an alcoholic; now doubly benighted, he alternates in his behavior between helplessness and violence. His sister, Emily, has now married, and he is sent off to stay with her. Though as an oversensitive adolescent Emily had once disturbed Cyril with her sheer vulnerability, he now views her, too, as a domineering and confident woman. Emily's husband, Tom Renshaw, a simple and healthy farmer, voluntarily bows to her authority. "I watched the tall, square-shouldered man learning with deference and tenderness towards his wife as she walked clearly at his side. She was the mistress, quiet and self-assured, he her rejoiced husband and servant" (p. 366). In this environment George is treated with contemptuous tolerance. Cyril, coming to visit, is shocked and saddened by the condition of his old friend: "His arms were thin, and he had bellied, and was bowed and unsightly." Amid the rustic tranquillity of Emily's home Cyril is reminded of the early days in Nethermere. Watching the farmers at work, Cyril believes he realizes how George's disintegration could have been avoided. George should never have left the unified life of Nethermere; alienation from his pastoral roots has caused his tragedy.

In the stackyard, the summer's splendid monuments of wheat and grass were reared in gold and grey. The wheat was littered brightly round the rising stack. The loaded wagon clanked slowly up the incline, drew near, and rode like a ship at anchor against the scotches, brushing the stack with a crisp, sharp sound. Tom climbed the ladder and stood a moment there against the sky, amid the brightness and fragrance of the gold corn, and waved his arm to his wife who was passing in the shadow of the building. Then Arthur began to lift the sheaves to the stack, and the two men worked in an exquisite, subtle rhythm, their white sleeves and their dark heads gleaming, moving against the mild sky and the corn. The silence was broken only by the occasional lurch of the body of the wagon, as the teamer stepped to the front, or again to the rear of the load. Occasionally I could catch the blue glitter of the prongs of the forks. Tom, now lifted high above the small wagon load, called to his brother some question about the stack. The sound of his voice was strong and mellow.

I turned to George, who was also watching, and said:

"You ought to be like that." (P. 367)

The writing here, like much of the natural description in *The White Peacock*, is superlative. But Cyril's rhapsody to natural processes and labors creates a serious problem at the end of the novel. In the trajectory of George's development, unifying farm-labor takes us back to his beginning, to the unawakened self-involvement and near brutality he displays at the novel's opening. Unthinking unity between man and nature is envisioned as an ideal by the novel's narrator, yet when George actually partakes of such a state his condition is hardly idyllic. Inadvertently, Cyril suggests that regression is a solution for failure. Expressing his own psychological needs, Cyril offers Eden as a resolution for the wasted human potential in *The White Peacock*. Thus, though George fails to deal adequately with Lettie's challenges to him or, indeed, to develop a strong, resilient self, Cyril implies that the villain of the piece is the demand for consciousness and not George's inadequate response to it. Yet the problems raised by *The White Peacock* cannot be resolved by recourse to the old myth of pastoral perfection. As much great literature reminds us, the child-like sensibility that finds peaceful oblivion in an untroubled nature must progress to more complex moral and intellectual syntheses in the face of the actual world. The Bible, Milton, Blake, Wordsworth, each in a different way, insist on what the Lawrence of *The White Peacock* sometimes allows himself to forget: we cannot go back to the Garden.

Notes to Chapter 1

1. For a detailed discussion of the various functions of the persona-narrator see the chapter entitled "Telling as Showing: Dramatized Narrators, Reliable and Unreliable," in Wayne C. Booth, *The Rhetoric of Fiction* (Chicago: University of Chicago Press, 1961), pp. 211–40.

2. The evidence is that Lawrence would agree with my statement. Lawrence eventually tired of his narrator and regretted the existence of the character: "I will write the thing again, and stop up the mouth of Cyril—I will kick him out—I hate the fellow." *The Collected Letters of D. H. Lawrence,* ed. Harry T. Moore (London: William Heinemann, 1962), 1:25.

3. D. H. Lawrence, *The White Peacock* (1911; reprinted., Harmondsworth, Middlesex: Penguin Books, 1950), p. 41.

4. Michael Squires takes full note of the Nethermere/Eden parallel in his analysis of *The White Peacock:* "Eden was most certainly in Lawrence's mind when he wrote the novel. . . . In the final chapters of the novel, perhaps the most significantly repeated word is *exile*. The characters, except for Emily, feel that they have been expelled from their pastoral paradise. . . . The novel, though far more than mere allegory, nonetheless makes vivid use of the myth of the Fall." But when Squires describes the novel as an affirmation of the rustic ideal, he is uncritically allowing the teller to determine the meaning of the tale: "the novel is prorural and antiurban, even anticultural, in its denouement and conclusion." "Lawrence's *The White Peacock:* A Mutation of Pastoral," *Texas Studies in Literature and Language* 12, no. 2 (Summer 1970): 274–75, 272.

5. Writers who accept the antifeminist bias as fundamental to the novel's meaning include: Robert E. Gadjusek, "A Reading of *The White Peacock,*" in Harry T. Moore, ed., *A D. H. Lawrence Miscellany* (Carbondale, Ill.: Southern Illinois University Press, 1959), pp. 188–203; Keith Sagar, *The Art of D. H. Lawrence* (Cambridge: Cambridge University Press, 1966); Julian L. Moynahan, *The Deed of Life: The Novels and Tales of D. H. Lawrence* (Princeton, N.J. Princeton University Press, 1963); and Raney Stanford, "Thomas Hardy and Lawrence's *The White Peacock,*" *Modern Fiction Studies* 5 no. 1 (Spring 1959): 19–28. Gadjusek's article is notable for the high praise it lavishes on Lawrence's first novel. This can be understood as his exaggerated reaction to the underestimation of the work by most critics. But Gadjusek's attempts to give functional significance to nearly all of the novel's pretentious literary references are palpably labored.

6. W. J. Keith considers the bees' fate a foreshadowing of what George will suffer after he is forced out of his "shell" into consciousness. But this view, which is in accord with the male-as-victim approach to *The White Peacock,* is based on a logical flaw as it makes George, the literal perpetrator of destruction, its figurative object. "D. H. Lawrence's *The White Peacock:* An Essay in Criticism," *University of Toronto Quarterly* 37 (April 1968): 239.

7. The equation is a standard one, appearing all through Lawrence's writings, and particularly notable in his seminal essay, "Study of Thomas Hardy." The following is chosen from a great many possible examples: "In its own degree, the prickly sow-thistle I have just pulled up *is*, for the first time in all time. It is itself, a new thing. And most vividly it is itself in its yellow little disc of a flower: most vividly. In its flower it issues something to the world that never was issued before. Its like has been before, its exact equivalent never. And this richness of new being is richest in the flowering disc of my plant." *Phoenix: The Posthumous*

Papers of D. H. Lawrence, ed. Edward D. McDonald (1936; reprinted., New York: Viking Press, 1968), p. 402.

8. One of the very few critics to discern the force and complexity of Lettie's character is David Cavitch: "Through Cyril's filmy *Weltschmerz* only Lettie's powerful but misdirected self-assertiveness strikes a spark of convincing vitality for the reader." *D. H. Lawrence and The New World* (Oxford: Oxford University Press, 1969), p. 20.

9. For all of Lawrence's reservations toward him, Cyril is an autobiographical figure who dimly foreshadows that far more powerful character, Paul Morel in *Sons and Lovers*.

10. Many critics have agreed, explicitly or implicitly, with F. R. Leavis' pronouncement that *The White Peacock* is "painfully callow," and dismissed the book. *Lawrence the Novelist* (New York: Clarion, 1955), p. 19.

11. The moon-scene has been examined by Stanford, but his analysis of Lettie's conduct as a liberation by the "traditional, sentimental mask of moon" tells us little. "Thomas Hardy and Lawrence's *The White Peacock*," p. 22.

12. Sagar, p. 10.

13. Graham Hough, *The Dark Sun: A Study of D. H. Lawrence* (London: Duckworth, 1970), p. 30. Frank Kermode goes even further and calls Annable "the first recognizable Lawrencian character." But considering the fairly clear parallels between Leslie and Gerald Crich, Lettie and Gudrun Brangwen, Cyril and Paul Morel, Emily and Miriam Leivers, and George and Walter Morel, it would seem that Kermode refers to the intensity and nature of Annable's ideas rather than to the type of character he is. *Lawrence* (Fontanta/Collins, 1973), p. 14.

14. My discussion of symbolism is particularly indebted to Eliseo Vivas' notion of "The Constitutive Symbol" in *D. H. Lawrence: The Failure and the Triumph of Art* (Bloomington, Ind.: Indiana University Press, 1960), pp. 273–82. I am aware of a more general debt to Susanne K. Langer's *Philosophy in a New Key: A Study in the Symbolism of Reason, Rite and Art* (New York: Mentor, 1951), and William York Tindall's study *The Literary Symbol* (Bloomington, Ind.: Indiana University Press, 1955).

15. George H. Ford has pointed out that peacocks are connected, in some of Aubrey Beardsley's drawings, to the figure of "Salome, the prophet-slayer." *Double Measure: A Study of the Novels and Stories of D. H. Lawrence* (New York: W. W. Norton & Co., 1965), p. 54.

16. Hough speculates that killing off the elder Beardsall was Lawrence's way of banishing his own father from the novel: "Cyril Beardsall the narrator is, rather feebly, Lawrence himself as a youth. Beardsall was his mother's maiden name. Even in his nomenclature Lawrence wishes to deny the share of the father in his being, just as by a simple piece of wish-fulfillment, he removes him from the plot." *The Dark Sun*, p. 25.

17. Daleski makes the important point that George and Annable are "disguised father-figures." Daleski realizes that for Lawrence to remove his father from his first novel is no mechanically simple matter. The Lawrence-persona, Cyril, thus has a need to find men on whom he may project his frustrated but passionate filial emotions. *The Forked Flame* (Evanston, Ill.: Northwestern University Press, 1965), pp. 312–15. Lawrence, it is clear from *The White Peacock*, could not escape his vexed and intense feelings about his father, but could only displace them (a similar process occurs in *Sons and Lovers*).

18. Squires notes the elegaic tone Cyril uses in his description of Annable's funeral. "A Mutation of Pastoral," p. 273.

19. Edward Nehls, *D. H. Lawrence: A Composite Biography*, 3 vols. (Madison, Wis.: The

University of Wisconsin Press, 1957), 1:63. Mary Freeman finds more in common between Lawrence and Lettie than between Lawrence and Cyril. As evidence she makes the comparatively superficial point that Lettie's arguments against socialism (on pp. 335–36 of the novel) are precisely those of the youthful author. Taking this a step further, it might be fair to say that Lettie articulates Lawrence's strength and clarity of mind while Cyril is the expression of the author's pained, confused emotions. *D. H. Lawrence: A Basic Study of His Ideas* (Gainesville, Fla.: University of Florida Press, 1955), pp. 22, 27. Anais Nin locates another source for the superior characterization of Lettie; she points out Lawrence's "complete realization of the feelings of women." Lawrence demonstrates this ability in his—as Nin terms it—"androgynous writing." *D. H. Lawrence: An Unprofessional Study* (Denver, Colo.: Swallow Press, 1964), p. 57. Nin's point is supported by an early review of *The White Peacock* which considers the book "characteristic . . . of the modern fiction . . . written by the feminine hand." The review is reprinted in W. T. Andrews, ed., *Critics on D. H. Lawrence* (London: George Allen and Unwin, 1971), p. 14.

2

The Merger Fallacy: *The Trespasser*

In *The Trespasser* Lawrence's characteristic omniscient narrator replaces the mishandled first person narrator of *The White Peacock*.[1] Distinguishing the tale from the teller accordingly becomes more complex than it was in the earlier novel. Now instanced is a far more typical and difficult form of the problem: for we must make the essential separation when *both* elements are introduced by the same omniscient narrative voice. We move toward resolving the issue by realizing that commentary is subsidiary to symbol and incident, and that the teller betrays himself by making editorial remarks that *contradict* rendered events and the significance arising naturally from those events.

The teller's commentary therefore creates an ideological and aesthetic discordance. In Lawrence's first two novels the teller introduces an attitude that is in conflict with the larger meanings of the work, and that is also self-contradictory, revealing itself as an ideal masking a disorder. The false or misleading conception is based on a romantic fallacy, a simplified and sentimental vision of man's ideal fate. The fallacy is developed by commentary, but symbolic action belies this commentary and shows the weakness underlying the glorification. Hence the narrator of *The White Peacock* establishes peaceful harmony between man and nature as an ultimate value, while the narrative demonstrates the evasion of conscious life-responsibility that escape into pastoral unity involves. In *The Trespasser* a related romantic notion motivates the male protagonist Siegmund.[2] He is obsessed throughout by an ecstatic merger-vision, a dream of unifying with his environment by melting into nature and removing the painful division between inner world and outer to make subject and object one. (The merger fallacy differs from the pastoral fallacy in that it concerns unification instead of unity and replaces peace with ecstasy.) Descriptions of Siegmund's merger-ecstasies flaw the novel with their overcharged grandiloquence.[3] One problem is that Lawrence handles the theme with heavy portentousness, indicative of a perhaps regrettable Wagnerian influence.[4] But the matter goes beyond exterior influences.

The ecstasy-prose is overripe and turgid because it is a discordant interpolation, demanding conclusions that the novel itself refuses to support. In general, problems of style in fiction cannot be separated from problems of conception any more than technical ineffectiveness can be divorced from failure of insight. In the case of *The Trespasser*, overwriting compensates for lack of control; unable to find the correct distance from Siegmund, the teller undertakes to overwhelm the reader into sympathy for his protagonist irrespective of what the character reveals about himself. (Cyril's pastoral prose, beautiful as it often is, also frequently appears exaggerated, indicative of a sentimental nature worship; as in *The Trespasser*, a conceptual fallacy surfaces in stylistic excess, and the excess occurs when the teller attempts to simplify the novel's complex issues.)

Since tale and teller come into direct conflict in Lawrence's second novel, the omniscient narrator must simultaneously move in opposite directions. Descriptions of Siegmund's experiences in nature are perceptibly admiring; there is a sympathy for his will to lose himself in the universe, and a vision of Siegmund as a man of soaring, transcendent soul. Yet the tale reverses this authorial approval of Siegmund and points the other way, showing that his nature-ecstasties are closer to disintegration than transcendence. His loss of the self in nature is revealed as part of a death-movement. Beginning with a naive acceptance of romantic myth, *The Trespasser* ends as a profound critique of the self-destructiveness inherent in certain forms of romanticism.

Helena, the female protagonist, is also presented in a contradictory manner. Her character and situation recall *The White Peacock*'s Lettie Beardsall, just as Siegmund reminds us of George Saxton. As in the earlier novel, the man is sometimes placed in the role of victim, his intense vitality sacrificed to the woman's rejection—the woman is put in a correspondingly oppressive position. But, and again the parallel with *The White Peacock* is striking, Helena cannot be limited to the role of villainness: if the teller charges her with being destructively emasculating, the tale shows her to be justifiably self-protecting. Indeed, her actions show that on the deepest levels of life-capacity and strength-of-being Helena is a far more vital character than Siegmund.[5] This is not to deny Helena's sexual coldness: her frigidity is an undeniable facet of her personality. Hence the plausibility of regarding Siegmund as a passionate man indirectly destroyed by Helena's repulses. Most critics of *The Trespasser*, accordingly, sympathize with Siegmund's sufferings and view the novel as the story of his victimization.[6]

But if tale and teller concur about Helena's frigidity, only the teller depicts her as being irreparably so. The incidents which actually compose the relationship between Siegmund and Helena tell a different story. Their encounters show Helena encouraging Siegmund out of genuine feeling, mitigated by her sexual coldness. The holiday they take together gives her an insight into the life of the body and she works tentatively to overcome her obstacles to passion. Furthermore, far from being cruelly emasculating, she shields herself from Siegmund's intensity because she intuits its annihilating quality. Bearing out her fears, her gradual movement toward increased human and sexual responsiveness is shattered by the unexpected suicide of Siegmund—a man doomed by his overweening needs.

The tale of the novel is figured forth by events; these give us a dynamic Helena, a character who develops and changes, and a Siegmund whose life follows a repetitive, unchanging pattern. Combining with action, intrinsic symbolism furthers the tale: the novel's cosmic symbolism, particularly the two key-images of sun and mist, is especially significant. The static, irredeemably frigid Helena and the heroic Siegmund are created by the narrator's commentary. Additional simplifying commentary is contributed by a *commentator*, a figure whose function is to introduce didactic editorial matter into the narrative. Hampson, a minor character who is analogous to Annable in *The White Peacock*, makes remarks that reverse the tale's inherent meanings.

The novel opens after Siegmund's death (the main action takes place in an extended flashback) in Helena's gloomy apartment. She is entertaining Cecil Byrne, her current suitor. The reason for the general mournfulness is the recent death of Siegmund. Now that Siegmund, her violin teacher before becoming her lover, is dead, Helena plays her instrument with its mute on, for the full force of the music would be "unendurable." Outstanding among the room's decorations is "a small soapstone Buddha . . . locked in his renunciation."[7] The rooms, with their "bare wall-spaces of dark green" and "scanty furniture" give assurance of "unwelcome." The funereal quality of the flat is intensified by the morbid presence of Louisa, a girl slavishly dedicated to Helena (the friendship has an unhealthy quality, and does not receive the approval that Lawrence gives to various homoerotic relationships in his work). Intent on her mourning, Helena has turned her home into a monastic retreat: "The room was very quiet, silent even of the ticking of a clock. Outside, the traffic swept by, and feet spattered along the pavement. But this vulgar storm of life seemed shut out of Helena's room, that remained indifferent, like a church" (p. 8). Cecil makes an attempt to revitalize her but his remarks are inane in the extreme: "After all . . . if you're alive you've got to live" (p. 9), and "Folk are good; they are good for one" (p. 11). In vivid opposition to her ghostly present life, Helena still bears the sunburn she received during a vacation on the Isle of Wight with Siegmund; its preternaturally deep imprint functions, throughout the novel, as a sign of her intense experiences on the Isle of Wight—the apex of her life. Because it is a further token of the vividness that preceded her current aridness of spirit, Helena longs for Siegmund's violin, now in the keeping of his insensitive widow, Beatrice.

The chapter is a qualified success and the novel never escapes from the stilted prose that marks its opening. Cecil, like Cyril before him, barely exists, and the vagueness of these two autobiographical characters suggests again that fictional self-mirroring—the creation of a fully realized autobiographical character—was difficult for Lawrence early in his career.[8] Yet despite their weaknesses, the introductory pages successfully employ imagery, in an organic coherent manner, to create an aura of numbed indifference following severe loss. This numbness has a negative dimension, since Helena rejects the living Cecil in her obsession with the dead Siegmund, but to see Helena as a purely destructive figure is to ignore the near-tragic depth of grief revealed in this chapter.

As developed in the long Isle of Wight flashback, the relationship of Helena and Siegmund is a paradoxical mixture of interdependence and conflict. Both characters idealize their holiday, distinguishing their illuminative time together from the routine of their lives. But if they agree on the importance of the experience, they envision opposed idealizations.

The island represents escape to Helena, but it promises transcendence to Siegmund. The controlling motifs of escape and transcendence are each symbolized by a natural force. Lawrence creates a richly metaphorical landscape on the Isle of Wight; sun, moon, sea, mist, stone, and sand are all figuratively charged.[9] Some of the symbolism is vague and overloaded, its implications blurred because its literal references are imprecisely articulated. But there are at least two natural images in the book that have consistent and coherent implications; each of these bears an intrinsic relation to one of the novel's protagonists. Helena's flight from reality is incarnated by the mist that surrounds the island,[10] while the sun signifies Siegmund's consuming desire to rise above his old life. The characters' differing concepts of deliverance makes the clash between them inevitable.

Helena states that the enveloping mist shields her, for a short time, from the exigencies of the outside world: "The mist is Lethe. It is enough for us if its spell lasts five days" (p. 27). Siegmund views the mist with another kind of favor; he sees it as an encouragement toward exclusive intimacy: "It couldn't have happened better for us than this mist. . . . There is nothing else but you, and for you there is nothing else but me" (p. 25). But Siegmund is typified by the sun-imagery diffused through the book, from the sunburn that is so slow to leave Helena's arms, to the early discussion of "sunset" (p. 27) that foreshadows Siegmund's death. The feeling associated with the sun in *The Trespasser* is of a revitalizing physical penetration that burns away stagnation. The sun brings the possibility of that deeper "relation between man and his circumambient universe"[11] Lawrence believed in, and is connected to the general principle of passion. Siegmund and Helena have contrasting, and indicative, attitudes toward the sun and its effects: " 'It is quite warm enough here,' she said, nestling in to him. 'Yes; but the sting is missing. I like to feel the warmth biting in.' 'No, I do not. To be cosy is enough.' 'I like the sunshine on me, real and manifest, and tangible. I feel like a seed that has been frozen for ages. I want to be bitten by the sunshine!' " (p. 47).

It is a special form of escapism, based on the mental faculty of fancy, that Helena indulges on the island.[12] Helena reorders the world in her mind so that it becomes a source of delight exclusively. The mist blocks out intrusions, allowing her to create a private reality; she tries to stay self-enclosed and assert the dominance of her mind over the surrounding world: "She wanted to see just as she pleased, without any of humanity's previous vision for spectacles. . . . She clothed everything in fancy. . . . The value of all things was in the fancy they evoked. She did not care for people; they were vulgar, ugly, and stupid, as a rule" (p. 43).

Their first physical encounter takes place in a natural setting analogous to what occurs between them: "The gold march of sunset passed quickly, the ragged curtains of mist closed to" (p. 29). Under this corresponding topography, Helena rejects Siegmund just at the point where he threatens to intrude on her fantasy life: "When Helena drew away her lips, she was exhausted. She belonged to that class of 'dreaming women' with whom passion exhausts itself at the mouth. . . . With her the dream was always more than the actuality. . . . For centuries a certain type of woman has been rejecting the 'animal' in humanity, till now her dreams are abstract, and full of fantasy, and her blood runs in bondage, and her kindness is full of cruelty" (pp. 30–31). These lines provide an accurate enough description of Helena's frigidity and fancifulness at this early point in the novel. But it is essential to notice that the lines are spoken by the narrator;[13] this authorial commentary categorizes Helena, but the living character (as the ensuing scenes show) goes beyond the imposed category.

The sun is perhaps most notable for its overpowering force, its fiery capacity to consume the separate sense of self. The desire to be absorbed typifies Siegmund, who wishes to transcend himself in order to lose himself. Hence, if Helena desires, through whimsy and imagination, to control the phenomenal world, Siegmund constantly seeks, and in the rhapsodic pages of the novel often finds, union with the cosmos: "Then the day flashed out, and Siegmund mated with joy. . . . he gave himself to the breeze and to the sea, feeling . . . as if he were part of it all. All his body radiated amid the large, magnificent sea-moon like a piece of colour" (pp. 20–21). The quotation is a good example of the novel's narrational self-division; tone suggests approbation for Siegmund's spiritual accomplishment, as imagery cautions that the man who subordinates himself to the moon courts dissolution in the stronger self of woman.

Moreover, though the narrator continues to conceive Siegmund as a hero of self-surpassing experience, the narrative action inexorably places him in a tradition of negative romanticism. The quality of Siegmund's obsession with losing himself in nature is of a very specific kind. It is not Wordsworthian; for Wordsworth nature is a moral force, deepening his understanding and love of man while, reciprocally, the "still, sad music of humanity" forces maturity upon him, causing him to look past the external world to the metaphysical presence beyond. Nor does Siegmund manifest Keats' rare ability to suspend himself and slide into the very essence of an external object. Rather, Siegmund descends from a creation of Byron: his literary progenitor is the *Weltschmerz*-filled persona of *Childe Harold*. That character's desire to mix with the most sublime manifestations of nature stems partly from a contempt for the ordinary life of man. Here, the desire to lose the self has a misanthropic, isolated, self-destructive quality; ordinary life becomes an impossibility—something hopeless, grand and untenable is sought:

> I live not in myself, but I become
> Portion of that around me; and to me
> High mountains are a feeling, but the hum
> Of human cities torture: I can see
> Nothing to loathe in nature, save to be
> A link reluctant in a fleshly chain,
> Class'd among creatures, when the soul can flee,
> And with the sky, the peak, the heaving plain
> Of ocean, or the stars, mingle, and not in vain.
>   Byron, *Childe Harold*, canto 3, stanza 7

After the kissing scene, which takes place on the foggy shore in the early evening, Siegmund and Helena return to their room. A fire (related to the sun, and hence to Siegmund)[14] is burning as the middle-aged musician finally seduces his young student. But their first intimacy is a failure. Helena has pity on his frustration, comes to him as if she were "offering herself" as a "sacrifice." Her antipathy toward sex undermines any chance for genuine sensuality. Relieved at her submission, Siegmund takes her with mixed feelings: "There was a good deal of sorrow in his joy" (p. 35).

They are isolated from one another afterward. He is nevertheless satisfied and lies "absolutely still," while she is "very hot, feverish and restless." She senses that some part of her being, previously unkown to her, has brought him this peace: "She had given him this new soft beauty. She was the earth in which his strange flowers grew. But she herself wondered at the flowers produced of her. He was so strange to her, so different from herself" (p. 36). Conceiving herself as intellectual and distant, even cold, she is suddenly cast in the role of "the earth." Unwilling to make this transition, Helena refuses Siegmund the dark, instinctual woman he reaches for, and asserts her abstract, separate self; this assertion coincides with the appearance of the moon.

In many of Lawrence's fictions, moon is associated with the spirituality and separateness of the female protagonist. (This is in direct opposition to the sun, which burns away the ego to allow entrance to the greater forces of nature.) Thus, as she feels Siegmund's oppressive tranquillity upon her, Helena is drawn by her "restlessness" toward the window, where she draws back the curtain and sees "The moon . . . wading deliciously through shallows of white cloud. . . . The moon was there to put a cool hand of absolution on her brow" (p. 36). She brings Siegmund to share the scene with her but, as always, his eyes see very differently from hers: " 'I like the moon on the water,' she said. 'I can hardly tell the one from the other,' he replied simply. 'The sea seems to be poured out of the moon, and rocking in the hands of the coast. They are all one, just as your eyes and hands and what you say, are all you' " (p. 37). These lines reaffirm the two characters' antithetic ways of perceiving the world. She distinguishes between moon and water (the sea had earlier been figuratively linked to Siegmund), while Siegmund unites them. Siegmund blurs the natural image, synthesizing its discrete elements into an amorphous whole with which he can identify; he blurs distinctions and makes the world contiguous with himself, conceiving of the universe as a huge complex of sympathetic response: "the darkness is a sort of mother, and the moon a sister, and the stars children, and sometimes the sea is a brother" (p. 37).

It is moon-symbolism, one of his techniques for the objective realization of meaning, that enables Lawrence to show that Helena remains unattainable, despite her physical submission, during this first sexual experience. She is the one thing isolated from Siegmund's reassuring sense of universal oneness. Though he finds a separate satisfaction, he fails to penetrate her hermetically private world.

Nor does he do so in the next sexual scene. Here, she gives herself willingly, but cannot overcome her frigidity; she uses sex as a gift, a sign of her favor, a way of putting him in the position of importunate need her imagination desires: "That night she met his passion with love. It was not his passion she wanted, actually. But she desired that he should want *her* madly, and that he should have all—everything. It was a wonderful night to him. It restored in him the full 'will to live.' But she felt it destroyed her. Her soul seemed blasted" (p. 56).

Though her lingering puritanism restricts her ability to react during sex, afterward there is a dramatic and significant change in her feelings; correspondingly, there is a shift in the imagery that surrounds her: "All things . . . were made of sunshine. . . . everything ran with sunshine, as we are full of blood, and plants are tissued from green-gold glistening sap. . . . Sunlight poured on the large round world. . . . Sunlight liquid in the water made the waves heavy, golden, and rich" (pp. 56–57). She looks at Siegmund with "love and gratefulness" and says "I saw the sunshine in you." The movement from the cold isolation of the moon to the interconnecting warmth of the sun implies a definite growth in Helena's capacity for response. The new warmth suffusing her extends her sensitivity to the surrounding world. Under the sun, the symbol for self-escaping physical intensity, Helena feels part of a hot, replenishing, unified natural scene. This shows a movement toward the forces the novel generally holds in opposition to her. By incorporating these opposing forces, Helena shows signs of a capacity for both spiritual and sensual experience. Her strong sensations of post-sexual pleasure and love indicate her inner growth.[15]

But the experience causes no parallel development in Siegmund. Afterward, he immerses himself in the sea, expressing the obsessive desires that underlie his attraction to Helena: "When Siegmund had Helena near, he lost the ache, the yearning towards something, which he always felt otherwise. She seemed to connect him with the beauty of things, as if she were the nerve through which he received intelligence of the sun, the wind, and the sea, and of the moon and the darkness" (p. 44). When he attempts the same kind of immersion in the sand, however, his hand encounters an unexpected obstacle, a "deep mass of cold, that the softness and warmth merely floated upon" (p. 58). This coldness, like the rock that scratches him while he is swimming (p. 41), is a reminder of the alien dimension in the universe. Despite his self-persuading illusions, he is being informed that nature is indifferent or antagonistic as often as it is sympathetic. The coldness is also analogous to Helena's frigidity: woman and nature both erect blocks to absolute unification. The romantic quest for a disintegration of the ego and a dissolution into the external world provides Siegmund's entire modus vivendi while on the island. But since his self-eradicating union is inevitably frustrated Siegmund is generally in a state of inconclusive ecstasy, that frenzy for the unattainable one critic has described as "nympholepsis."[16] His desire is never tempered by reality and Siegmund is pushed steadily closer to death, a force he glorifies when he realizes that neither Helena nor nature will give his urge for union full satisfaction. Death is another implication of the cold under the earth—the one that will prove most prophetic.

The descriptions of Siegmund's irresolvable ecstasies create an exceptionally lush romanticism, with an emphasis on awesome, overwhelming experience that verges on self-abnegating death-worship and moves in its search for the most intense possible sensation from pleasure to self-sacrificing pain. Significantly, Siegmund and Helena are great admirers of Wagner; the book is full of Wagnerian references, including the name of its hero, taken from *Die Walküre*. Wagner's music dramas have many points of similarity to *The Trespasser*. Indeed, if we accept the description of one music historian, Wagner's operas parallel Lawrence's second novel in one essential regard: "[Wagner's] music . . . was able . . . to suggest . . . that all-embracing state of ecstasy, at once sensuous and mystical, toward which all romantic art had been striving."[17]

This "all-embracing state of ecstasy" has the effect of freeing the ego from its singularity, and in this sense can be related to self-destruction. An aura of ecstacy and disintegration combined permeates the novel because its hero demonstrates how the two states of being may fuse into one.

This duality underlies his increasing attraction to the sun, whose rays grow steadily hotter as the novel progresses, melting distinctions to release Siegmund from his own specificity, his status as a separate organism. Helena, however, fails to parallel Siegmund's rapturous self-destructiveness. Having moved toward a sun that suggested warmth and vital response, she recoils from a *burning* sun that reduces and dissolves her entire personality: "It seems to her as if all the lightness of her fancy and her hope were being burned away in this tremendous furnace, leaving her, Helena, like a heavy piece of slag seamed with metal" (p. 92). Yet even this annihilating intensity of sun barely satisfies Siegmund, who cannot be sufficiently overwhelmed: " 'It is really a very fine sun,' said Siegmund lightly. 'I feel as if I were almost satisfied with heat' " (p. 93).

Siegmund believes that the sun cleanses him, burning away the years of mediocre imperfection that preceded his current transcendence: "he had washed away all the years of soilure in this morning's sea and sun and sand. It was the purification. Siegmund became again a happy priest of the sun" (p. 59). His ordinary life, as the later scenes with Beatrice will show, makes demands on him and hampers the absolute freedom he wants. On the Isle of Wight he can establish an egocentricity that is infantile in its totality. Siegmund has the kind of paradoxical egotism, found in Byron as well as other romantics, wherein the ego appears very weak, since it seems so willing to dissolve into the objective world, but also enormous, since the whole world is seen as an ego extension, and all the love for nature is difficult to distinguish from love of self. Siegmund's is a narcissistic personality: self-concentrated, yet blurred in self-conception and easily violated by other people: " 'I tell you . . . it remains tied tight round something inside me . . . for hours . . . what everyone else's opinion of me is.' 'If you feel [sure of] yourself, is not that enough?' she said brutally. . . . 'What is myself?' he asked. 'Nothing very definite,' she said, with a bitter laugh' " (p. 89).

Yet Siegmund's frail ego can enlarge gigantically and subsume the world. Siegmund and Helena reach their closest intimacy when the young woman describes the whole rocking universe as a pale reflection of her lover: "gorse and the stars and the sea and the trees, are all kissing Siegmund. The sea has its mouth on the earth, and the gorse and the trees press together, and they all look up at the moon, they put up their faces in a kiss, my darling. But they haven't you—and it all centres in you, my dear, all the wonder-love is in you more than in them all Siegmund—Siegmund!" (p. 73). The passage is maudlin, but it deeply moves Siegmund and Helena. He is gratified by the indulgence of his egocentricity, and from somewhere in his unconscious comes the relationship that seems to mean most to him—that of mother and child: "Yet as he lay helplessly looking up at her some other consciousness inside him murmured: 'Hawwa-Eve-Mother!' . . . This woman, tall and pale, drooping with the strength of her compassion, seemed stable, immortal, not a fragile human being, but a personification of the great motherhood of women" (p. 74).

This strange passage provides an important clue to Siegmund's psychology; he wants Helena to provide him with an all-gratifying, egocentric world, to remove from him all problems of adult responsibility. Moreover, the transformation of Helena to a *magna mater* figure suggests an Oedipal source for Siegmund's weakness of self. The cosmic and natural phenomena with which he wishes to merge can thus be understood as analogues for that same great mother Helena also embodies. At the same time Helena enjoys the maternal role that supplies emotion without the demands of passion.

Nevertheless, while Siegmund continues throughout the novel to manifest characteristics associated with the sun, Helena's relationship to the mist is considerably more complex. On the beach she sees an invalid with "pain-sunken eyes"; frightened by this intrusion of suffering into her idyll, she invokes the full force of the protective mist: " 'The Mist Spirit,' she said to herself. 'The Mist

Spirit draws a curtain round us—it is very kind. A heavy gold curtain sometimes; a thin, torn curtain sometimes. I want the Mist Spirit to close the curtain again. I do not want to think of the outside. I am afraid of the outside, and I am afraid when the curtain tears open in rags. I want to be in our own fine world inside the heavy gold mist-curtain' " (p. 94). These words explain Helena's attachment to the mist, but they contain a note of desperation; the "mist-curtain" is in the process of coming apart. Shortly thereafter, with the suddenness of a Joycean epiphany, the mist slides away from her eyes to reveal an unclouded reality. She finally realizes Siegmund's ordinariness, perceiving him as a man instead of a character in an escapist fantasy: "Was that really Siegmund, that stooping, thick-shouldered, indifferent man? Was that the Siegmund who had seemed to radiate joy into his surroundings, the Siegmund whose coming had always changed the whole weather of her soul? . . . She looked at him again. His radiance was gone, his aura had ceased. She saw him a stooping man, past the buoyancy of youth, walking and whistling rather stupidly—in short, something of the 'clothed animal on end,' like the rest of men. She suffered an agony of disillusion. Was this the real Siegmund, and her own only a projection of her soul?" (pp. 99–100).

By no longer seeing Siegmund as an object for her fancy, Helena forsakes the mist-principle of avoidance; yet she fails to handle her new knowledge well. Helena's epiphany is authentic, but her reaction is to intensify her defensive avoidances. (This is in contrast to a character like Gabriel in Joyce's "The Dead" who is stunned out of blindness and complacency by his vision into truth.)[18] In response to her revelation Helena realizes that love is not a panacea, but something selfish and actual, with a "brute" element; since Siegmund cannot "save" her, she rejects him violently, struggling against the "prison" of his embrace. Siegmund's "consciousness is dark" after the rebuff; he realizes Helena offers no simple life-resolution, so he looks elsewhere, deciding that Helena is just a stage in a journey toward a more ultimate goal: "If he were 'an infant crying in the night', it was crying that a woman could not stil. . . . But he needed to know what was right, what was the proper sequence for his acts. Staring at the darkness, he seemed to feel his course, though he could not see it. He bowed in obedience" (p. 103). At this point in the narrative, both characters are confirmed in their prevailing flaws. Helena displays her sterile rejection of physical reality; Siegmund is despairingly unable to deal with her resistance to intimacy; he is too desperately in need of psychic union to overcome her fear of sexual union. Neither character receives what he desires from the other: a magical transformation of reality.

In the aftermath of this climactic scene, Siegmund remains unchanging, but Helena demonstrates a genuine development. She is apologetic and physically demonstrative, and she behaves this way after the mist-curtain is removed to allow the emergence of the actual Siegmund. She faces her guilt for the "crying of lives," men wounded by her coldness, and ventures to say "It shall not be any more." Helena's reform should not be exaggerated, she is a contradictory character, and the text is often frustratingly vague; still, after her insight she accepts shortcomings and moves toward a possible, limited relationship. Siegmund, however, misjudges the situation, addresses himself to neither her problem nor her transformation, and castigates himself for not forcing her into submission: "I can't bear to compel anything, for fear of hurting it. So I'm always pushed this way and that, like a fool" (p. 106). But force cannot overcome the imperfections in their relationship, just as illusions and misconceptions had been no solution.[19]

Both characters suffer from Siegmund's absolutist approach to experience. He demonstrates this quality when, as the time to leave the island draws near, he reveals his secret impulse entirely to abandon his family. He hesitates before notifying them of his return: " 'Shall I?' he asked, meaning, should he wire to Beatrice. His manner was rather peculiar. 'Well, I should think so,' faltered Helena" (p. 128). Readers who see *The Trespasser* as a novel about the destruction of Siegmund might argue that Helena is sealing his doom here. But it is more likely that she simply hesitates before making irrevocable decisions at this inconclusive stage. His absoluteness is revealed once again as, near its end, they retrospectively discuss their trip. " 'I wish we might never go back,' he said. . . . 'It would be too much for life to give. We have had something, Siegmund.' . . . 'Everything!' . . . 'You are everything,' he said" (p. 116).

His fatal need to possess her totally, to merge his being with hers in some impossible oneness, causes Helena's tentative uncertainty toward him. The objective realization of this issue through symbol and action creates a level of meaning in *The Trespasser* that most critics have not descried. This level, the tale itself, affirms the female character, as the teller of the tale, operating in the explicitly ideological passages of the novel, attacks her. The teller makes himself felt, first, in the narrational sympathy directed at Siegmund, a sympathy that is out of proportion to the stature of the created character. (This excessive empathy is woven into the novel's prose and cannot be adequately demonstrated by a single passage—all quotations instance it.) Furthermore, on the island Siegmund meets a more articulate version of himself, Hampson, a composer. This *Doppelgänger*'s relationship to Siegmund strikingly parallels the connection of George and Annable in *The White Peacock*. Like Annable, Hampson is hostile to women, and his diatribes have been taken too readily as a definitive explanation of Siegmund's and Helena's conflicts:

> "The best sort of women—the most interesting—are the worst for us," Hampson resumed. "By instinct they aim at suppressing the gross and animal in us. Then they are supersensitive—refined a bit beyond humanity. We, who are as little gross as need be, become their instruments. Life is grounded in them, like electricity in the earth; and we take from them their unrealized life, turn it into light or warmth or power for them. The ordinary woman is, alone, a great potential force, an accumulator, if you like, charged from the source of life. In us her force becomes evident.
>
> "She can't live without us, but she destroys us. These deep, interesting women don't want *us*; they want the flowers of the spirit they can gather of us. We, as natural men, are more or less degrading to them and to their love of us; therefore they destroy the natural man in us—that is, us altogether." (P. 84)

Annable's view of the sexes, which sees woman as a predator, man as her victim, is repeated and amplified here. Hampson's statements, though far from uninteresting or unintelligent, simplify and distort the conclusions that are created organically within the novel. Indeed, his speech reverses such inherent implications: where *The Trespasser*'s imagery and action reveal Siegmund's death-attraction, Hampson finds a "natural" life-power in the musician. Hampson inverts Siegmund's dependency on Helena, suggesting that women cannot live without men. His suggestion concerning a passive force in women requiring interaction with men for vitalization appears valid. But the composer misleads when he accuses Helena of destroying Siegmund, contradicting the conclusive textual evidence that Siegmund is self-destructive.

For the opinions expressed in the static speeches of Hampson and Annable contrast with the inherent implications of the dramatized scenes in Lawrence's first two novels. Obligated to different romantic myths, the male protagonists of the two books avoid the task of constructing adult identities. George is associated with the seeming safety of pastoral escape, while Siegmund is attracted to the rapturous union with the cosmos. The women they are involved with intuit the negativity encapsulated in the romantic visions and decline invitations to regression. George's melancholia and alcoholism, Siegmund's *Weltschmerz* and eventual suicide, demonstrate that Lettie and Helena were right to be tentative, for the two men evade the challenges of consciousness and responsibility; in the end they simply cannot cope with the world. Passages in *The White Peacock* and *The Trespasser* that blame women for destroying men, though they seem to have the teller's own sympathetic *imprimatur* (and the teller speaks for some *part* of Lawrence's personality that was hostile to women), clash with the three-dimensional portrayals that show the female characters as self-preserving and sexually cautious, but not deliberately undermining of masculinity.

The White Peacock and *The Trespasser* share a peculiarity of structure—bearing on style as well as plot. In each of the works the male protagonist is relegated to a life of domestic tawdriness after the failure of his relationship with the woman he genuinely desires: George's miserable marriage to the bar-girl, Meg, follows his rejection by Lettie; Siegmund returns to his accusing and hostile wife, Beatrice, after his trip to the Isle of Wight. In both novels this section forms a kind of denouement; it is too long, as it is less interesting than the earlier doomed-love-affair sequences, and it strengthens the prevailing tone of despairing pessimism. The exposition of the central action—the love affair whose grand redemptive possibilities are gradually transmuted into failure—is presented through figuratively significant settings. The pastoral landscapes of *The White Peacock* and the vast cosmic backdrop in *The Trespasser* are both richly symbolic. The denouement, however, with its scenes of anticlimactic, petty domesticity, employs a style closer to social realism. This makes the second half of *The White Peacock* comparatively pallid; it is harder to make an aesthetic judgment about the stylistic division in *The Trespasser*—the first half of the novel is so overblown that the naturalist section, though only moderately skillful, comes as something of a relief.

The movement back to London, to Beatrice and his family, entails an extreme narrowing of perspective for Siegmund. He goes from the broad seascapes of the Isle of Wight to the cramped atmospheres of English lower-middle class life. His emotional being, which had reflected the spatial largeness of his environment, is now correspondingly diminished: he feels caught in a domestic trap, and on the defensive before the acrid hostility of his wife and children. The scenes of family strife are marked by a tension between the facts of the case, which on the whole justify the antagonism of Siegmund's wife and children, and the authorial sympathy that continues to be aimed at him. Beatrice is carping and shallow, yet the novel vindicates her bitterness. She condemns Siegmund for his utter self-involvement and though she makes her points in the clichéd accents of the shrewish wife, it is undeniable that his extreme subjectivity obscures his awareness of other people. Her exasperation at his failure to realize that "there's more than one person in the world" (p. 168) is supported by his behavior throughout the novel. Siegmund answers her in a contemptuous tone: "Don't I know what you are? Listen to yourself!" But he has, evidently, nothing of substance to say. Like Aaron in *Aaron's Rod*, Siegmund feels more hostility toward his wife than she objectively earns; his resentments are stated, and implicitly approved, but their causes are not convincingly dramatized.

Refusing to justify himself, Siegmund moves about his house in a mood of mute, hurt victimization. Neither his thoughts nor his emotions are clear to him; he is in a general state of blurred confusion. He recognizes his state of uncertainty and it brings out a pathetic and helpless self-pity: "I used to think that, when I was forty . . . I should find everything straight . . . walking through my affairs as easily as you like. Now I am no more sure of myself, have no more confidence than a boy of twenty. What can I do? It seems to me a man needs a mother all his life" (p. 159). Siegmund has

been overwhelmed by his sun-experiences on the island; both
Siegmund and Helena return from their excursion with brilliant
sunburns, a sign of the intensity they shared, but the sun also
reaches Siegmund's mind: " 'I suppose this is the result of the
sun—a sort of sunstroke,' he said, realizing an intolerable stiffness
of his brain, a stunned condition in his head" (p. 159). The orgy of
romantic merging, the confusion between objective and subjective
status that he had undergone on the island, makes his former life
irrecoverable. The desire to lose the self in the greater world has
become so constant and intrinsic a part of Siegmund's personality
that suicide appears the inevitable solution. Both nature itself and
Helena resist his need for merger: nature by returning him to
himself after his ecstasy-experiences, Helena by insisting on some
degree of separation between them. Death, the final merger, exerts
an irresistible draw.[20]

Siegmund achieves his long-sought union in a scene marked by
both an ecstasy of suffering and the suspense of independence
before a greater will: "He was hardly conscious of anything he did;
try as he would, he could not keep his hands steady in the violent
spasms of shuddering, nor could he call his mind to think. . . . In
every particular he was thorough, as if he were the servant of some
stern will" (p. 188). Siegmund's death mirrors and culminates his
life.

Beatrice complacently flourishes after her husband's death. She
acquires a boardinghouse, takes up music and generally prospers.
She thus resembles Meg, in *The White Peacock*, who becomes a
stout, respectable matron while George turns into a pitiful alcoholic. The strong implication is that women profit from male
suffering. In *The Trespasser* this implication is strengthened by
Beatrice's indifference toward Siegmund's death. But the full force
of the tale is absent from the pat, manipulated endings of Lawrence's first two novels. It is indicative that when Lawrence's
narrative is most antifeminist it is most palpably contrived.[21]

Helena seems to be in a similar victimizing position. The last
chapter shows her moving, reluctantly but steadily, into a relationship with another man after Siegmund's death. Commentary by the
narrator, and by Cecil, her present suitor, places Helena in a
position of callous insensitivity toward Siegmund's fate, and im-

plies that she is initiating another destructive cycle by turning to a relationship that will have negative consequences for the man involved. However, in marked contrast to Beatrice's deliberate indifference, Helena's response to Siegmund's death is severe. It causes her to emulate Siegmund's own drifting, dissolving lack of focus: "It was no use her going . . . it was no use her going anywhere; the whole world was opened, but in it she had no destination, and there was no direction for her to take" (p. 198). But in Helena this state is temporary. Hers is not a disintegrative personality, and the acceptance of Cecil denotes a positive will-toward-life. To condemn her for turning to a new relationship is to condemn an affirmative movement.

Moreover, the chapter's imagery shows that Helena is something more complex than an undermining woman, establishing Cecil as her next object after having ruined Siegmund. A full year after her vertiginous experiences on the Isle of Wight the effects of that time, imaged by the sunburn, begin to fade at least. Helena now reacts favorably to Cecil's long-standing desire for greater intimacy. Her positive response comes just as they enter a strangely misty "larchwood:" " 'Have you noticed how the thousands of dry twigs between the trunks make a brown mist, a brume?' . . . 'That's the larch fog,' he laughed. . . . As they went along she caught swiftly at her hat; then she stooped, picking up a hatpin of twined silver. She laughed to herself as if pleased by a coincidence. 'Last year,' she said, 'the larch-fingers stole both my pins—the same ones' " (p. 213). There is a duality here: the "pins" are removed just as they had been before the intimacies of the vacation with Siegmund. The removal seems indicative of a withdrawal of defenses, divesting Helena of her destructive, emasculating qualities; yet the two characters are also moving into another version of the escapist world of the mist. The ambivalent imagery thus describes a disarmed Helena who still seeks the realm of forgetfulness and fantasy. The end result of her relationship with Cecil is uncertain.

Cecil himself encourages the view that Helena remains unalterably cold, and will destroy him in turn now that he is replacing Siegmund. He reflects on his predecessor with something of Cyril's admiration for George: "He always felt a deep sympathy and kinship with Siegmund; sometimes he thought he hated Helena."

This hatred is no true reflection of Helena's character, any more than Hampson's speeches do justice to her development in the course of the novel.

On one level, *The Trespasser* is about the failure and destruction of men, innocent victims of an unjust world within which women thrive. But this story is told by a teller of the tale; more a fiat of ideology than a realized fiction, the imposed story regulates and narrows the significance of the work. The novel's ideology contains maudlin and hostile elements, and the ideologue in Lawrence diminished the force of his art; but the artist in him, writing with a freedom of insight beyond predetermination, neither villified women nor glorified men, and wrote different novels.

Notes to Chapter 2

1. Robert Scholes and Robert Kellogg make the provocative point that Lawrence's use of omniscient narrative "is a function of his attempt to be rebel, prophet, and artist, attacking the old verities but accepting the notion of verity." Regrettably, Scholes and Kellogg go on to be ironic at Lawrence's expense, establishing their own normative standards for narrative art and rebuking the novelist for failing to follow guide-lines he would have indignantly rejected: "[Lawrence] insists on omniscience in a world where omniscience is an anachronism. . . . He fought with the Time Spirit, insisting on using esthetic materials which were not truly usable, and the Time Spirit was revenged by the failure of the tools." *The Nature of Narrative* (Oxford: Oxford University Press, 1966), p. 279.

2. "Romantic" is an ambiguous word, of course, that has been defined in any number of contradictory ways. Yet the importance of merging for the romantic poets has been discussed by various critics. Albert Gérard for example notes that romantic theories of epistemology are based on the belief that "perception is a *tertium quid* resulting from the action of the mind on sensory data, i.e., from a merging of subjective and objective. In what Coleridge calls 'vital knowledge' an intimate fusion takes place between the consciousness and its object, and the percept becomes an integral part of the percipient's mind. "On the Logic of Romanticism," *Essays in Criticism* 7 (1957), reprinted in Robert F. Gleckner and Gerald E. Enscoe, eds., *Romanticism: Points of View* (Englewood Cliffs, N.J.: Prentice-Hall, 1970) p. 263.

3. Baruch Hochman is one critic who notices how pervasive the theme of merging is in *The Trespasser*. Hochman argues that "*The Trespasser* embarrasses with its excess of sensibility. It appals with a sort of overwriting that comes of the effort to represent the hectic world of subjectivity at the point of its disintegrative interaction with the natural world of sun, sand and sea." *Another Ego* (Columbia, S.C.: University of South Carolina Press, 1970), p. 29.

4. The novel contains manifold internal references to Wagner and some critics notice Lawrence's conscious and deliberate use of Wagnerian themes and techniques. Thus Harry

T. Moore finds that "in *The Trespasser* Lawrence revealed a familiarity with the methods of that . . . *symboliste* idol, Richard Wagner." *The Life and Works of D. H. Lawrence* (New York: Twayne, 1951), p. 152.

5. Only one critic that I know of agrees with this minority view. David Cavitch speaks of Helena as "the only fully actualized figure" in *The Trespasser* and calls Siegmund a "half-created character." Cavitch generally believes in the centrality and predominance of the female characters in Lawrence's earliest novels. He maintains that "in his first two books Lawrence attends principally to the female reality." *D. H. Lawrence and the New World* (London: Oxford University Press, 1971), pp. 18–21.

6. For examples see: E. W. Tedlock, Jr., *D. H. Lawrence: Artist and Rebel* (Albuquerque, N.M.: University of New Mexico Press, 1963), p. 50; Mary Freeman, *D. H. Lawrence: A Basic Study of His Ideas* (Gainesville, Fla.: University of Florida Press, 1955), pp. 30–35; R. E. Pritchard, *D. H. Lawrence: Body of Darkness* (London: Hutchinson University Library, 1971), p. 28; Herbert Howarth, "D. H. Lawrence from Island to Glacier," *University of Toronto Quarterly* 37, no. 3 (April 1968): 215–29 and Michael C. Sharpe, "The Genesis of D. H. Lawrence's *The Trespasser*," *Essays in Criticism* 11, no. 1 (January 1961): 34–39.

7. *The Trespasser* (1912; reprint ed., Harmondsworth, Middlesex: Penguin Books, 1969), p. 6.

8. Cecil's pursuit of Helena parallels quite closely Lawrence's own interest in Helen Corke, a fellow schoolteacher he met in the winter of 1908–9. Helen Corke experienced the events upon which the plot of *The Trespasser* is based and wrote about them in a novel of her own, *Neutral Ground*. Lawrence's friendship with Miss Corke consisted largely of "his efforts to revive her" from "a personal disaster." Harry T. Moore, *The Intelligent Heart* (New York: Farrar, Straus and Young, 1954), p. 81. As for Cyril, the general circumstances of his life-situation are very similar to Lawrence's own. Among commentators who have pointed out the connection is Graham Hough, *The Dark Son* (London: Duckworth, 1956), p. 25.

9. In a useful comment, Pritchard notes the centrality of cosmic symbolism in the novel: "The lovers' affair is dominated by three images: the sea, akin to the underground cold, the great 'brute force' that is the unliving source and destroyer of life; the moon that embodies the primacy of the individual self; and the ambivalent sun, life-giver and life-consumer, that burns up Siegmund with its passion and even marks Helena," *Body of Darkness*, p. 29.

10. Helen Corke herself invented the phrase "The Mist Spirit." She uses the term in the journal she kept during her vacation with the musician on whom the character of Siegmund is based. The information is revealed in "The Freshwater Diary" section of her book: *In Our Infancy: An Autobiography* (Cambridge: Cambridge University Press, 1975), pp. 222–35.

11. The phrase is taken from "Morality and the Novel," in *Phoenix: The Posthumous Papers of D. H. Lawrence*, ed. Edward D. McDonald (New York: Viking Press, 1936), p. 527. The concept pervades Lawrence's writing.

12. That which Lawrence calls "fancy" in Helena, her mental preference for rearranging objects, though without synthesizing them into new, original forms, is nearly identical to Coleridge's famous definition of the "Fancy." Coleridge considers this faculty vastly inferior to the creative powers of the imagination: "The Fancy is indeed no other than a mode of Memory emancipated from the order of time and space. . . . the Fancy must receive all its materials ready made from the law of association." *Biographia Literaria*, chap. 13.

13. Charles Rossman observes that these notions are "explained editorially." " 'You are the call and I am the answer': D. H. Lawrence and Women," *The D. H. Lawrence Review* 8: no. 3 (Fall 1975): 260. In his long and generally fine article Rossman discerns a division in

The White Peacock and *The Trespasser*. On the one hand we perceive that the novels are filled with destructive women, and we are brought near to apprehending "the books . . . as little more than vehicles for [Lawrence's] personal animus against women" (p. 261). But, Rossman goes on to argue, Lawrence's art transcends such tendentious purposes. We ultimately realize that "although it is true in *The White Peacock* that women undermine the men's hold on life and often reduce them to the state of 'captive, slave, or servant,' the complete truth is that men invite such treatment because of their weak grip on life in the first place. The major struggle of the man in these novels is to achieve self-responsibility, and in fact, Lawrence focuses not on the barrier posed by women but on the *self*-destruction of the men. . . . George is destroyed less by Lettie, and Siegmund less by Helena or Beatrice, than by their own inabilities to grow into self-responsibility, to become their own master" (pp. 262–63).

All of which is extremely plausible, and it seems to me that Rossman has a very precise understanding of the nature of the *tale* in the two novels. But Rossman, I submit, has failed to ask an essential question: how is it that we frequently have the impression the novels are antifeminist tracts? Obviously we do perceive them as such on some level, many a critic has based his discussion of the books on this perception, and Rossman could not describe this element if it were not there. And this is just the point: transcended or not the misogyny is *there*, and we are simplifying matters and giving Lawrence the benefit of too many doubts when we minimize it.

In a word, making these divided, flawed novels into unified works of art is Rossman's mistake.

14. Throughout Lawrence's work sun and fire imagery is associated with males. In a relevant example, the short story "The Witch a la Mode," contemporaneous with *The Trespasser* and closely related to the novel in theme and characterization, the Siegmund-figure, Bernard Coutts, attempts to overcome the cold detachment of Winnifred, the Helena of the story, by resorting to the fire principle in a blatant, desperate way. When, like Helena, she refuses to manifest her passion in anything more than a kiss, Bernard gives her "ivory . . . lamp" (indicative, like the moon in *The Trespasser*, of the woman's remoteness) an "involuntary" kick that starts a blazing fire in Winnifred's living room.

15. This capacity for growth inspires Cavitch's praise of Helena and allows Richard Aldington to remark that it is " 'Helena' whose personality gives its special and haunting quality to . . . *The Trespasser*." *Portrait of a Genius But* . . . (1950; reprint ed. New York: Collier Books, 1961), p. 62.

16. See Leo Gurko, *"The Trespasser*: D. H. Lawrence's Neglected Novel," *College English* 24 (October 1962): p. 29.

17. Donald Jay Grout, *A History of Western Music* (New York: W. W. Norton, 1964), p. 388.

18. James Joyce, *Dubliners* (New York: Compass Books, 1967), pp. 220–24.

19. In his article (see note 7), Howarth willingly accepts Siegmund's conviction. For this critic, Helena's problem is that she does not submit, and Siegmund suffers because he does not insist on his natural superiority: "Helena never commits herself to Siegmund wholeheartedly, never becomes a real woman, never capitulates and trusts and follows the man. . . . *The Trespasser*'s record of the male-female relationship is that men are nicer than women, and wiser than women, but have abdicated their leadership." Pp. 21–22. It is unclear that Howarth means by "a real woman," but the capitulation he calls for requires

Helena to deny her integrity as it demands that she blind herself to the destructive flaws in Siegmund's being.

20. Siegmund's morbid state—including the thoroughgoing dependency on another ego for the will-to-live—is apparently something Lawrence understood and, at one extremely vulnerable point, shared. Lawrence's mother died in 1910; the following year was one of the bitterest in his life, he was imbued and fascinated with the idea of death during this period: "Then, in that year, for me everything collapsed, save the mystery of death in life. I was twenty-five, and from the death of my mother, the world began to dissolve around me, beautiful, iridescent, but passing away substanceless. Till I almost dissolved away myself." "Preface to *The Collected Poems of D. H. Lawrence*," *Phoenix*, p. 253. Lawrence rewrote *The Trespasser* while still under the influence of this mood, and it clearly affected his portrait of Siegmund.

21. The endings of both novels communicate a sense of hurriedness, as though Lawrence were tired of them himself. This is especially true of *The Trespasser*, rewritten after Lawrence had already begun *Sons and Lovers*.

3
The Underlying Pattern: *Sons and Lovers*

1

The pastoral and merger fallacies of *The White Peacock* and *The Trespasser* provide ways of *not* revealing and communicating realities. Escape mechanisms for the male characters with whom they are identified, these romantic myths are also methods of evasion for the narrator of the story. Presenting George and Siegmund in long and elaborate passages of prose poetry, the narrator never specifically defines the difficulties that trouble his protagonists. The passages obscure more than they clarify; we never learn precisely why George and Siegmund wither in the course of their relationships with women; nor, conversely, do we learn the source of the power and endurance the women show. What we do know, after studying the two early novels, is that the narrator works to transfer all the grandiose resonance of the pastoral and merger fallacies to his male characters. There is a simultaneous attempt, therefore, to amplify these characters and to obfuscate their actual problems. Putting the two purposes together, we can legitimately conclude that the teller of the tale avoids male weakness.

In *Sons and Lovers* Lawrence moved from an art of evasion to an art of confrontation. Without abandoning the symbolically charged landscapes of his first two novels, in his third Lawrence also employs a psychological realism that unites a character's experience with his history, so that his perceptions of the world accord with the facts of his past. Mystical or escapist experiences are now given a basis and a rationale, and are no longer panaceas, instant answers to anguished circumstance. The subject of *Sons and Lovers* is equally unevasive; the novel is autobiographical,[1] and a creative triumph[2]—the achievement emerges from Lawrence's struggle with the pained memories that contained the primary images of his consciousness.

The overshadowing phenomenon revealed by this exploration was Lawrence's destructively intimate relationship with his mother. The connection, as Lawrence himself wrote, included Oedipal feelings, and was so intimate as to blur the line between their respective egos: "We have loved each other, almost with a husband and wife love, as well as filial and maternal. . . . [We were] like one, so sensitive to each other that we never needed words. It has been rather terrible and has made me, in some respects, abnormal."[3] These lines, written shortly after Lawrence had begun *Sons and Lovers*,[4] do more than provide a fundamental insight into that novel: they cast revealing light on a great many of the male-female relationships described in Lawrence's first five novels. Seeing such relationships as figurative recapitulations of an Oedipal attachment helps explain the form they frequently take: they are unbalanced, juxtaposing a dominating woman with a disintegrative man, threatening to culminate in the man's dissolution and some obscure victory of the woman. This would suggest an element of womb-reversion, of the man seeking to be enveloped by the woman. Hence the novels give us (and the matter is vague, perhaps unconscious, in the first two books) indirect re-creations of the attachment between a domineering mother and her dependent son. Since Lawrence profoundly experienced an Oedipal attachment himself, the male-female relationships in his fiction very often show signs of this formative influence.

The opening chapters of *Sons and Lovers* examine the genesis of the overintimate mother-son relationship between Gertrude and Paul Morel (based directly on Lawrence's experience with his own mother, Lydia Beardsall Lawrence). The examination is performed with an exceptional sensitivity, particularly notable in the portrayal of Gertrude. This sensitivity may be understood as the result of the events Lawrence describes in the novel. That is, having himself suffered the near-fusion with the mother he depicts in Paul, Lawrence developed his extraordinary empathy for the inner life of women. Thus the teller of the tale and its protagonist share a preternatural intimacy with one of its characters—Gertrude Morel. And the *teller's* special relationship with Gertrude is one of the striking characteristics of *Sons and Lovers* throughout. Partly for this reason, the "abnormal" mother-son relationship is presented with a rich comprehensiveness: we learn its history, its sources, and its implications for the members of the violently unhappy Morel family.

The central issue in the initial sections of *Sons and Lovers* is not the vexed question of which of the mutually hostile parents is the morally superior.[5] The teller describes both Gertrude and Walter Morel fairly, qualifying his commentary dramatically, to show the tragic, irreparable incompatibility of their union. (Closer to Gertrude, the narrator nevertheless succeeds in presenting an objective portrait of Walter.) More significant than the moral (or moralistic) question, is the effect the Morels' bitter, divisive marriage has on Paul. When he grows into a young man, Paul suffers from deficient vitalism: the result of having had an alienated father who remained in the distance and a mother who approached too close.

With no evasions to compensate for, the early section of *Sons and Lovers* shows a unity of technique and subject, and a harmony of tale and teller. Problems develop subsequently; unfailingly honest when analyzing the *source* of Paul's difficulties, Lawrence is less willing to confront all the *consequences* of Gertrude's influence on Paul. There are subtle distortions in the description of Paul's relationships with Miriam Leivers and Clara Dawes. These distortions refer to a problem inherent in Lawrencian narrative. Lawrence employs, in *Sons and Lovers*, his preferred omniscient narrator technique, and shows great skill in interweaving outer descriptions with his characters' inner thoughts. But Lawrence's style of internal narrative is characterized by the constant presence of a moderating, interceding author. He avoids actual stream-of-consciousness narrative with its implicit demand that the illusion (at least) of the characters' autonomy be created. In Lawrence's internal narrative the line between character and narrator is blurred, giving an interfering teller ample opportunity to weigh the scales.

This problem pertains to the portrayal of Miriam. Beginning with a fair description of both Paul's and Miriam's shortcomings, the narrator gradually places the blame for the failure of the relationship largely on Miriam. We detect a manipulation, an interference, when the narrative voice enters Miriam's thoughts, and she conceptualizes in ways that contradict her dialogue, her actions, her role in symbolic scenes. The manipulation exaggerates Miriam's responsibility for the unsuccessful involvement, and correspondingly diminishes Paul's guilt. The indirect effect of this is to minimize Gertrude's destructive influence on Paul's integrity of being—a negative influence that is nevertheless fully communicated by the tale itself.

There is also a manipulation of Clara's inner voice. Originally depicted as a proud young woman, the narrator gradually has Clara regret her defiant independence and become a submissive figure. Paul clearly lacks the requisite male force, and the obeisance takes place before her former husband, Baxter Dawes—a man paralleled, in appearance, manner, and social level with Walter Morel. The submission inverts the more usual pattern: here the woman is dominated. This occurs together with Clara's gradual transmutation into a general symbol for Woman, the *magna mater*. It is woman as abstraction and principle who is dominated. But the problem is that Clara's subservience to Baxter appears not only unjustified but unconvincing; indeed, her humble self-denigration is part of a process wherein Clara and Baxter become mere symbolic figures for the author (playing the role of substitute parents for Paul), and lose their integrity as separate characters. The novel suffers as the narrator forces a pattern upon it, for the domineering role of woman grows organically out of rendered events, while its inversion feels willed and forced. And what we learn, above all, from Clara's yielding to Dawes, is how deeply the teller resented, and wanted to reverse, the pattern the tale reveals.

2

In the opening section of the novel the implied author works, to miraculous effect, through a series of naturalistic scenes, commentary justified by the action, and a skillfully arranged pattern of imagery and symbolism that enriches the meaning of the sturdy structure of events. Thus a bifurcated imagery dominates the early part of the novel and plays a consistent role throughout. Gertrude and Walter are each connected to a characterizing image of color. Walter is characterized through images of redness, from the blood that brings the ruddiness to his features, to the fire that frequently accompanies his appearances. The pallid and intense Gertrude is associated with whiteness, the color of Madonna lilies, and the moon, and her strained, livid face. As the characters develop, the significance of the colors related to them expands accordingly: a series of values accrues to each of the image-clusters. To Morel's red-hued vividness are connected his own vitality, sexuality and warmth; conversely, Morel's redness eventually suggests violence and lack of control. The pallor that typifies Gertrude is initially connected to the stern, threadbare respectability of her puritanical upbringing; in the context of the novel the implications of the color gradually extend to include values related to her: domination, mental and spiritual consciousness and, as well, responsibility and control. But at the beginning of *Sons and Lovers* Walter's coloring predominates.

Vivifying and brilliant, his verve is manifested in his abundance of blood: "He had wavy black hair that shone again, and a vigorous black beard that had never been shaved. His cheeks were ruddy, and his red, moist mouth was noticeable because he laughed so often and so heartily" (pp. 16–17).[6] His irresistible virility is something unprecedented in Gertrude's experience. With a sense of her inherited shortcomings, Gertrude is drawn toward her own antithesis, to the mystery of the miner's radiance: "She was a puritan, like her father, high-minded, and really stern. Therefore the dusky, golden softness of this man's sensuous flame of life, that flowed off his flesh like the flame from a candle, not baffled and gripped into incandescence by thought and spirit as her life was, seemed to her something wonderful, beyond her" (p. 18).

Walter Morel fulfills the sexual promise of his vitality, but bitterly disappoints his wife in other ways. Gertrude's tentative movement toward Walter's values, made in defiance of her genteel upbringing, meets no corresponding flexibility. He is an enclosed man, sharing very little with her. Morel is authentically self-sufficient (he is indomitable as almost no other Lawrencian male is), but if this is admirable on one level, it also leaves his bride fearfully isolated in a social milieu beneath her own.

Moreover, the other side of his gallant spontaneity is a heedless avoidance of responsibility. Though he often does "the right thing by instinct," financial problems perplex and frustrate him. His reaction to these irritating matters is indicative: he tries to bury them, stuffing unpaid bills into his pockets, and covering the flimsiness of his finances with lies. Irresponsibility affronts Gertrude's deeply-ingrained self-respect. He, sense of decency demands monetary independence and she is horrified by the sudden withdrawal of her security: "I don't like sitting on another man's chairs and eating from an unpaid table" (p. 20). She goes "rigid" when she learns about the unpaid furniture. Later, she becomes pallid as she learns that Walter's mother owns the house they live in; feeling herself helpless and deceived, Gertrude asserts her puritan instincts, a now-sought reservoir of strength. She goes "white to the lips," sits "white and silent," becomes "her father." (Her father, George Coppard, is described as a harsh, "fair" man of Pauline temperament, "haughty," "proud," and filled with "integrity.") All Walter's allurements seem mere facades for weakness: "There was nothing at the back of all his show." His influence loses its hold on her; in the face of challenge, she reverts to her roots: "Something in her proud, honourable soul had crystallized out hard as rock" (p. 22).

She begins the long process of turning from him, and now sees the other side of his energetic vigor: the mental and moral darkness that so often overwhelms his natural warmth and gentleness. He had inadvertently described himself when first amusing Gertrude with his imitation of miners stumbling in their black environment: " 'Yi, an' there's some chaps as does go round like moudiwarps.' He thrust his face forward in the blind, snout-like way of a mole, seeming to sniff and peer for direction" (p. 19). This is really self-parody, for Morel is blind in his thoughtlessness, benighted in his inability to see beyond himself to the needs of other people. Therefore, despite their surviving on the wages his strength makes possible, his family receives little additional support or pleasure from his force. The paradox in the Morel family is that the powerful father is curiously irrelevant to the people who depend on him.

In another paradox, Gertrude rejects, with increasing fury, the very qualities in Morel that had originally appealed to her. Having wanted him because he was different from her, she now wants to make him the same as her: "His nature was purely sensuous, and she strove to make him moral, religious. She tried to force him to face things. He could not endure it—it drove him out of his mind. . . . in seeking to make him nobler than he could be, she destroyed him" (pp. 23, 25). Here the narrator—telling us things that he elsewhere demonstrates—points to the opposing principles that animate them: Morel has an *energy* that exists regardless of the people around him; Gertrude has a *will* that strives to make self-duplications of the people around her. His dark, ruddy force stays to itself; her pallor spreads and engulfs.

The antimony between his warm color and her cold pallor continues as its emotional resonance changes from an attracting difference to a discordant opposition. The tension between them erupts over their eldest child, William. Coming "just when her own bitterness of disillusion was hardest to bear," the son assuages her. She grapples him to her own values, dressing him in a "little white hat" and "white coat," nurturing his long blond locks. In short, she overmothers her child in a potentially emasculating way. One morning she comes down to the parlor to find her cherished son "cropped like a sheep," his hair spread out in front of the hearth in "a myriad of crescent-shaped curls, like the petals of a marigold scattered in the reddening firelight" (p. 24). In the presence of the "reddening firelight" Morel makes a gesture of masculine assertion. His objection to Gertrude's pampering of their son is reasonable enough ("Yer none want ter make a wench on 'im"), but his manner of interference is bound to be ineffective. A sudden, nearly-brutal action, neither anticipated nor followed by any subtler demonstrations of concern, his is a remarkably bungled attempt to provide a male influence.

An early climax to the "fearful, bloody battle" of their marriage occurs when Morel returns from an unsuccessful attempt at an escapist holiday with a comrade. The Morels are immediately engaged in a vicious verbal struggle. In the end, losing the war of words, Morel goes into an inarticulate rage, and violently thrusts his pregnant wife out of the house. Now the ruddy coloring that had held such sensual promise becomes the sign of uncontrolled brutality: "He came up to her, his red face, with its bloodshot eyes, thrust forward, and gripped her arms." His abundance of blood[7] indicates, not virility, but drunken stupor: "he went back into the kitchen, dropped into his armchair, his head, bursting full of blood, sinking between his knees" (p. 34). All of Morel's passionate heat is transformed into an oppressive force in a stifling house, a wildness of word and action "like a brand red-hot down on her soul."

Violence and vitality are each accompanied by imagery of red when manifested by Morel. The two characteristics are inextricably related in Morel's being. Gertrude accepts the one only to be violated by the other: later, rejecting his brutality, she also loses his intense life-force. Yet Gertrude does reject her husband's power over her, and triumphs over his ability to reach her.

In the symbolic scene that follows this incident of violence, the forces associated with Gertrude defeat those of Walter. Mrs. Morel is thrown into the midst of an outer nature that reflects and hypostatizes her heart's inner nature. The imagery that delicately unites Gertrude with her environment is of a cold pale light that brings her to a state of pristine independence:

> The moon was high and magnificent in the August night. Mrs. Morel, seared with passion, shivered to find herself out there in a great white light, that fell cold on her, and gave a shock to her inflamed soul. . . . For a while she could not control her consciousness; mechanically she went over the last scene, then over it again, certain phrases, certain moments coming each time like a brand red-hot down on her soul; and each time she enacted again the past hour, each time the brand came down at the same points, till the mark was burnt in, and the pain burnt out, and at last she came to herself. . . .
>
> She hurried out of the side garden to the front, where she could stand as if in an immense gulf of white light, the moon streaming high in face of her. . . .
>
> She became aware of something about her. With an effort she roused herself to see what it was that penetrated her consciousness. The tall white lilies were reeling in the moonlight, and the air was charged with their perfume, as with a presence. Mrs. Morel gasped slightly in fear. She touched the big, pallid flowers on their petals, then shivered. They seemed to be stretching in the moonlight. . . .
>
> Mrs. Morel . . . melted out like scent into the shiny, pale air. After a time the child, too, melted with her in the mixing-pot of moonlight, and she rested with the hills and lilies and houses, all swum together in a kind of swoon.
>
> When she came to herself she was tired for sleep. . . . the clumps of white phlox seemed like bushes spread with linen. . . . She passed along the path, hesitating at the white rosebush. It smelled sweet and simple. She touched the white ruffles of the roses. (Pp. 34–35)

Here we have the teller of *Sons and Lovers* at his best. Close to his character's inner affective life, he balances intimacy with tactful distance, and the character's experience has an integrity of its own. In a passage as vividly transcendent as it is convincingly naturalistic we are shown how Gertrude is relieved of Morel's tyrannical, passionate heat, and comes back to herself in a cold light that frees her mind and spirit. She simultaneously overcomes her isolation and merges with surrounding nature. Yet this self-loss contains no element of human passion but is a merger with outer forces that confirm her own cold integrity. A mixture of whites, the moon, the roses, the lilies, repurify her soul: Gertrude thus embraces a self-reflecting nature, and the union highlights a victory for her kind of being. Nor is the nature with which she unites descriptive of the "phallic power"[8] or "dark forces of life"[9] that some critics find in this passage. On the contrary, Walter's "dark forces of life" and "phallic power," in their negative embodiment, are precisely what Gertrude escapes and overcomes in this scene. Rather than showing Gertrude unaccountably immersing herself in the very forces she rejects, the passage depicts her in a curiously virginal encounter, an intoxicating assertion of her inviolable femaleness.

The controlling symbol of the scene's events is the moon, which governs and dominates the kinetic movement of light. Moon is the queenly incarnation of the female, independent state that streams into her. Also Gertrude is not, quite, alone during this occurrence—she is accompanied by her still-unborn child. The scene shows us a merger of mother, nature, and infant. And the infant is a subsidiary element, entirely enfolded into a great maternal being. This binding in white between mother and foetus is the beginning of their Oedipal tie.

But as the child, Paul, will find in later life, the attempt to live only by a perverse connection, or by a bond with immutable nature, is doomed to failure. The human relation is always essential. Thus Gertrude begins to shiver; the pristine night is chillingly cool: "Fearful always for the unborn child, she wondered what she would do for warmth. She went down to the coal-house, where was an old hearthrug she had carried out for the rag-man the day before. This she wrapped over his shoulders. It was warm, if grimy" (p. 36). She cannot do without Walter completely; the ragged "hearthrug" is not dispensable. So she comes back into the house, doing warming, homely tasks for him, and comes to a compromise. She will continue to live with him, to be *near*, but not *of*, his warmth; but in some deeper way she belongs to the events of the weird night, and the unborn son who shared them.

Subsequently, the marriage degenerates steadily as Morel asserts, with increasing desperation, the manhood Gertrude spurns. Relatedly, his drunkenness is a descending spiral wherein the more he tries to escape her contempt, the more he arouses it. Theirs is an early version of the Lawrencian conflict between consciousness and unconsciousness, but in *Sons and Lovers* (previous to the Lawrencian doctrine that makes regenerative claims for the unconscious)[10] the unthinking Morel seems wholly self-absorbed, a kind of natural solipsist. Compassionate in his sentiments, admirably energetic and hardworking, he is far from being an evil man. But things outside his immediate sphere, his repetitive round of mine and pub, are unreal to him. Gertrude is left to struggle with the details of poverty and accept all the human and emotional responsibility for the family.

Yet there is another side to Morel's isolation. Once having found him guilty of irresponsible acts Gertrude, with Calvinistic unforgivingness, will not be mollified by appeasing actions. Even when Walter displays natural gentility and delicacy she is unwilling to relent: it is almost as if she were pleased at the excuse to banish him from the family inner-circle. We often resent her excessive harshness, and this suggests the objectivity of the teller in the early section of the novel. Though the narrational camera is far closer to Gertrude than to Walter, the teller carefully avoids displaying a *moral* bias against Mr. Morel. One rare close-up shot of Morel describes him with comprehensive sympathy, showing both his *joie de vivre* and his impervious enclosure: "[Morel] sat down to an hour of joy. He toasted his bacon on a fork and caught the drops of fat on his bread; then he put the rasher on his thick slice of bread, and cut off chunks with a clasp-knife, poured his tea into his saucer, and was happy. With his family about, meals were never so pleasant. He loathed a fork. . . . He preferred to keep the blinds down and the candle lit even when it was daylight; it was a habit of the mine" (Pp. 38–39). The Morel children resent him because they feel his capacity for enjoyment has no relation to them. On the other hand, their judgmental regard (learned from the mother) stifles Morel's intrinsic warmth: "As he bent over, lacing his boots, there was a certain vulgar gusto in his movement that divided him from the reserved, watchful rest of the family" (p. 57). He seals the alienation by never stopping to consider the problem: "He always ran away from the battle with himself."

Gertrude's attitude toward her alternately brutal and childish husband changes gradually from antagonism to indifference: "There were many stages in the ebbing of her love for him, but it was always ebbing" (p. 62). Withdrawing from Walter, her strongest emotions are transferred to the children she must protect and reinforce against him. She especially singles out her two older sons as recipients of her frustrated love. Accordingly, the focus of the novel shifts, after the first two superlative chapters, to William and Paul. There is a lessening of intensity because the sons, as characters, lack the vividness of the parents.[11]

They lack fully delineated clarity as literary characters just as, in their function as representations of human beings, they lack independence of self. For Gertrude's sons' separateness of being is challenged by their involvement with her destiny. Thus, at points, Paul and William operate merely as agents of Gertrude's ambition, realizing her hunger for larger experience: "she had two sons in the world. . . . She could think of two places, great centres of industry, and feel that she had put a man into each of them, that these men would work out what *she* wanted" (p. 127). The sons willingly play this unhealthy role because they feel their mother's pain of deprivation so strongly; having been fully drawn into Gertrude's way of being, they identify with her completely. For Paul, particularly, the urge to compensate his mother for her unhappy life is a basic *raison d'être:*

> Once roused, he opened his eyes to see his mother standing on the hearthrug with the hot iron near her cheek, listening, as it were, to the heat. Her still face, with the mouth closed tight from suffering and disillusion and self-denial, and her nose, the smallest bit on one side, and her blues eyes so young, quick, and warm, made his heart contract with love. When she was quiet, so, she looked brave and rich with life, but as if she had been done out of her rights. It hurt the boy keenly, this feeling about her that she had never had her life's fulfilment: and his own incapability to make up to her hurt him with a sense of impotence, yet made him patiently dogged inside. It was his childish aim. (P. 85)

This image of the deserving woman denied dominates Paul's childhood impressions. It interferes, finally, with his normal development, for his determination to better his mother's fate diminishes his ability to successfully shape his own. Moreover, the ego-damaging effects of the overidentification with the mother are increased by the psychically absent father who makes identification with a male impossible.

The older son shows his over-involvement with his mother in various ways: his white-collar job in London gives great vicarious gratification to a woman trapped in a provincial, lower-class environment. He tries to reverse his mother's social descent by becoming engaged to a girl, "Gyp" Western, whose only discernible virtues are middle-class snobbery and taste for luxury. Still more revealing of an exaggerated intimacy between mother and son is the way William treats Gyp when they are in Gertrude's presence. When William brings Gyp home to the Morel house for a vacation, he evinces an attitude of increasing harshness and intolerance toward his fiance. Though his criticisms of the light-headed girl are not unfair, the brutality of his tone, and the sudden reversal in his feelings, suggest the dissolution of the separate man who had been Gyp's admiring lover. He now sees with Gertrude's eyes and abuses Gyp with the words that Gertrude feels but is not in a position to express. It is almost as though his personality were usurped, though the more important point is that there is a hidden constant rivalry between mother and lover which the mother must win because she is the son's image of perfection.

Hence there is ample justification for the claim Lawrence made, in a letter that is a near-perfect summary of the psychological action of *Sons and Lovers*, that "William gives his sex to a fribble, and his mother holds his soul."[12] But the split between mind and body ultimately destroys William since he is in reality suppressing his passion by diverting it from its true object. Thus the disease which literally kills him has a symbolic function. He dies of "a peculiar erysipelas, which had started under the chin where the collar chafed" (p. 169). More than once in *Sons and Lovers* Lawrence uses collars to represent control,[13] and the erysipelas (a disease that turns the infected area a deep red) suggests that the effort had exacted a fearful price. In the end, the rebellious passion erupts. William's death leaves us with the tacit question of whether life is viable when deepest feelings are incestuous.

Disease often has thematic significance in Lawrence's work. Gertrude reacts to William's illness and death by cleaving all the closer to his memory, indifferent to everyone else. Paul responds by becoming deathly ill himself; he threatens to dissolve without the mother who has energized him from prenatal existence: "One night he tossed into consciousness in the ghastly, sickly feeling of dissolution, when all the cells in the body seem in intense irritability to be breaking down" (p. 175). The illness has the desired effect: it arouses his mother's deepest love, and this restores Paul to life. Moreover, Paul and Gertrude "[knit] together in perfect intimacy" during his convalescence. Rising in a "white and fragile" condition from his sickbed, Paul reenters Gertrude's sphere: a sphere that, judging from William's case, contains a disturbing element of vexed incestuous feeling.

The imagery of white broadens in implication as it is applied to Gertrude's relationships with William and Paul. (We observe how often the mother and sons are "pale" or "white" when in proximity to one another—see pages 164, 171, 175.) Not only does color imagery help clarify that the young men are dominated by the values of will and mind, represented by the mother, and divided from the passionate qualities associated with the father. Beginning with the moon-lit garden scene, the imagery of white is gradually imbued with the suggestion of incestuous love.

3

Paul's intimate connection to his mother disrupts both his capacity for passion and his independent hold on life: together these form one of the reasons his adolescent relationship with Miriam Leivers fails. The other is Miriam's fear of sexuality, manifested in a painful alienation from her natural environment.

The teller carefully traces the backgrounds to Miriam's problem. Mrs. Leivers, though the mother of several children, is an eternal virgin. She tries to float above the realities of farm life, "of birth and begetting," in unsullied religious superiority. Her air of pained saintliness encourages the worst in basically decent men, for it implies that they are irredeemably coarse: "The over-gentleness and apologetic tone of the mother brought out all the brutality of manner in the sons" (p. 182). Her hypersensitive daughter cannot help being influenced; Miriam spurns the things of the actual world, too involved with her fantasy life to deal effectively with outer reality. Miriam, we are told, prefers her dreams. Her imagination turns to the two traditional outlets of frustrated women: religion and romance. Heroes out of Walter Scott fuse with Jesus in her mind; she daydreams about men, but they must be exalted enough to transcend their natural, physical beings.

Yet this Miriam who lives entirely in an unreal dream world is presented by commentary. The commentary is deft and sensitive, but we should be wary of it—its tone is a bit too confident, its revelations too categorical. Lawrence employs the absolutes he disbelieved in when he portrays the farm girl whose life is all make-believe and idealization: "So to Miriam, Christ and God made one great figure, which she loved tremblingly and passionately when a tremendous sunset burned out the western sky, and Ediths, and Lucys, and Rowenas, Brian de Bois Guilberts, Rob Roys, and Guy Mannerings, rustled the sunny leaves in the morning, or sat in her bedroom aloft, alone, when it snowed. That was life to her" (p. 177). We wonder, is it the character or the narrator who is being too stock and literary, who is taking images from art rather than life? The teller too facilely equates a traditional literary figure with his own original character. For, to use Lawrencian terminology, the "living" character, Miriam, cannot be "nailed down"[14] to the narrator's description of her. Miriam the dramatic character is opposed to Miriam the static portrait, and her actions do not describe a girl who is incapable of visceral feeling, or who deliberately rejects physical life in favor of her fantasies: she is rather engaged in an intense struggle with her debilitating fears of the natural world. She has been indocrinated into such fears by a mother who teaches her that the actual world, with its cycles of reproduction, is low and coarse and brutal: it is a lesson in superiority that inevitably teaches trepidation. As a result her responses are stifled and distorted, but not cancelled; in her encounters with her environment she is paralyzed, in fact, by an abundance of feeling.

One such encounter suggests that her fears can be conquered. The scene depicts Paul Morel at his best, characterized by a tense, energetic, delicate masculinity. Miriam correspondingly achieves control over her fears. The encounter (which takes place as Miriam tries, with awkward timidity, to feed her chickens) delineates the constructive potential in the relationship:

> As he went round the back, he saw Miriam kneeling in front of the hen-coop, some maize in her hand, biting her lip, and crouching in an intense attitude. The hen was eyeing her wickedly. Very gingerly she put forward her hand. The hen bobbed for her. She drew back quickly with a cry, half of fear, half of chagrin.
> "It won't hurt you," said Paul.
> She flushed crimson and started up.
> "I only wanted to try," she said in a low voice.
> "See, it doesn't hurt," he said, and, putting only two corns in his palm, he let the hen peck, peck at his bare hand. . . .
> "Why, I'd let her take corn from my face," said Paul, "only she bumps a bit. She's ever so neat. . . ."
> He waited grimly, and watched. At last Miriam let the bird peck from her hand. She gave a little cry—fear, and pain because of fear—rather pathetic. But she had done it, and she did it again.
> "There, you see," said the boy. "It doesn't hurt, does it?"
> She looked at him with dilated dark eyes.
> "No," she laughed, trembling. (P. 159)

With the forbearance of a patient lover, Paul coaxes her into the sharp physical contact. Encouraged by his firm confidence, Miriam's rigidity before natural experience gives way. Paul, a man refined enough to trust, shows her that the pecking need not be painful, and so she suffers the penetrating thrusts of the hen's beak. At the end, unprecedented sensation fills her "dilated dark eyes." The scene's symbolism, with its strong sexual undertone, suggests that Miriam's resistance is not absolute, and that Paul is the one who can make her relax and yield.

But we should not fall into a reverse simplification: while hardly indifferent to it, Miriam is profoundly afraid of the physical world. She shows something close to cowardice before bodily contacts. In a scene where Paul pushes her ever higher on a swing, the exuberant freedom of the motion, combined with the rhythmic intimacy of Paul's proximity, nearly cause her to lose consciousness: "She felt the accuracy with which he caught her, exactly at the right moment, and the exactly proportionate strength of his thrust, and she was afraid. Down to her bowels went the hot wave of fear. She was in his hands. Again, firm and inevitable came the thrust at the right moment. She gripped the rope, almost swooning" (pp. 187–89). Surely Miriam's "swoon" results from the repression of sexual response, not its absence. She is unable to lose herself in a larger physical experience because she is constantly resisting natural impulses and, as a consequence, is always self-conscious.

Resisting natural impulses becomes increasingly difficult as she becomes aware of her own physicality, the "serpent in her Eden." She painfully acknowledges that her attraction to Paul is sexual: "Full of twisted feeling, she was afraid she did want him. She stood self-convicted. Then came an agony of new shame. She shrank within herself in a coil of torture. Did she want Paul Morel, and did he know she wanted him? What a subtle infamy upon her! She felt as if her whole soul coiled into knots of shame" (p. 212). Because of her training the admission requires tortuous rationalization. She sanctifies her feeling by making a specious equation between her passion and the sacrificial passion of Christ: "How could it be wrong to love him? Love was God's gift. And yet it caused her shame. . . . 'But, Lord, if it is Thy will that I should love him, make me love him—as Christ would, who died for the souls of men.' " The thought of physical love can only be accepted if it is misidentified as Christian suffering and self-sacrifice.

Miriam suggests more than she realizes by linking her fervent dedication to Christ and her feelings about Paul Morel. Surely the teller distracts us from the central issue when he generalizes the significance of Miriam's emotions: "She remained kneeling for some time, quite still, and deeply moved. . . . Then she fell into that rapture of self-sacrifice, identifying herself with a God who was sacrificed, which gives to so many human souls their deepest bliss." More to the point is the intensity of spiritual and physical love that Miriam feels, with agape and eros merging into one confused and overwhelming force in her mind. For if her religious ecstasy is authentic, it is also designed to mask her sexual passion even from herself.

If Miriam cannot face her feelings directly, her actions, once she has assuaged her guilt with religion, reveal her desires. She makes physical overtures—"Sometimes, as they were walking together, she slipped her arm timidly into his"—that *he* cannot accept: "But he always resented it" (p. 214). It is Paul who restricts their relationship to the spiritual-intellectual plane. He prefers them to keep to their artist/audience and teacher/student roles; in both cases he keeps himself above her, intact, superior to emotion.[15] He enjoys teaching her algebra, avoiding the tensions between them through this most abstract of subjects. Yet she infuriates him during the math lesson: "She was poring over the book, seemed absorbed in it, yet trembling lest she could not get at it. It made him cross" (p. 194). Paul is angered, ostensibly, by her incongruous piety: "What do you tremble your *soul* before it for?" he cried. 'You don't learn algebra with your blessed soul. Can't you look at it with your clear simple wits?' " But this does not explain the violence of his reaction: "in spite of himself, his blood began to boil with her. It was so strange that no one else made him in such fury. He flared against her. Once he threw the pencil in her face" (p. 195). Paul is threatened because he knows her concern for the algebra is but the mildest reflection of her intense feeling for him. He refuses to let their connection become physical or emotional, rarifying it totally into the realm of the mind: "With Miriam he was always on the high plane of abstraction, when his natural fire of love was transmitted into the fine stream of thought" (p. 214). He convinces himself that he is thus bowing to her will: "She would have it so." Yet, Miriam is anxious for the touch that he finds unbearable: "Then, if she put her arm in his, it caused him almost torture. His consciousness seemed to split" (p. 214). The question becomes whether he resents her spiritual possession, or whether he is merely afraid of emotional and physical contact.

The cause of Paul's agony is a source of disagreement among critics of *Sons and Lovers*. They can be divided, roughly, into two camps: "Freudians," who trace the problem to Paul's paralyzing Oedipal-tie to his mother; and "vitalists," who consider Miriam one of the obstacles to Paul's full manhood. Each category of critic simplifies matters by favoring either Paul or Miriam, and placing the blame for their unhappy relationship on one character only. (The Freudian critics perhaps come closer to the heart of the issue, but the truth is that the failure of the relationship between Paul and Miriam culminates their mutual reinforcement of one another's weaknesses.) There are also critics who believe that Lawrence himself was confused, and the indecision is a source of problems in the novel.[16] This seems valid since there is a large amount of narrative uncertainty in the sections of the novel dealing with Paul and Miriam's relationship. The teller's attitudes are not satisfactorily clarified, and his ambivalencies are often manifested in tale/teller division around the character of Miriam.[17]

Consequently, within the tale Miriam's spirituality is an integral part of her inner struggle, functioning as a disguise for her vital feeling, but for the teller Miriam's religiousness is a static element, a spectre to be raised whenever Paul's emotional blocks become evident. Paul attributes his frequent hostilities toward Miriam to a sort of silent accusation, a sexual guiltiness she emanates: "she seemed in some way to make him despise himself." But this is vague, and seems more in response to what is said about Miriam than to what she actually does. What the novel actually *shows* Paul resenting is Miriam's persistent, silent demand for union: "Always something in [his] breast shrank from these close, intimate, dazzled looks of hers" (p. 189).

It might be objected that at this point I am reversing the teller by being unfair to Paul. Many critics have argued that the "union" Paul fears is a horrible fusion he is right to reject.[18] And Miriam does betray a dominating spirituality: when she loves something she wants its soul to submit to her own. Her enveloping embraces of her younger brother indicate a smothering possessiveness. Revealingly, Miriam lavishes her attentions on such passive recipients as children and flowers. She prefers to control her object, avoiding the equal and mutual contact that might force her to yield and endanger her domination. This tendency supports—though it does not entirely justify—Paul's observation that Miriam "always wanted to embrace him, so long as he did not want her."

Yet rarely does the psychic violation of one person by another occur without the tacit consent of both partners. For domination to take place, someone must be willing to be dominated. More to the point in this particular relationship, *Miriam could not possess and absorb Paul, unless he had a desire to be possessed and absorbed.* Indeed, between the two motivations it is Paul's will to be enveloped that is more clearly evidenced by the action. In the following passage the teller describes Miriam's devouring designs, but the tale shows us Paul wishing to be consumed:

All his strength and energy she drew into herself through some channel which united them. She did not want to meet him, so that there were two of them, man and woman together. She wanted to draw all of him into her. It urged him to an intensity like madness, which fascinated him, as drug-taking might.

He was discussing Michael Angelo. It felt to her as if she were fingering the very quivering tissue, the very protoplasm of life, as she heard him. It gave her her deepest satisfaction. And in the end it frightened her. There he lay in the white intensity of his search, and his voice gradually filled her with fear, so level it was, almost inhuman, as if in a trance.

"Don't talk any more," she pleaded softly, laying her hand on his forehead.

He lay quite still, almost unable to move. His body was somewhere discarded.

"Why not? Are you tired?"

"Yes, and it wears you out."

He laughed shortly, realizing.

"Yet you always make me like it," he said.

"I don't wish to," she said, very low.

"Not when you've gone too far, and you feel you can't bear it. But your unconscious self always asks it of me. And I suppose I want it."

He went on, in his dead fashion:

"If only you could want *me*, and not want what I can reel off for you!"

"I!" she cried bitterly—"I! Why, when would you let me take you?"

"Then it's my fault," he said, and, gathering himself together, he began to talk trivialities. He felt insubstantial. In a vague way he hated her for it. And he knew he was as much to blame himself. This, however, did not prevent his hating her. (Pp. 239–40)

The difference between the authorial and dramatic voices here is instructive. The teller's remarks, and Paul's accusations, insist that Paul's spilling forth of self answers Miriam's unspoken will. Yet his "inhuman . . . trance" suggests that the loss of being fulfills an inner compulsion, something beyond consciousness. We are told that she is urging his soul into her own, but we see her acting to ease and restore him. She is physical and tender in this encounter, while he is perfervid, abstract and bodiless. Her disclaimers sound sincere, and her bitterness at his statements seems spontaneous and justified. There is an attempt at fairness and balance at the end, but nevertheless the passage illustrates the narrator's consistent identification with Paul's attitudes: hence Paul's subjective impressions receive an authorial certification that makes them appear as objective statements of fact. Behind this uncertainty is a vagueness of narrative attribution that leaves unanswered critical questions such as the identity of the speaker and the amount of credence he deserves. The result is a slanting of the narrative against Miriam, with Paul and the teller united in a formidable alliance against her.

Still more marked is the contradiction between narration and incident in regard to Miriam's forswearing of her body, her "purity." For Miriam does not finally behave like a physically frigid girl. The aforementioned embraces of her brother, for example, hardly evidence revulsion from physical contacts. Yet throughout *Sons and Lovers*, the teller exaggerates the degree to which Miriam's virginal fear of sex cripples her relation to Paul. As in *The White Peacock* and *The Trespasser*, the narrator inflates the puritanism of the woman to mitigate the problem of devitalization in the man. The following passage provides an instance of the distortion: "The fact that [Paul] might want [Miriam] as a man wants a woman had in him been suppressed into a shame. When she shrank in her convulsed, coiled torture from the thought of such a thing, he had winced to the depths of his soul. And now this 'purity' prevented even their first love-kiss. It was as if she could scarcely stand the shock of physical love, even a passionate kiss, and then he was too shrinking and sensitive to give it" (p. 221). As R. E. Pritchard has pointed out, the passage refers to an event that could never have taken place.[19] Intent on faulting Miriam, the narrator forgets that it is impossible for Paul to react to her secret thoughts. Never in the novel does Miriam verbally articulate the contents of her Christian-sacrifice reverie. Yet this unexpressed and undisplayed "purity" is presented as the chief obstacle to their sexual fulfillment. Lawrence's final remark about Paul's "shrinking" attempts impartiality but has the quality of a brief afterthought, and fails to alter the basic tenor of the commentary which militates against Miriam.

Reinforcing the view of Miriam communicated by editorial comment is Gertrude Morel's opinion of the girl. Gertrude describes Miriam as entirely possessive and, tellingly, she perceives Paul's availability for a devouring relationship: "She is one of those who will want to suck a man's soul out till he had none of his own left . . . and he is just such a gaby as to let himself be absorbed. She will never let him become a man; she never will" (p. 199). Yet Gertrude's words are more revealing of her unconscious designs than descriptive of Miriam's desires. Implicit herein is the issue of projection: indeed it is a good example of tale/teller division in *Sons and Lovers* that while the tale implies projective transferences of various kinds—both Gertrude seeing herself in Miriam and Paul seeing Gertrude in Miriam—the teller seems entirely incognizant of the problem.

Yet we can best understand the unjustified resentment toward Miriam as a deflection to a third party of accusations that Paul and Gertrude dare not make against one another. For this reason, among others, a Freudian approach to *Sons and Lovers* has much to recommend it.[20] It adds to the coherence of the novel if we understand that an unresolved Oedipal relationship causes within Paul his frequent feelings of being incomplete or uncreated. (Lawrence's language of psychic metaphor has the advantage over Freudian terminology in that it can describe inner states with poetic, if not scientific, precision.) Because his mother unconsciously encourages a regressive relationship and because he has no father with whom he can authentically identify, Paul fails to close the circle of his ego and lacks integrity of self. His connection to his mother is based on mutual dependency, and one source of his antagonism to Miriam is the threat she presents to this essential union: "why did he hate Miriam, and feel so cruel toward her, at the thought of his mother?. . . . Why did she make him feel as if he were uncertain of himself, insecure, an indefinite thing, as if he had not sufficient sheathing to prevent the night and the space breaking into him?" (p. 238). Though deprived of discrete being by the attachment to his mother, only the continuance of that attachment can create wholeness and protect him against chaos and nothingness. At times Miriam replaces Gertrude in this dependent relationship, at others she is most attracted to him when he is most independent: "Seeing him so, she loved him; he seemed so simple and sufficient to himself" (p. 274). Either way, as a potential obstacle to Gertrude, Miriam gives him existential vertigo.

Exacerbating the situation further, Miriam demands that Paul duplicate with her the complex connection he is only capable of with his mother. The similarities between Miriam and Mrs. Morel have been exaggerated by overprogrammatic critics;[21] there are many differences between the embittered, practical woman and the otherworldly, dreamy girl. But there is a crucial parallel: each woman unites emotion and sexuality in her attitude toward Paul. Miriam hides passion under her religious fervor, while Gertrude's maternal possessiveness is incestuous. But Paul is only able to return the dual feeling to his mother.[22] Miriam learns this whenever she tries to get too close.

Paul's refusal of physical intimacy with Miriam, and the reason behind such a refusal, becomes manifestly clear in two adjacent scenes—both of them taking place one evening in the Morels' cottage. In the first scene, Paul and Miriam are studying French together while some bread bakes in the oven. Paul allows the bread to burn when another girlfriend, Beatrice, enters the cottage and involves him in a trivial, yet sexual, flirtation, a coy kissing-game. Paul allows the scorching of the food because, in a very minor way, he forgets himself and releases his usual inhibitions toward sensuality. After Beatrice leaves, the atmosphere is tense with erotic suggestion, and Miriam's usual restraint is weakened. She feels a visceral pull toward Paul: "Why might she not press his body with her two hands?" and appeals to him in a look that ambiguously combines soulfulness and fearful sexual desire: "Suddenly she looked up at him. Her dark eyes were naked with their love, afraid, and yearning. . . . She lost all her self-control, was exposed in fear. And he knew, before he could kiss her, he must drive something out of himself. And a touch of hate for her crept back again into his heart" (p. 256).

The lines are subject to opposing interpretations: perhaps Paul is resentful because Miriam is silently pleading for a purely spiritual intimacy, an emasculating soul-union; conversely, Paul's "touch of hate" may arise because her "yearning" demands a full physical response he cannot provide. The ambivalence is resolved, I believe, by Paul's subsequent action: "Suddenly he flung down the pencil, and was at the oven in a leap, turning the bread. For Miriam he was too quick. She started violently, and it hurt her with real pain. Even the way he crouched before the oven hurt her. There seemed to be something cruel in it, something cruel in the swift way he pitched the bread out of the tins, caught it up again." Paul's saving the bread from burning is a symbolic action that communicates a rejection of uncontrolled heat, of wild fire. Such imagery, as we have seen, is suggestive of characteristics associated with Walter and spurned by Gertrude. Preventing the bread from burning, then, Paul is not only attending to a task set by his mother: he is showing that he will not forget himself in passion and lose consciousness of his mother's will, while subtly adumbrating both his continuing separation from Walter's sometimes destructive vitality and his cleaving to Gertrude's control and restraint. More than rejecting Walter, he rejects Miriam: hence the significance of his turning the bread just after Miriam makes her intense, unspoken gesture toward him. Paul turns from both the principle of passion and its potential object, so that the most important fact revealed by this action is the strength of his loyalty to Gertrude.

Indeed, the ensuing scene makes it clear that Gertrude takes this bread-burning as a symbolic assault on herself, and her relationship with her son. Seeing the ruined loaves, Gertrude mistakenly assumes they were burned because Paul was "engrossed with Miriam." Bitterly criticizing the girl, the mother inadvertently describes her own engulfing attachment to Paul. Her words outline the parallels between the two women, though Paul responds to his mother's need with a pliant vulnerability withheld from Miriam. In her fear of losing him, Gertrude makes a disturbingly explicit, physical movement toward her son:

> He had taken off his collar and tie, and rose, bare-throated, to go to bed. As he stooped to kiss his mother, she threw her arms round his neck, hid her face on his shoulder, and cried, in a whimpering voice, so unlike her own that he writhed in agony:
> "I can't bear it. I could let another woman—but not her. She'd leave me no room, not a bit of room—"
> And immediately he hated Miriam bitterly.
> "And I've never—you know, Paul—I've never had a husband—not really—"
> He stroked his mother's hair, and his mouth was on her throat.
> "And she exults so in taking you from me—she's not like ordinary girls."
> "Well, I don't love her, mother," he murmured, bowing his head and hiding his eyes on her shoulder in misery. His mother kissed him a long, fervent kiss.
> "My boy!" she said, in a voice trembling with passionate love. (Pp. 261–62)

Divested of his restraining collar, Paul reveals some of the repressed incestuous feeling toward his mother (we realize that he suppresses his passion partly to avoid learning its actual nature).

Yet Gertrude is the more insistent and active partner here, while Paul is full of "misery." Whether the misery develops from guilt toward Gertrude or dismay at his general situation is not certain, but Paul is in a cruel dilemma: there can hardly be peace or satisfaction for him in a possessive relationship with Gertrude, yet neither can he find fulfillment outside his perverse connection.

As it is increasingly clear that Miriam is not the object of his love, protracting the relationship would seem useless. Yet the older, experienced Clara Dawes convinces Paul to try passion with Miriam. The down-to-earth Clara refuses to believe that Miriam is only interested in a "spiritual" relationship: "she doesn't want any of your soul communion. That's your own imagination. She wants you." The chapter following Clara's injunction, entitled "The Test on Miriam," is an agony of cross-purpose and contradiction wherein it is very difficult to separate Paul's failures from Miriam's. There is an almost unendurable feeling that Paul and Miriam have mutually exclusive ends, that each asks for something the other cannot give: Paul seeks a release, a self-forgetting in sexuality,[23] while Miriam wants a guilt-assuaging security. Yet a scrutiny of the text supports the view (reinforced by the various poems and stories about the Paul-Miriam, or Lawrence-Jessie Chambers, affair) that Miriam for her part, is willing to yield and change, while Paul pursues a repetitive, unbending path.[24]

The chapter first presents a causal link between the problems of Walter and those of Paul. Vitality of an insensitive type leads to devitalization; in *Sons and Lovers*, specifically, Walter's unconscious brutality creates Paul's ontological dependency:

> A good many of the nicest men he knew were like himself, bound in by their own virginity, which they could not break out of. They were so sensitive to their women that they would go without them for ever rather than do them a hurt, an injustice. Being the sons of mothers whose husbands had blundered rather brutally through their feminine sanctities, they were themselves too diffident and shy. They could easier deny themselves than incur any reproach from a woman; for a woman was like their mother, and they were full of the sense of their mother. (P. 341)

What the passage implies is perhaps more important than what it states: the problem is not so much that the son is "diffident and shy," but that he identifies so completely with his mother's feelings

of violation. At the same time he is utterly alienated from his
father's vitality—a divorce from the male-figure that is bound to
damage his development.

Because of this twofold vitiation of Paul's ego, he is unable to
overwhelm Miriam's sexual fears with the sheer vital life-force that
characterizes Walter. Yet it becomes increasingly clear that a
power of this kind is necessary if Miriam is to fully overcome the
hysterical prudery of her upbringing: " 'all my life, Mother said to
me, "There is one thing in marriage that is always dreadful, but you
have to bear it." And I believed it' " (p. 355). Even so, Miriam
determines to try for physical love: " 'I am only afraid.' . . . she
gripped his arms round her, and clenched her body stiff. 'You *shall*
have me,' she said through her shut teeth" (p. 346). The teller does
no justice to the turmoil Miriam is undergoing when he weighs the
scales against her in passages like the following: "She was sorry for
him; it was worse for him to have this deflected love than for
herself, who could never be properly mated" (p. 344). The sudden
assumption that Miriam is irreparably frigid is unjustified, yet
typical of anti-Miriam passages scattered through the novel. These
unfairly delimiting judgments of a dynamic character can only be
understood as expressions of Lawrence's own hostility—the result,
perhaps, of his not having fully mastered the emotions raised in
parts of *Sons and Lovers*.

Despite the teller's premature adjudications, in the action of
Sons and Lovers Miriam makes the physical gestures toward Paul
while he shrinks away from her. For example, one evening when
the two are picking cherries, Miriam makes a tentative movement
that Paul evades in a particularly crushing way. The fruits,
"crimson and scarlet drops," suggest both sexuality and blood,
mixing passion and death. Lawrence paints a skyscape that captures just this duality: "She went to the fence and sat there,
watching the gold clouds fall to pieces, and go in immense,
rose-coloured ruin towards the darkness. Gold flamed to scarlet,
like pain in its intense brightness. Then the scarlet sank to rose,
and rose to crimson, and quickly the passion fell out of the sky. All
the world was dark grey" (p. 349). As Miriam watches the dusk
turn from warmth to pain to darkness she has a prevision of Paul's
false fire, his hollow masculinity.

But she herself has a rare moment of abandon under the trees, hanging the "fine red pairs" of cherries over her ears in an unusually free and sensual action. Coming down from his cherry-picking, Paul tears the sleeve that protects his arm. Miriam draws nearer to him: "It was near the shoulder. She put her fingers through the tear. 'How warm!' she said." Sexual tension heightens as they walk toward a grove of trees; but Paul withdraws, destroying Miriam's feelings, and showing the real nature of the "sacrifice" she must make to approach him: "He stood against a pine-tree trunk and took her in his arms. She relinquished herself to him, but it was a sacrifice in which she felt something of horror. This thick-voiced, oblivious man was a stranger to her" (pp. 349–50). Paul fades into an anomymous blackness, demanding that she follow him in this bleakly impersonal passion.

This impersonality is a complex matter. We may believe that Paul moves to a plane of experience beyond Miriam's consciousness and individuality, that he suspends his personal ego and achieves an intuition of the greater "darkness," the living universe. Yet in the context of *Sons and Lovers* Paul's self-cancellation is more closely related to lack of ego than transcendence of the ego. On the level of essential being, Paul is too intermingled with Gertrude to establish his own singleness. It is as though there were no separate male for Miriam to meet in a passionate encounter. Divided from his mother Paul faces disintegration, yet he now avoids the anguished Oedipal relation. Therefore Paul seeks to escape from his white mother-bound reality into the darkness of nonbeing, his only alternative: "To him now, life seemed a shadow, day a white shadow; night, and death, and stillness, and inaction, this seemed like *being*. To be alive, to be urgent and insistent— that was *not-to-be*. The highest of all was to melt out into the darkness and sway there, identified with the great Being" (p. 350). Such a passage, again, can be interpreted as showing Paul's superiority to merely personal experience: but this is to ignore the negativity and weakness of Paul's feeling, his death-related sense of an amorphous dissolution into the universe.

Miriam precisely needs the personal connection to put her deep fears at rest. Though she conceives of sexuality as sacrificial during their contacts, cooperating with Paul's foreboding impersonality is as much her "sacrifice" as the sex itself. Paul wants to divest himself of all his tortured life in the embrace. She submits to his need, but keeps looking for a reassuring specific relation; this, surely, is a source of her compulsive urge to look in his eyes, and the passion-breaking fright at the back of her own. Her human demands interfere with the full life-escape, and he thinks more directly of his actual goal: "Why did the thought of death, the after-life, seem so sweet and consoling."[25] Miriam is just a means for him; it is impossible for Paul to join sexuality and individual feeling: "If he were really with her, he had to put aside himself and his desire. If he would have her, he had to put her aside" (p. 354). He remains frustratingly unavailable, the death-attraction is indicative of a general elusiveness, a not-being-there for Miriam. After a week of deadlocked lovemaking, they both realize there is no way out of the impasse.

The relationship between Paul and Miriam inevitably fails because it does not set its own unique terms. Rather, Paul and Miriam's involvement imitates the connection between Paul and his mother. Paul substitutes one possessive woman for another because Paul is a man who needs to be possessed.

The parallel between Miriam and Gertrude as symbolic figures for Paul is dramatized in a figurative scene. The scene recalls Gertrude's formative experience in the moonlit garden. Miriam, like the older woman, is often surrounded by imagery of white, particularly by light-colored floral imagery. On at least one occasion, moreover, the moon is connected to Miriam's devitalizing influence on Paul (see p. 220). The role this strand of imagery plays in the scene suggests that Paul simultaneously rejects both Miriam and Gertrude:

> Through the open door, stealthily, came the scent of madonna lilies, almost as if it were prowling abroad. Suddenly he got up and went out of doors.
> The beauty of the night made him want to shout. A half-moon, dusky gold, was sinking behind the black sycamore at the end of the garden, and the air all round seemed to stir with scent, as if it were alive. He went across the bed of pinks, whose keen perfume came sharply across the rocking, heavy scent of the lilies, and stood alongside the white barrier of flowers. They flagged all loose, as if they were panting. The scent made him drunk. He went down to the field to watch the moon sink under.
> . . . . The moon slid quite quickly downward, growing more flushed. Behind him the great flowers leaned as if they were calling. And then,

like a shock, he caught another perfume, something raw and coarse. Hunting round, he found the purple iris, touched their fleshy throats and their dark, grasping hands. At any rate, he had found something. They stood stiff in the darkness. Their scent was brutal. The moon was melting down upon the crest of the hill. It was gone; all was dark. . . .

Breaking off a pink, he suddenly went indoors. . . .

"I shall break off with Miriam, mother". . . . The male was up in him, dominant. [Gertrude] did not want to see him too clearly.

. . . .

"On Sunday I break off," he said, smelling the pink. He put the flower in his mouth. Unthinking, he bared his teeth, closed them on the blossom slowly, and had a mouthful of petals. These he spat in the fire. (Pp. 358–59).

The disappearance of the moon (but not before it had grown "flushed"), and the domination of the madonna lilies and pinks by the "brutal" scent of the purple iris, are signs of the eclipsing of Miriam and Gertrude by some force that opposes them— presumably, the force of passion. Paul does break with Miriam shortly after this incident to turn to the sensual Clara Dawes. Nor is it coincidental that Paul incinerates the flower-petals. He figuratively sacrifices Miriam (rather clearly associated with the pinks)[26] to the image for Walter's forceful masculinity. This indicates the curious transference of loyalty, from his mother to his father, implied by Paul's change of love-object: as Miriam recapitulated Gertrude, so the relationship with Clara signifies Paul's unconscious movement toward his father's maleness and independence. Through Clara, Paul attempts to belatedly reinforce the being weakened by a lack of paternal influence. The attraction toward Clara thus includes a desperate questing for erotic fulfillment.

4

Paul abruptly turns toward sexuality, exaggerating its powers of redemption. The notion of passion as all-redeeming contradicts the realized action of *Sons and Lovers*, and Paul claims therapeutic properties for sexuality that much of the novel belies. Though some fibre of the bond between Gertrude and Walter Morel is never severed, basically their story demonstrates that even a full sexual connection cannot compensate for a lack of "finer intimacy." Paul denies this when he discusses Gertrude with Miriam: "my mother, I believe, got *real* joy and satisfaction out of my father at first. I believe she had a passion for him; that's why she stayed with him. . . . That's what one *must have*, I think . . . the real, real flame of feeling through another person—once, only once, if it only lasts three months. See, my mother looks as if she's *had* everything that was necessary for her living and developing. There's not a tiny bit of feeling of sterility about her. . . . once it has happened to you, you can go on with anything and ripen" (pp. 386–87). Despite these incongruous comments, most of *Sons and Lovers* testifies that Gertrude did not "ripen." Paul forgets this because, having been divorced from passion, he inflates its significance.

The path he discovers to salvation seems delusory, but this is not immediately apparent, and for a time Paul dedicates himself to sexual experience. His powerful desires are embodied in the person of Clara Dawes. Her female identity is firm and developed, as is communicated by her silent, womanly self-assurance, and by the erotic, nearly overripe, outlines of her body: "a certain heaviness, the heaviness of a very full ear of corn that dips slightly in the wind, that there was about her, made his brain spin." She replaces Walter as an embodiment of strong, sexual being and, accordingly, is frequently characterized by imagery of red. The color plays a role in many of her encounters with Paul; we note the rich earth of the river bank beside which they first consummate their relationship, and the "scarlet brick-red carnations" Paul buys Clara at the outset of this important excursion.

But Paul is too wounded by his past to emulate Walter's flame of achieved manhood and duplicate the sexual fulfillment of his parents' early period. Unable to come to Clara as an equal partner, he reverts to a mother-child relationship by apprehending her as a *magna mater* figure. She is perceived as a giantess, a great and overarching archetype of woman.[27] Relatedly, the desire for self-annihilation Miriam felt in Paul becomes the essence of his love for Clara. Clara overwhelms Paul with a sense of self-reduction that recreates mother-infant proportions as it instances his obliteration by women: "He was Clara's white heavy arms, her throat, her moving bosom. That seemed to be himself. . . . There was no himself. The grey and black eyes of Clara, her bosom coming down on his, her arm that he held gripped between his hands, were all that existed. Then he felt himself small and helpless, her towering in her force above him" (p. 403).

Losing his being in a greater force, the body of woman or the universe itself, contains a suggestion of death. Scattering flowers over the kneeling Clara, at one point, Paul chants the grim old rhyme that begins "Ashes to ashes, dust to dust." Clara glances up at him with "pitiful, scared grey eyes," in a premonition of the death that is an inseparable part of his love. Indeed Paul often seems singled out for a tragic fate, a premature dying. (Most of the characters in *Sons and Lovers* are intimate with disease, physical or psychic, and with death by disease.) Yet to ephemerally "die" and dissolve into outer forces is not a purely negative matter, not indicative only of a pathology.

In Lawrence, as in the Romantic poets, loss of self is an extremely complex phenomenon; it may suggest rapturous trans-cendence, self-destruction, or both simultaneously. In his relation-ship with Clara Paul's problems lead (the connection is obscure but inescapable) to supreme and liberating experiences of unity. The break in his being leaves an opening entered by the universe. Starting as less than a fully formed man, he can also become "more" than an individual. Paul seems to be one of those who are compensated for suffering and injury by capacities unavailable to ordinary people: he partakes of the paradox Edmund Wilson has described as "the conception of superior strength as inseparable from disability."[28] Paul is thus capable of powerful fusion-experiences, at once erotic and mystical, that carry him and Clara into a principle of energy and sexuality far beyond their individual selves:

> Clara was not there for him, only a woman, warm, something he loved and almost worshipped, there in the dark. But it was not Clara, and she submitted to him. The naked hunger and inevitability of his loving her, something strong and blind and ruthless in its primitive-ness, made the hour almost terrible to her. She knew how stark and alone he was, and she felt it was great that he came to her; and she took him simply because his need was bigger either than her or him, and her soul was still within her. . . . What was she? A strong, strange, wild life, that breathed with his in the darkness through this hour. It was all so much bigger than themselves that he was hushed. They had met, and included in their meeting the thrust of the manifold grass-stems, the cry

of the peewit, the wheel of the stars. . . . And after such an evening
they both were very still, having known the immensity of passion. They
felt small, half afraid, childish. . . . To know their own nothingness, to
know the tremendous living flood which carried them always, gave
them rest within themselves. If so great a magnificent power could
overwhelm them, identify them altogether with itself, so that they knew
they were only grains in the tremendous heave that lifted every
grass-blade its little height, and every tree, and living thing, then why
fret about themselves? They could let themselves be carried by life (Pp.
429–31)

The passage brilliantly dramatizes ideas we think of as pro-
totypically Lawrencian. The notion that the most fulfilling
lovemaking occurs in sympathetic relation to the living, surrounding universe comes vividly alive: Paul and Clara's experience of
being carried away by the darkness contains the immensity critics
have attributed to it.[29] Yet there are problems within this very
moving description: why does intuiting the hugeness and life of the
universe cause a parallel intuition of individual "nothingness"?
Apprehending the life around us does not enlarge the self, but
diminishes it; going beyond taking pleasure in peaceful self-
indifference, Paul finds satisfaction in self-cancellation.[30] Why,
we wonder, is this the manner of Paul's transcendence, and why
does he present Clara, at last, with the sense of her own insignificance.

This self-diminishment leads to another problem in the encounter. Paul and Clara have merged with the universe but not with
one another. We might say that theirs is a "higher" experience than
the union of two people, yet Clara desires not the universe but a
man. Though carried away by his desperation into the "tremendous
living flood," Clara cannot be "satisfied" by their union. She is not
content with apprehensions of the "tremendous heave that lifted
every grass blade"; she wants what Miriam wanted, the human
connection: "She had not got him; she was not satisfied. She had
been there, but she had not gripped the—the something—she
knew not what—which she was made to have" (p. 431). She turns
to Paul for reassurance, wondering whether she is just a means for
passional experience: "is it *me* you want, or is it It?" The lack of
personal emotion begins to ruin even their sex: "Gradually, some
mechanical effort spoil their loving, or, when they had splendid

moments, they had them separately and not so satisfactorily" (p. 443). The inhumanness takes it toll.

Lovemaking is not the end of his meetings with Clara: like Miriam she is a means to experiences of self-loss. Clara allows loss of self in sexuality, while Miriam encourages abandonment of self to her possessive spirituality. Both relationships create versions of Paul's original fusion with his mother; relatedly, Paul's merger-experiences with the universe can be viewed as a replacement for maternal engulfment. Paul's relationships with the two young women therefore recapitulate his primal attachment; Miriam and Clara function as substitutes, making Paul's eventual return to the maternal matrix inevitable.

Hence, it is not altogether surprising that Paul displaces some of his vexed emotions toward Gertrude onto Clara. Paul's intense and sentimental reactions toward Baxter Dawes constitute an equally coherent transference. More specifically, Paul displaces onto Clara and Baxter emotions toward his parents *he is unable himself to accept*.

In a man with Paul's background, hidden guilt toward his father, felt alongside hidden hostility toward his mother, would be natural.[31] Part of the Oedipal pattern is hatred toward the mother who keeps one in bondage and guilt towards the father whose woman one wants to "steal." (Indeed, a self-hating guilt toward the wronged father may explain Paul's frequent death wishes.) But in *Sons and Lovers* such feelings only surface indirectly—manifesting themselves in regard to the Dawes couple. This is one of the reasons why Clara and Baxter can legitimately be approached as surrogate parents for Paul.[32] Indeed, a connection between the two couples is made in the text. When Paul describes the conflicts that had existed in the Dawes' marriage, Miriam notes the crucial parallel: "It was something like your mother and father" (p. 386).

Paul's "peculiar feeling of intimacy" towards Dawes, a man who is outwardly his enemy, can therefore be explained as a displacement of frustrated filial emotions. (Though weaker in character, on the surface Baxter is strikingly similar to Walter—both men are vital, rough, and incipiently brutal.) The parallel may also account for Paul's sudden release of Baxter after he succeeds in establishing a deadly hold on the larger man's throat during their fistfight over Clara. Not only might Paul relent out of some unconscious intimation of a symbolic parricide,[33] but allowing Baxter to defeat and maul him is a playing out of a punishment ritual, a satisfaction of filial guilt feelings.

In relation to Clara and Baxter, Paul is enabled to reverse his habitual attitudes, and express the emotions and impulses repressed in his contacts with his actual parents. In the substitute relationship, Paul is sympathetic toward the man and hostile to the woman. The first faint sign of this reversal is Paul's odd reluctance to accept Clara's version of the marriage: " 'But why did you leave him?' . . . 'he sort of degraded me. He wanted to bully me because he hadn't got me. . . . And he seemed dirty.' 'I see.' He did not at all see. . . . 'But did you . . . ever give him a chance?' " (pp. 335–36). After his violent encounter with Baxter, Paul's favorable view of him intensifies; when Dawes comes down with typhoid Clara, in another of the novel's feverish emotional transitions, also draws closer to him. She feels an enormous sense of guilt toward Baxter, though nothing in the novel contradicts her earlier estimate of him as a bullying, degrading man. There now takes place a justification of Baxter, a vilification of Clara. Abruptly, and without convincing actual or psychological cause, Clara almost revels in a guilt Paul corroborates: " 'I *have* been *vile* to him!' she said. 'I've said many a time you haven't treated him well,' he replied. . . . 'And I *made* him horrid—I know I did! You've taught me that. And he loved me a thousand times better than ever you do.' 'All right,' said Paul" (p. 466).

We are not informed of what actually took place during the Dawes' marriage, but observing the two characters in action it seems extraordinarily unlikely that their separation was entirely Clara's fault. Yet through Paul's accusations and Clara's self-recriminations the teller of the tale endeavors to convey such an impression. The narrator, then, working through various characters, communicates a subjective empathy for Baxter and a biased antagonism toward Clara. (We may speculate that Lawrence had his own repressed hostility toward women and sympathy toward men to release.) The Clara who is revealed to us by the tale is warm, insightful, and defiantly self-protective, while the tale's Baxter is loweringly hostile and dull-witted. At points, the narrator ignores these objectively demonstrated characteristics and places

Clara in a position of inferiority, having her literally and figuratively kneel before Baxter. As in Miriam's case, the teller interferes with Clara's inner voice. Her thoughts and impulses toward Baxter grow increasingly discordant with her fundamental character. The distortion that results looks ahead to a problem that becomes common in Lawrence's later fiction: a woman submits to a man in a compliance that reverses our gradually formed impression of their relative strengths-of-being, so that the weaker character seems forced (by the narrator) into a dominating position. Thus, filled with her unexplained guilt, Clara suddenly bows to Dawes in a subservience that conflicts with the character as we know her: "She wanted to make restitution. . . . she wanted to humble herself to him, to kneel before him. She wanted now to be self-sacrificial. . . . She wanted to do penance. So she kneeled to Dawes, and it gave him a subtle pleasure" (p. 466).

I should not wish to be accused of simplification here. One of Lawrence's general achievements is his creation of characters who are open, flexible, and authentically self-contradictory. Certainly it is possible for Clara to have a momentary urge for self-prostration. But Clara's submission to Baxter culminates a process: it is a notably artificial fictional moment, but the whole sequence of which it is a part—describing the Paul-Clara-Baxter triangle—is comprised of willed and hollow occurrences. During this section of *Sons and Lovers* the author manipulates his *dramatis personae*, and there is an attenuation of the full, rendered life we expect, and receive, from the Lawrencian tale.

The novel returns to nearly its original force when Gertrude Morel returns to a central role within it. After Gertrude is stricken with cancer, Paul turns to her with passionate feelings of pity and adoration. He helps arrange a final reconciliation between Clara and Baxter, and is enabled to concentrate on the relationship that is most essential to him. The last scenes between Paul and Gertrude are love-scenes—the strangest the novel has to show: "His face was near hers. Her blue eyes smiled straight into his, like a girl's—warm, laughing with tender love. It made him pant with terror, agony and love" (p. 468). Now that it has been rendered harmless, they acknowledge their fearful bond: "They were both afraid of the veils that were ripping between them." At the same time, in the crucible of her dying feelings Gertrude is

utterly unforgiving toward her husband: "Now she hated him. . . .
She could not bear him to be in the room. And a few things, the
things that had been most bitter to her, came up again so strongly
that they broke from her, and she told her son" (p. 469). If this
seems harshly vengeful, it also shows the depth of warping disillu-
sionment she suffered from Walter.

Again, the hostility Paul has toward Gertrude is covert, emerg-
ing in the triangle, Paul-Clara-Baxter. But the young man's empathy toward his mother is dominant: the emotional cornerstone of
Sons and Lovers. Therefore, tempting as it is to see Paul's mercy
killing of his mother as liberating, a necessary euthanasia leading
to his vitalization, there is no clear evidence that Paul frees himself
from Gertrude at the end of the book. On the contrary, during the
waning of her life they share a sickly death-intimacy. And while it
is true that their painfully intense final intimacy does not preclude
unconscious hostility to Gertrude on Paul's part, it is also undeniable that on the conscious, deliberate level he decides to take his
mother's life because, in his unlimited empathy, he virtually shares
her pain: "he knew the unutterable misery of her nights that would
not go." It is an authentic case of killing with love.

After her death, he sees again the face that had always moved
him, that had held his loyalty and love: "She lay like a girl asleep
and dreaming of her love. The mouth was a little open, as if
wondering from the suffering, but her face was young, her brow
clear and white as if life had never touched it. He looked again at
the eyebrows, at the small, winsome nose a bit on one side. She
was young again" (p. 485). Now, without her, his world comes
undone: "His mother had really supported his life. . . . Now she
was gone, and for ever behind him was the gap in life, the tear in
the veil, through which his life seemed to drift slowly, as if he were
drawn toward death. . . . his own hold on life was so unsure,
because nobody held him [he was] feeling unsubstantial, shadowy"
(p. 495). These lines forcefully testify to the disintegration of being
Paul undergoes without his mother's support. The sense of purpose
and coherence in life is lost without her: "There seemed no reason
why people would walk along the street, and houses pile up in the
daylight" (p. 498).

Still, there is ambiguity at the end of *Sons and Lovers*, communicated by the contradictory titles of the last two chapters: "The Release" and "Derelict." Which is it? Is Paul released from Gertrude at the end? If so, there is another ambivalency: is he released into life or death? Or is Paul now, in the sense of abandoned and directionless, "derelict?" Lawrence gives no simple answer, and Paul's fate becomes, as the many critical altercations about the matter show, a debatable question.[34] Clearly, there is a tensile strength in Paul; he will not easily succumb: "He would not admit that he wanted to die, to have done. He would not own that life had beaten him, or that death had beaten him" (p. 501). Paul endures a fierce ontological struggle, but does not yield entirely to the forces of dissolution. He has inner resources: his artistic talent, a certain stubborn if delicate resiliency, a general capacity for survival. He looks outside his inner turmoil to the surrounding world. Small intimations of life come to him through the hopelessness: a donkey that nuzzles him under a "smoky red sunset," two mice scampering for food. He finds a life-force in the mechanical-industrial world, only regretting that he is not part of it: "Far away he could hear the sharp clinking of the trucks on the railway. No, it was not they that were far away. They were there in their places. But where was he himself?" (p. 499). This coincides with his earlier defense, to Clara, of industrial towns; he had argued that, for all its ugliness, the town will "come right."

But Paul's renewed life-urge takes its most serious form in a final search for a woman to save and restore him. He considers Clara first, but realizes she cannot accept the full responsibility of his despair: "Clara could not stand for him to hold on to. She wanted him, but not to understand him. He felt she wanted the man on top, not the real him that was in trouble" (p. 495). Surely, the answer to this is that he never offers Clara his "real" self; the inner man is absent from the relationship: "Even when he came to her he seemed unaware of her; always he was somewhere else." She prefers Baxter in the end, because he is *there;* however flawed, he is someone to encounter.

Paul then heads for the town, looking for hope in its gaslit lampposts. But the garish glare of the pubs gives him neither the escape his father finds in similar places nor a substitute for his mother's light. Within the pub he feels hopelessly alienated:[35]

"Everything suddenly stood back away from him. He saw the face of the barmaid, the gabbling drinkers, his own glass on the slopped, mahogany board, in the distance. There was something between him and them. He could not get into touch" (p. 501).

Finally, out of mounting desperation, he turns to the old relationship with Miriam. He is aware, as if for the first time, of her independent endurance. She seems the ideal person to save him; her spirituality now strikes him favorably: "She looked as if she had got something . . . some hope in heaven, if not in earth. . . . He would leave himself to her. She was better and bigger than he. He would depend on her" (p. 502). But she refuses to be his deliverance, to let him regress to this new form of infant/mother relation. Miriam concentrates on Paul's strength, not his weakness. She returns to her perennial encouragement of his creative work, his painting and drawing:[36] "He felt again all her interest in his work. . . . Why was she always most interested in him as he appeared in his work?" (p. 504). Though sensing his silent need, she is unable to overwhelm him in his distress. She is accused, in these last pages, of wanting to smother Paul, to own him, but she is actually timorous, reticent. Miriam will not make the decision for him now, like a mother doing what is best for her child regardless of its will: "She had borne so long the cruelty of belonging to him and not being claimed by him. . . . She pleaded to him with all her love not to make it *her* choice" (pp. 507–8).

Evidently, there are limitations to Miriam's possessive instincts, for she refuses to ingather the shattered man who comes to her for salvation. Paul wordlessly calls out to her to be stronger and more domineering than she ever was: to envelop him with surety and be more like Gertrude than Miriam. This is the "strong demand" of the "unknown thing in him"—the demand before which she is impotent.[37] For in the moment of crisis, she cannot "take him and relieve him of the responsibility of himself," even if Paul wants "her to hold him and say, with joy and authority: 'Stop all this restlessness and beating against death. You are mine for a mate'" (p. 508). Paul cannot take, he can only be taken. But Miriam's actions show her refusing to enfold Paul and be a mother to an annulled man.

Walking away from Miriam, Paul's last thoughts and feelings are rendered in a famous passage of astonishing beauty. Paul's fate, as anticipated in these final sentences, hovers perilously between being and nothingness, his soul caught between the beckoning extinguishing universe and the insistent continuous life of man.

> The town, as he sat upon the car, stretched away over the bay of the railway, a level fume of lights. Beyond the town the country, little smouldering spots for more towns—the sea—the night—on and on! And he had no place in it! Whatever spot he stood on, there he stood alone. From his breast, from his mouth, sprang the endless space, and it was there behind him, everywhere. The people hurrying along the streets offered no obstruction to the void in which he found himself. They were small shadows whose footsteps and voices could be heard, but in each of them the same night, the same silence. . . . Little stars shone high up; little stars spread far away in the flood-waters, a firmament below. Everywhere the vastness and terror of the immense night which is roused and stirred for a brief while by the day, but which returns, and will remain at last eternal, holding everything in its silence and its living gloom. There was no Time, only Space. Who could say his mother had lived and did not live? She had been in one place, and was in another; that was all. And his soul could not leave her, wherever she was. Now she was gone abroad into the night, and he was with her still. They were together. But yet there was his body, his chest, that leaned against the stile, his hands on the wooden bar. They seemed something. Where was he?—one tiny upright speck of flesh, less than an ear of wheat lost in the field. He could not bear it. On every side the immense dark silence seemed pressing him, so tiny a spark, into extinction, and yet, almost nothing, he could not be extinct. Night, in which everything was lost, went reaching out, beyond stars and sun. Stars and sun, a few bright grains, went spinning round for terror, and holding each other in embrace, there in a darkness that outpassed them all, and left them tiny and daunted. So much, and himself, infinitesimal, at the core a nothingness, and yet not nothing.
>
> "Mother!" he whispered—"mother!"
>
> She was the only thing that held him up, himself, amid all this. And she was gone, intermingled herself. He wanted her to touch him, have him alongside with her.
>
> But no, he would not give in. Turning sharply, he walked towards the city's gold phosphorescence. His fists were shut, his mouth set fast. He would not take that direction, to the darkness, to follow her. He walked towards the faintly, humming, glowing town, quickly. (Pp. 509–11)

This evocative statement conceives a dominating principle of death, eventually enfolding everyone in its blackness. Paul had been protected against this "immense dark silence" by the mother who fused with him into a whole and resisting unit. Since she has gone into the darkness, he seems destined to follow, his being inevitably drawn after hers. We realize that Paul's chance for survival is precisely equal to the degree of his differentiation from Gertrude. Having been one with her in life, it seems tragically probable that he will be one with her in death.

Still, we believe Lawrence when he tells us that Paul, so nearly nothing, is "yet not nothing." It would be altogether too fatalistic to deny Paul's capacity to defeat the past that has battered him so. Paul somehow maintains himself, the source of his strength mysteriously intertwined with his weakness.

But the last paragraph of the passage presents a problem, as it undercuts the tension and balance of the writing that precedes it. Having carefully described an annihilating universe, whose encroachments Paul is just barely able to withstand, the teller interposes lines that seem too entirely positive. Where the "endless space" had reduced all illumination to insignificance, the darkness is now countered with a power of light. Hence the "town" is given a potency at the end of the passage that is signally lacking from it at the beginning. More importantly, it is now suggested that Paul can triumph over the surrounding gloom absolutely, and that he can achieve the victory simply through an application of his defiant will.

We cannot say with certainty whether or not Paul will endure and escape the extinction that hangs over him. But we do know, contrary to the last paragraph of *Sons and Lovers*, that Paul Morel is too wounded and bereaved a young man to experience a beginning so hopeful and so new.

Notes to Chapter 3

1. Almost all critics of *Sons and Lovers* acknowledge its basis in Lawrence's personal history. This is particularly true of the first (Gertrude-Walter) and second (Paul-Miriam) sections. The third part (Paul-Clara-Baxter) is more of a fictional construct. According to Harry T. Moore, for example, Lawrence himself pointed out both the closeness of life and art in the novel, and the distinction between the two parts: "Lawrence said toward the end of his life that the first half of the book was all autobiography." *The Life and Works of D. H. Lawrence* (New York: Twayne, 1951), p. 94.

2. The quality of *Sons and Lovers*, I would suggest, parallels the degree of autobiography in any given section. Thus the first part is superlative, the second uneven and the third,

contrived. The reasons for these inconsistencies include the tale/teller problem and the artificial handling of the Paul-Clara-Baxter triangle. Frank O'Connor expresses a related view: "Absolutely, the opening half [*of Sons and Lovers*] is the greatest thing in English fiction." *The Mirror on the Roadway* (Peters, 1955), reprinted in Gamini Salgado, ed., *A Casebook on "Sons and Lovers,"* (London: Macmillan & Co., 1969), p. 145.

3. *The Collected Letters of D. H. Lawrence*, ed. Harry T. Moore, 2 vols. (London: William Heinemann, 1962), 1:69.

4. The letter describing Lawrence's "abnormal" relationship with his mother was dated 26 October 1910. In a letter dated 18 October 1910 Lawrence mentioned that he had completed "about one-eighth" of his new novel, *Paul Morel* (an early title for *Sons and Lovers*). *Collected Letters*, 1:66.

5. Most critics deal with this moral question. Keith Sagar decides that Gertrude is to be preferred in her conflict of values with her husband: "Gertrude Morel is right, though the novel qualifies her rightness—it is not absolute, but relative to the alternatives offered." *The Art of D. H. Lawrence* (Cambridge: Cambridge University Press, 1966), pp. 21, 23. But views sympathetic to Walter are encountered more frequently. Mark Schorer defends Mr. Morel in a loaded rhetorical question: "Which of these characters is given the real sympathy—the hard, self-righteous, aggressive, demanding mother who comes through to us, or the simple, direct, gentle, downright, fumbling, ruined father?" "Technique as Discovery," in *The World We Imagine: Selected Essays by Mark Schorer* (New York: Farrar, Straus and Giroux, 1948), p. 13. More subtly, H. M. Daleski convincingly shows Gertrude to be far coarser than her husband during the scene where Walter tries, pathetically, to make her a present of a coconut (*Sons and Lovers*, p. 14). *The Forked Flame: A Study of D. H. Lawrence* (Evanston, Ill.: Northwestern University Press, 1965) p. 44. Daleski, like Schorer, charges Lawrence with tale/teller discrepancy in relation to the character of Walter: "The weight of hostile comment which Lawrence directs against Morel is balanced by the unconscious sympathy with which he is presented dramatically, while the overt celebration of Mrs. Morel is challenged by the harshness of the character in action." Ibid., p. 43. If this is so, how to account for the widely held opinion that the first part of the novel is the best?

6. D. H. Lawrence, *Sons and Lovers* (1913; reprint ed., Harmondsworth, Middlesex: Penguin Books, 1943).

7. Daniel A. Weiss, equating Walter directly with the phallus, argues that in his original proud, ruddy state Morel was "tumescent," but that the various violent, humiliating incidents he has with Gertrude cause his "progressive detumescence." This overly synecdochic view of Walter makes Gertrude a castrator by ignoring who is oppressing whom in 'the violence-scenes. *Oedipus in Nottingham: D. H. Lawrence* (Seattle, Wash.: University of Washington Press, 1962), pp. 21–23.

8. Dorothy Van Ghent, *The English Novel: Form and Function* (1953; reprint ed., New York: Harper & Brothers, 1961), p. 249.

9. Mark Spilka, *The Love Ethic of D. H. Lawrence* (Bloomington, Ind.: Indiana University Press, 1955), p. 44. Both Van Ghent and Spilka, perhaps because they are working retrospectively from Lawrence's later ideas, attribute characteristics to Gertrude's experience that directly contradict the imagery pervading the scene.

10. An exaggeration of the redeeming powers of the unconscious or vital self is the source of the tale/teller split in Lawrence according to John E. Stoll in *The Novels of D. H. Lawrence: A Search for Integration* (Columbia, Mo.: University of Missouri Press, 1971).

Stoll believes that Lawrence considers the conscious mind "incestuous"; for Lawrence, therefore, wholeness of being can only come with the destruction of consciousness. But, Stoll argues, "Lawrence never shows how (social) consciousness which up to this time has conditioned, if not determined, the entire psychic life of his heroes, can be uprooted without destroying the entire organism" (p. 5). Stoll makes his case strongly, but his conception of the basic contradiction in Lawrence is narrow. The argument loses in scope what it gains in concentration.

11. In regard to Paul, this is a fairly radical view, but David Cavitch, with some justice, connects Paul to some of the weaknesses that marred the depictions of Cyril and Cecil in *The White Peacock* and *The Trespasser:* "When Lawrence turned to writing *Sons and Lovers* a good deal of Cyril and Cecil persisted into his characterization of Paul, for Paul retains some of their vague transparency through which we view more substantial figures, especially Mrs. Morel."*D. H. Lawrence and the New World* (London: Oxford University Press, 1969), p. 21.

12. The value of the letter is not that it was written by the author of the work in question. But in describing his just-completed book to Edward Garnett Lawrence outlines the core of the novel; this is the tale *Sons and Lovers* has to tell:

> It follows this idea: a woman of character and refinement goes into the lower class, and has no satisfaction in her own life. She has had a passion for her husband, so the children are born of passion, and have heaps of vitality. But as her sons grow up she selects them as lovers—first the eldest, then the second. These sons are *urged* into life by their reciprocal love of their mother—urged on and on. But when they come to manhood, they can't love, because their mother is the strongest power in their lives and holds them. . . . As soon as the young men come into contact with women, there's a split. William gives his sex to a fribble, and his mother holds his soul. But the split kills him because he doesn't know where he is. The next son gets a woman who fights for his soul—fights his mother. The son loves the mother—all the sons hate and are jealous of the father. The battle goes on between the mother and the girl, with the son as object. The mother gradually proves stronger, because of the tie of blood. The son decides to leave his soul in his mother's hands, and, like his elder brother, go for passion. He gets passion. Then the split begins to tell again. But, almost unconsciously, the mother realizes what is the matter, and begins to die. The sons casts off his mistress, attends to his mother dying. He is left in the end naked of everything, with the drift towards death.
>
> *Collected Letters,* 1:160–61.

13. Surprisingly, Lawrence's use of the collar is quite close to its emblematic traditional-Christian significance. In another example, note that Morel tears off his collar on the night he thrusts Gertrude from the house. *Sons and Lovers,* p. 37.

14. "Morality and the Novel," in *Phoenix: The Posthumous Papers of D. H. Lawrence,* ed. Edward D. McDonald (1936; reprint ed., New York: Viking Press, 1968), p. 528.

15. A. B. Kuttner points out that Paul's method of approaching Miriam are "self-defensive . . . barriers . . . to keep his real self . . . inviolate." "A Freudian Appreciation," *Psychoanalytic Review* (July 1916), reprinted in Salgado, ed., *Casebook,* p. 74.

16. The leading Freudian critics of *Sons and Lovers* are Kuttner, Louis Fraiberg, and Weiss. Among the most significant "vitalists," so termed because they consider Paul full of vital being that he must, and does, redeem from interfering forces, are Van Ghent, Spilka, Daleski, and Julian Moynahan in *The Deed of Life: The Novels and Tales of D. H. Lawrence* (Princeton, N.J.: Princeton University Press, 1963). I borrow these terms, but not necessar-

ily the definitions or writers I place under the headings, from Stoll, *The Novels of D. H. Lawrence*, p. 66. One important critic who sees aesthetically harmful confusion in Lawrence's handling of Paul's and Miriam's relationship is Schorer, *The World We Imagine*, pp. 13–14.

17. Various critics have detected an unfairness to Miriam. Graham Hough expostulates that "it seems on the face of things that it is Miriam's reluctance which stands in the way. We may read between the lines that her reluctance is the consequence of his earlier inhibitions. . . . And from this time on the suspicion intrudes itself that the author is identifying too closely with Paul. . . . less than justice is done to Miriam's side, and Paul's *ex parte* explanations have it too much their own way." *The Dark Sun: A Study of D. H. Lawrence* (1956; reprint ed., London: Duckworth, 1970), p. 51. R. E. Pritchard talks about the frequent "authorial misrepresentation to which Miriam is subjected, either by unsubstantiated assertions or by the blurring of the supposedly impartial narrative voice with the thoughts and comments of the characters." *D. H. Lawrence: Body of Darkness* (London: Hutchinson University Library, 1971), p. 40. Jessie Chambers' own comments about sexuality, positive and not overassertive, fit the Miriam that tentatively gestures toward Paul, not the frigid figure created by the commentator: "I had no desire to be a nun. My instinct was to achieve some understanding of life, not to evade it. Neither could I believe in his division of life into the spiritual and the physical. It seemed to me entirely mistaken. For divided in this manner 'physical love' became an insult, and 'spiritual love' an abstraction." Jessie Chambers (E.T.), *D. H. Lawrence: A Personal Record*, 2nd ed. (London: Frank Cass & Co., 1965), p. 139.

18. His terminology seems exaggerated, but Mark Spilka expresses a fairly common view when he calls Miriam "a decided forerunner of those feminine creatures of intellect and will whom Lawrence would later deplore as spiritual vampires." *The Love-Ethic of D. H. Lawrence*, p. 68.

19. Pritchard, *D. H. Lawrence: Body of Darkness*, p. 40.

20. Lawrence's knowledge of Freud went beyond the superficial acquaintance that might be expected of any intellectual of his generation. His wife, Frieda, was involved with a leading Freudian psychologist before she met Lawrence; she was therefore in a position to transmit Freudian theory to the English writer: "I had a great friend, a young Austrian doctor who had been a pupil of Freud's and had worked with him. Consequently he had been fundamentally influenced by Freud, and through him I was much impressed too. So Lawrence through this friend and me had an almost direct contact with these new ideas." Frieda Lawrence, *The Memoirs and Correspondence*, ed. E. W. Tedlock, Jr. (New York: Knopf, 1964), p. 460. Martin Green tells us that this Freudian disciple was the brilliant but unstable psychoanalyst, Otto Gross. *The von Richthofen Sisters: The Triumphant and the Tragic Modes of Love* (New York: Basic Books, 1974), pp. 32–62.

21. See for example Weiss, *Oedipus in Nottingham*, p. 41.

22. Many critics have noted that this follows the disturbance Freud outlines in his essay "The Most Prevalent Form of Degradation in Erotic Life." Freud argues that sons with an incestuous attachment to their mothers cannot combine emotional and sexual love. *The Collected Papers of Sigmund Freud*, trans. Joan Riviere (London: Hogarth Press, 1953), 4: 203–16.

23. J. M. Murry refers to this tendency when he says that in *Sons and Lovers*, "Woman is the means to oblivion, the sexual connection the only waters of true Lethe." *Son of Woman* (1931; reprint ed., London: Jonathan Cape, 1954), p. 54.

24. The two short stories that rework Paul and Miriam's relationship have opposing points of view, showing how much difficulty Lawrence had in locating the partner responsible for its failure. The earlier story, "A Modern Lover" (1909), takes an anti-Miriam line. When Cyril Mersham, the Paul-figure, sexually approaches Muriel (a name that alternated with "Miriam" in Lawrence's fictional references to Jessie Chambers), she shies away, making Cyril feel "as if she had tipped over the fine vessel that held the wine of his desire, and had emptied him of all his vitality." *The Complete Short Stories of D. H. Lawrence* (1922; reprint ed., New York: Viking, 1961), 1: 21–22. But this story is a weak effort, suffering from vague self-pity and facile anti-feminism. The later story on the same theme, "The Shades of Spring" (1912), shows a considerable advancement in technique and honest self-confrontation. In this work the young man, Syson, comes back after several years to his old girl friend, Hilda (Miriam-Muriel), to find her happily involved in a physical relationship with a gamekeeper. Shocked, he realizes he had dramatically misjudged the young woman: "He was startled to see his young love, his nun, his Botticelli angel, so revealed. It was he who had been the fool." *Complete Short Stories*, 1: 209. She, meanwhile, treats him with the specially wounding scorn of a knowledgeable older woman, looking back on an inadequate former lover: "*we* can't walk in *our* wild oats—we never sowed any." Ibid. The same self-blame comes through in the important poem "Last Words to Miriam." Here the poet accuses himself of insufficient power to love. The controlling metaphor, as in much of *Sons and Lovers*, is heat or fire, which suggests that the poem refers specifically to sexual love. Yet I think it would be reductive to see the poem as only about the physical connection. After all, there is nothing in *Sons and Lovers* suggesting that Paul is, *per se*, sexually feeble. Rather, "the last/Fine torture" the girl in the poem deserves, but does not receive, is the emotional and sexual love that could reassure her intense soul and frightened body. *The Collected Poems of D. H. Lawrence*, eds. Vivian de Sola Pinto and F. Warren Roberts (New York: Viking Press, 1964), p. 111.

25. Fraiberg considers Paul's attraction to death instrumental in the destruction of his relationship with Miriam: "the cause of [Paul's] failure [is] his association of love with death and the beginning of a positive pleasure in the equation." "The Unattainable Self," in *D. H. Lawrence and "Sons and Lovers": Sources and Criticism*, ed. E. W. Tedlock (New York: New York University Press, 1965), p. 229. Judith Farr makes a connection between Paul and Childe Harold, noting that both characters are driven by a sense of (probably incestuous) sin, and that "Paul's difficulty, like Harold's, results in a sporadic quest for inanition, a loss of self in Nature." Judith Farr, ed., *Twentieth Century Interpretations of "Sons and Lovers"* (Englewood Cliffs, N.J.: Prentice-Hall, 1970), p. 12.

26. Though not referring to the madonna lilies (surely linked to Gertrude), Julian Moynahan makes good sense when he says: "the raw coarse scent of the iris evokes Clara, as the pinks whose petals he soon spits into the fire evoke Miriam." *The Deed of Life*, p. 28.

27. Weiss points out: "To Clara, Lawrence applies the images of giantism. . . . Lawrence gathers the attributes of the Great Mother par excellence . . . what Freud calls 'the memory picture of his mother as it has dominated him since the beginning of childhood.'" *Oedipus in Nottingham*, p. 60.

28. See the title essay of Wilson's *The Wound and the Bow: Seven Studies in Literature* (New York: Oxford University Press, 1965), p. 235.

29. Mark Spilka, for example, considers this experience "an actual immersion in the 'fourth dimension.'" *The Love-Ethic of D. H. Lawrence*, p. 71. Spilka borrows the phrase from Lawrence himself, who uses it to describe experience at its irradiated best: "By life, we mean something that gleams, that has the forth-dimensional quality." *Phoenix*, p. 528.

30. At this point *Sons and Lovers* is developing a theme first worked out in *The Trespasser*. The light the character of Siegmund throws on Paul Morel is one of the reasons *The Trespasser* deserves more critical attention than it has generally received. (Paul and Siegmund may be compared, but not equated. Paul finds life and death in merger, while Siegmund finds only self-destruction.)

31. Karl Menninger contends that the son who is overattached to his mother feels more hatred and fear than love toward her. Menninger makes the (highly debatable) assumption that Lawrence consciously deals with this paradox in *Sons and Lovers:* "One might say that persons who have 'a mother fixation' fear their mothers more than their fathers. . . . By a pretense of attachment to her such a boy can conceal his hostility to her, eliminate the necessity of any fear of her, and avoid the consequences of attempting to express his masculinity in a normal way. (D. H. Lawrence described this classically in *Sons and Lovers*.)" *Love Against Hate* (New York: Harcourt, Brace and World, 1942), reprinted in Farr, p. 97. That Paul may be suffering from repressed guilt toward Walter is substantiated by Freud's ideas about the "fear" and concern sons with Oedipal problems have toward their fathers. Richard Wollheim has succinctly summarized Freud's thoughts on the subject: "On account of the loving wish for the mother and the hostile wish against the father, the child feels itself threatened by the father, and this threat is represented in his mind as the threat of castration. The child, however, also loves his father; and so along with fear of the father goes some measure of fear for the father—fear, that is, for the father on account of his, the child's, hostility." *Freud* (Fontana/Collins, 1971), p. 120.

32. Though not the only critic to make this point, Frank O'Connor may have been the first. Salgado, ed., *Casebook*, p. 150.

33. See Weiss, *Oedipus in Nottingham*, p. 32.

34. Every critic of *Sons and Lovers* must decide whether its ending is life- or death-affirming. Summarizing the opinions this critical matter has elicited would make an elephantine footnote. The following lists illustrate how critics divide on the issue. There is no pretense at being comprehensive. I regret this procrustean method, since any serious commentator brings his own nuances and details to his view:

Toward Life
Maurice Beebe
Harry T. Moore
Mark Spilka
Graham Hough
H. M. Daleski
Keith Sagar
David Cavitch
John E. Stoll
Julian Moynahan
Daniel A. Weiss
Judith Farr
E. W. Tedlock Jr., *D. H. Lawrence, Artist and Rebel: A Study of Lawrence's Fiction* (Albuquerque, N.M.: University of New Mexico Press, 1963).
Yudishtar, *Conflicts in the Novels of D. H. Lawrence* (Edinburgh: Oliver & Boyd, 1969).

Stephen J. Miko, *Toward Women in Love: The Emergence of a Lawrentian Aesthetic* (New Haven, Conn.: Yale University Press, 1971).

Toward death
Dorothy Van Ghent
Louis Fraiberg
A. B. Kuttner
R. E. Pritchard
J. M. Murry
Eliseo Vivas, *D. H. Lawrence: The Failure and the Triumph of Art* (1960; rpt. Bloomington, Ind.: Indiana University Press, 1964).

For Mark Schorer, who condemns the entire novel for confusion, the ending is harmfully self-contradictory: "in the last few sentences of the novel, Paul rejects his desire for extinction and turns toward 'the faintly humming, glowing town,' to life—as nothing in his previous history persuades us that he could unfalteringly do." *The World We Imagine*, p. 12. Donald E. Mortland provides an original twist. He finds more death than life-direction at the end, but reasons that dissolution leads toward a greater existence: "Paradoxically, Paul's vitalism becomes not a force to sustain him in life but instead one working toward the extinction of self: that which is vital and eternal is the darkness—the 'great Being'—and only by surrendering his identity to it can he truly become a part of this greater force." This is a clever resolution, but no amount of critical legerdemain can make death life. "The Conclusion of *Sons and Lovers:* A Reconsideration," *Studies in the Novel* 3, no. 3 (Fall 1971): 313.

35. Paul exemplifies R. D. Laing's concept of "the divided self" during this scene, according to David J. Kleinbard. Paul only experiences the bar with his protective, false "outer self"; the vulnerable "inner self," locus of a shaky identity, is hidden away from a world that threatens to overwhelm it and, consequently, cannot "get into touch." "Laing, Lawrence and the Maternal Cannibal," *The Psychoanalytic Review* 58, no. 3 (Spring 1971): 6.

36. In an article that generally overrates the redeeming power of artistic creativity in *Sons and Lovers*, Maurice Beebe claims that Miriam's concern for Paul, even vis-à-vis his art, is covertly possessive, hence selfish: "even as muse [Miriam] is false. She gives herself to him as a kind of sacrifice, but her aim is to possess by giving, without realizing that she must either keep her distance like a true muse or really be sacrificed if Paul is to move one phase of his artistic development to another." Yet Miriam's encouraging interest in this most separate, individual aspect of Paul acknowledges distance, and is neither sacrificial nor proprietary. "Lawrence's Sacred Fount: The Artist Theme of *Sons and Lovers*," *Texas Studies in Literature and Language* 4, no. 4 (Winter 1963), reprinted (in different form) in Salgado, ed., *Casebook*, pp. 177–90. Above excerpt from p. 182.

37. In his well-known and influential book, *The Love Ethic of D. H. Lawrence*, Mark Spilka entirely sympathizes with Paul. But the critic modifies his sympathies somewhat in a later article; referring to this last scene between Paul and Miriam Spilka is moved to write: "Yet why should Miriam relieve him of self-responsibility? What 'unknown thing' speaks *strongly* for such privileged weakness? Lawrence's lapse into special pleading reveals Paul's lapse into infantilism and self-negation." "Lawrence's Quarrel with Tenderness," *Critical Quarterly* 9, no. 4 (Winter 1967): 368.

4

Balance Through Imbalance: *The Rainbow*

In his heart of hearts I think [Lawrence] always dreaded women, felt
that they were in the end more powerful than men. Woman is so
absolute and undeniable. Man moves, his spirit flies here and there,
but you can't go beyond a woman. From her man is born and to her he
returns for his ultimate need of body and soul. She is like earth and
death to which all return.

Frieda Lawrence[1]

1

The Rainbow records man's inner life at a level beneath consciousness.[2] The centrally relevant comments Lawrence makes in a
famous letter indicate the "theme" of the novel: the exploration of
the hidden and obscure part of the self Lawrence calls the "carbon"
of character.[3] Lawrence's conception views man as existing most
vitally underneath the perceivable personality in an area indifferent to the will's power of self-formation and the conscious mind's
capacity for self-conception. It implies that the most significant and
universal dimension of human experience has been hitherto ignored by novelists. Lawrence describes the carbon-character as
"inhuman" because its nature is involuntary: entirely beyond
deliberate self-determination. This dark element in us determines
what and how we are. Invisible, the carbon of character is

nevertheless the final substance of our beings, just as carbon has no pure visible form in the universe yet is the constituent of all its manifest forms.

The highly ambitious and original subject requires an appropriate style. In an often disregarded remark from the same important letter, Lawrence calls for a carbon technique through a narrative voice that would impose neither an ethical nor an intellectual pattern on its characters: "that which is physic—non-human, in humanity, is more interesting to me than the old-fashioned human element—which causes one to conceive a character in a certain moral scheme and make him consistent. The certain moral scheme is what I object to. In Turgenev, and in Tolstoi, and in Dostoievsky, the moral scheme into which all the characters fit—and is nearly the same scheme—is, whatever the extraordinariness of the characters themselves, dull, old, dead."[4] Lawrence objects to the element in a novel formed by the author's ethical idea, just as he expresses disinterest in the part of an individual that is based on a "human conception." "Carbon" is to character, that is to say, as "tale" is to novel: the essential underlife more profound than any abstract imposition. The intruding author can play no role in a novel that successfully describes hidden being: his subject is the "diamond" of a predetermined scheme and he places an imposed abstract pattern on the underlife. The theme of *The Rainbow* forced Lawrence to discover a carbon-level of creativity in himself: he had to authentically realize the intuitions of his characters instead of formulating a pattern of idea and action for them to follow. The unified tone of *The Rainbow* and the reader's consistent sense of having penetrated to an unusually deep level of human existence demonstrate the absence of an interfering teller (for the final approbation of the writer is in the reader's consent). The achievement of carbon-narrative makes *The Rainbow* a seamless web wherein form is suited to content as both work toward the revelation of unknown facets of life.

Lawrence re-creates carbon-life through a technique we might call stream-of-unconsciousness. While certainly intent on reproducing his characters' thoughts, Lawrence is more concerned with the mysterious inner movement of their instincts, impulses and emotions. Lawrence works toward imitating this deeper existence partly by reproducing its rhythm. The central experiences of the novel's characters are structured, not in any neatly logical sequence, but in powerful contradictory waves. On the carbon-level, self-knowledge develops in a painful dialectic: perceptions occur, are contradicted, and are then re-formed: the characters move slowly, cumbersomely, toward advancing their inner selves. Thus Lawrence arrives at the elemental transformations ("allotropic changes") of carbon-being.

The teller plays a special role in *The Rainbow* and its symbolic action is of a unique kind. Stream-of-unconsciousness must be described by a narrator for only an authorial voice can translate nonverbal inner experience into language. Yet *The Rainbow* is in the inclusive Lawrencian tradition wherein being is figured by action. The difference is that the events are narrated from within, the teller describes the hidden causes and consequences of actions through a technique of *narrational inscape*.

Much of the novel focuses on the interaction of the carbon-personality and the exterior world. There is a blurring of time and space demarcations because the inward self lives in subjective time, Bergson's *la durée*,[5] and merges memory, emotion, and sensation with the objective realities of place, event, and object. Dialogue is almost irrelevant in a novel which penetrates to subverbal, subcognitive areas of life (indeed long passages of *The Rainbow* proceed without conversation). Words are often mere distractions for the novel's characters, false signals inadequate to the silent communication that takes place beneath verbalizations. Indeed, the entire surface-relationship between people is a comparatively unimportant matter in *The Rainbow*. ("What did it matter who they were, whether they knew each other or not?" says Lawrence about two of the novel's characters after their sexual union.[6]) The connections between characters that interest Lawrence are carbon-relationships, interaction on this deepest level.

The interaction ultimately reveals relative strengths-of-being. For more than the instinctive or affective or physical self (all of these are its components) the carbon is the very core of self—the part of us that distinguishes between being and nonbeing. The intuition of the self as whole or destroyed, integrated or disintegrated (a common occurrence in *The Rainbow*) takes place on the carbon level: a wordless realization, it arises mysteriously from beneath the consciousness and feels decisive.

The novel's relationships thus develop in the parts of the mind that are darkest yet most telling. The conflicts that pervade the connections would therefore express fundamental, if unarticulated, needs of the self—needs that betray whether independence or dependency is finally sought. Observing the nature of these conflicts we notice a major and central phenomenon: in all three of the generations chronicled by *The Rainbow* women are independent and integral on the deepest plane, while men are dependent and lacking separate being. The novel's men come to its women in an indirect search for strength-of-self, hoping to be saved from a threatening disintegration. The women also suffer from this inequality because their force isolates them as it destroys, or nearly destroys, the men. The ontological imbalance between men and women forms the tale of *The Rainbow*, as carbon-narrative allows Lawrence to tell his story with consistency, profundity and balance.

2

The overanalyzed opening pages of *The Rainbow* recapitulate a theme of *The White Peacock:* the untrammeled oneness of man and nature in the preindustrial British midlands.[7] The virtuosity of Lawrence's prose brings the reader into direct contact with the experience of unity: "They took the udder of the cows, the cows yielded milk and pulse against the hands of the men, the pulse of the blood of the teats of the cows beat into the pulse of the hands of the men." More than *mimesis*, the imitation of reality, this is linguistic approximation of *methexis*, the participation in reality: the reader seems to share the farmers' rhythmic intimacy with the animals.[8]

Within the farming family being described, the Brangwens, it is specifically the males who are satiated, in mute, sensory gratification; they live immersed in the heart of nature and are so overwhelmed by her sheer cyclical force that they fail to develop any identity differentiated from the surrounding natural processes: "It was enough for the men, that the earth heaved and opened its furrows to them. . . . So much warmth and generating and pain and death did they know in their blood, earth and sky and beast and green plants, so much exchange and interchange they had with these, that they lived full and surcharged, their senses full fed, their faces always turned to the heat of the blood, staring into the sun, dazed with looking towards the source of generation, unable to turn round" (pp. 8–9). *The Rainbow*, unlike *The White Peacock*, is free of pastoral sentimentality; the life depicted is hardly idyllic, and the barely individuated state of the Brangwen men is too rudimentary to be desirable.[9]

Opposed to their earthbound men, the Brangwen women look above to the church steeple and beyond to the creations of civilization. Their husbands are identified entirely with nature, but the women long for culture: "the women wanted another form of life than this, something that was not blood-intimacy. . . . She faced outwards to where men moved dominant and creative, having turned their back on the pulsating heat of creation, and with this behind them, were set out to discover what was beyond, to enlarge their own scope and range and freedom" (p. 9). In an unconscious expression of the need for balance, the Brangwen women admire the male principle,[10] the church-tower of Ilkeston, the outward thrust of ambition, while the men invest themselves in the female principle, the furrowed soil, the inert and fertile land.

Despite this initial distinction, Tom, the first Brangwen male Lawrence examines at length, is not satisfied with "blood-intimacy": Tom's mother's influence uproots him from a life of thoughtless oneness with the land. But if female ambition urges him toward a more complex existence, it rapidly becomes clear that the well-intentioned Tom is unable to meet the challenge. When he is sent, "forcibly," to school he is "an unwilling failure from the first." Unable to approach books conceptually, he comes to them with feeling and instinct, as if he might have the same intimate relationship with literature as his ancestors had with the earth. But learning through *Anschauung* leaves him feeling helpless and uncertain in the world of culture: "He sat betrayed with emotion when the teacher of literature read. . . . Tom Brangwen was moved by this experience beyond all calculation. . . . But when . . . he came to take the book himself . . . the very fact of the print caused a prickly sensation of repulsion to go over his skin, the blood came to his face, his heart filled with a bursting passion of rage and incompetence" (p. 16). The description of Tom is compelling, and he is a finer character than George Saxton, because Lawrence has objectified his own attitude toward this fumbling, sensuous type of man. Tom's difficulty is that while his mother has driven a wedge between him and the land, he only incorporates enough of the outer world to become disoriented. Yet we are not encouraged (as in *The White Peacock*) to condemn the woman who tears the man away from his roots.

Tom, like the other Brangwen males, is dependent on women for guidance in all abstract matters. He seems to have no inner source of life-values and goals, but follows the imperatives of his mother and sister. Receiving direction from women turns his developing sexuality into a problem, since his exaggerated respect for them leads him to make the old Christian division of women into Madonnas and whores. Mere "carnal contact" is "nothing, so dribbling and functional," but with a "nice girl" he is "incapable of pushing the desired development." His upbringing paralyzes him. The good sexual experience he finally does have occurs because the woman, "a handsome reckless girl" with no cheapness about her, is the initiator.[11] Afterward, when he cannot "tear himself away," we can safely assume it is her self-confidence, as well as the pleasure that she gave, that holds him. Molded by women, Tom lacks confident maleness, let alone assertive sexuality. The overinfluence of women in his formation leads to a deficiency not only of manhood but of being. Tom relies on women for his "stability"; he is like all the Brangwen males who need women in order not to feel "like straws in the wind, to be blown hither and thither at random" (p. 19).

From a distance, Tom sees the girl's lover, a "foreigner" with strange, polished manners and "cold, animal intelligence." The man invokes all the exotic unknown the Brangwen women teach Tom to desire. A vague longing overcomes him: "Brangwen went up to his room and lay staring out at the stars of the summer night, his whole being in a whirl. What was it all? There was a life so different from what he knew it. What was there outside his knowledge, how much?" (p. 25). Clearly there are two things "outside his knowledge": how to be a man with a woman, and how to cope with the complex world beyond his sphere. Tom's ineffective reaction to feeling inadequate is to turn to brandy—his drinking makes him feel happily "at one with the world" but further reduces a self he already apprehends as insufficient: "he had achieved his satisfaction by obliterating his own individuality, that which it depended on his manhood to preserve and develop" (p. 28).

After this despairing, self-destructive experience, Tom first sees Lydia Lensky, the widow and Polish refugee. He is impressed by her mysterious aura of independence: "her curious, absorbed, flitting motion, as if she were passing unseen by everybody . . . arrested him." She, too, brings him into contact with the alluring unknown world.[12] But whereas earlier the beyond has sent him into a confused "whirl," the woman gives him a place in the darkly mysterious "far world": "He moved within the knowledge of her, in the world that was beyond reality" (p. 29). Unsure that she shares his subterranean "recognition," he returns to the state of unreality and nonexistence from which she somehow saves him. "The doubt was like a sense of infinite space, a nothingness, annihilating" (pp. 29–30). The novel's prose makes us intimate with Tom's inner apprehensions, exposing the stark contradictions that exist on the irrational level of emotional intuition.

Tom's immediate, complete desire for mental intimacy with Lydia suggests transferred dependency, since he meets Lydia soon after his mother's death. But if transferred dependency is the psychology beneath the metaphysic, it is more relevant to observe that Tom does not so much see Lydia as absorb the inmost sense of the unknown woman. When Tom's sister calls Lydia "plain" the comment sounds false, exposing the paltriness of seeing. The teller's technique throughout is to explore the visions of the inner eye, to reify the emotional knowledge beyond the senses. Tom neither knows nor cares whether Lydia is "plain." She connects him not only to the mysterious sphere without, but to unconceived centers within. Through Lydia Tom moves toward self-discovery as well as the "world beyond reality." (For Tom, there is an implicit connection between certainty in the outer unknown and knowledge of an equally unknown inner self.) Awareness of her culminates for him in a "daze . . . another centre of consciousness. In his breast, or in his bowels, somewhere in his body, there had started another activity. It was as if a strong light were burning there . . . this transfiguration burned between him and her, connecting them, like a secret power" (p. 39). For the man of dark consciousness, the unfathomable communion with Lydia paradoxically brings with it the possibility of light.

But he cannot come to Lydia as an equal. She makes him feel his social and intellectual inadequacy: "he himself was her inferior in almost every way." Moreover, Tom brings Lydia his feeling of disoriented insignificance before the universe. The feeling of nonexistence in a vast darkness is one Tom shares with characters like Cyril Beardsall, Siegmund, and Paul Morel, all of whom sometimes experience themselves as minuscule and threatened by an implosive universe. Tom, however, finds a clear and direct solution: Lydia is his source of stability, a woman can prevent his feeling nullified:[13] "Unless she would come to him, he must remain as a nothingness. . . . after he had raged and tried to escape, and said he was good enough by himself, he was a man, and could stand alone, he must, in the starry multiplicity of the night humble himself, and admit and know that without her he was nothing. . . . But with her, he would be real. . . . she would bring him completeness and perfection" (p. 41).

Thinking about Lydia or taking her in his arms, Tom feels created. But his achievement of self is too dependent on her to be enduring or profound. She grants him a fleeting moment of integration, taking him to her in a carbon-meeting that brings him into a "fecund darkness"; from this darkness come the "light" and "dawn" wherein he feels newly made. But she is indifferent to the surface man, uninterested in any but the most unspoken and impersonal kind of intimacy. He, on the other hand, is not satisfied with connection on the deepest level and separation on the shallower levels of personality. The continuing distance between them and her inescapable foreignness throw him back on himself in a torment. Walking away from her embraces he returns to his former insecurity and confusion. Tom's reversion is depicted symbolically; he steps out into a night-scene whose slightly sinister morphology figuratively reflects Tom's disturbed state of mind:

> He went out into the wind. Big holes were blown into the sky, the moonlight blew about. Sometimes a high moon, liquid brilliant, scudded across a hollow space and took cover under electric, brown-iridescent cloud-edges. Then there was a blot of cloud, and shadow. Then somewhere in the night a radiance again, like a vapour. And all

the sky was teeming and tearing along, a vast disorder of flying shapes and darkness and ragged fumes of light and a great brown circling halo, then the terror of a moon running liquid-brilliant into the open for a moment, hurting the eyes before she plunged under cover of cloud again. (P. 49)

The lines are very beautiful, and the mood they express need not be overelaborated. But in this imagery of torn chaos briefly irradiated by moonlight it is possible to see a parallel with Tom's unformed being and its recent exposure to Lydia's light.[14] The moon is elusive, only intermittently illuminating, and threatening, and these characteristics apply to Tom's perception of Lydia as well. (The phrase "terror of the moon" is applicable to Lydia because the challenges and demands and mysteries associated with the foreign woman make her frightening.)

It is necessary at this point to make a distinction between the integrating effect Lydia has on Tom and what she is in herself. The fact is that when we meet the two characters they are *both* in a dark state, lacking in self-realization. In their union they bring one another into a mutual "new birth." Lydia's darkness however is very different from Tom's; she is not ignorant but blank as after a deliberate spurning of consciousness. Deculturated and deprived of her language, she is very nearly a person without a surface personality—one who is all inarticulable carbon. Even on the deepest level she has gone into retreat. She is in her position partly because of external circumstance—and partly as a result of choice. She has recoiled from the affairs of men and withdrawn into apathy. Her first husband, Paul Lensky, was a dedicated doctor and fierce, patriotic Polish revolutionary who "worked very hard, till nothing lived in him but his eyes." An embodiment of the male-principle, he lived only to extend his will and abstract ideas into the outer world. Even the death of his children barely interrupted his labors. The world of intellect and ideals Lydia shared with her husband gradually grew meaningless. From having her femaleness brutally, utterly ignored, she withered into a "darkness . . . like remorse, or like a remembering of the dark, savage, mystic ride of dread, of death, of the shadow of revenge" (p. 51). She remains in this strange state, afraid, resentful, and, finally, in a "heavy oblivion," after Lensky dies and until she meets Tom.

Lydia's darkness (it is essential to make distinctions among the many ways Lawrence uses this word), then, is of thwarted, neglected life, of sterility. Like Lettie in *The White Peacock,* Lydia has a vital response to the sight of some flowering snowdrops. She is painfully stirred into personal life by the experience of life in nature and drawn toward Tom because she wants him to continue the process of renewal: "He was the man who had come nearest to her for her awakening." But Lydia's desire for revitalization is not equivalent to Tom's need for completion. Lydia is quiescent, but Tom is not fully created.[15] The difference is that between the life that lies dormant and the life that has only begun. Nor is it difficult to understand why Lydia accepts Tom: his "fresh" vitality and intimacy with natural life-forces engage her instinct for self-renewal.

Yet he seems inadequate to her unspoken demand that he meet her and take her on the carbon-level. He is self-conscious and rather conventional, unable to abandon himself and join her in the unknown element. In contrast, Lydia almost always lives and functions within her deepest self, perceiving Tom from within her "radically-unchanged element" and gradually undergoing an "allotropic" change from passiveness to receptivity. But Tom's misplaced emphasis on outer considerations ruins the consummation she now seeks: "she opened and turned to him . . . new as a flower that unsheathes itself and stands always ready, waiting, receptive. . . . He forced himself, through lack of understanding, to the adherence to the line of honourable courtship and sanctioned, licensed marriage. . . . She gave herself to the hour, but he could not, and he bungled in taking her" (pp. 56–57). Only after they marry and social sanction is given to natural attraction can Tom join Lydia in "an elemental embrace beyond their superficial foreignness." Now "his eyes opened on a new universe," and he can, through her, come into "contact with the unknown, the unaccountable and incalculable" without being overwhelmed.

The marriage-struggle, the search for accommodation of differences, now first begins. Tom is often in "a raging fury" because there is so much of Lydia he fails to reach. Lydia, a triumph of Lawrence's characterization, is an intriguing woman. Her pride, hardened by pain, makes her isolated, and her separateness draws on private sources of strength. There is a curious potency about her blankness, as if suffering had burned away excrescence and left only a deep and feminine essence. Her background of revolutions, pogroms (which she had observed with vague, amoral amusement), and violence is utterly foreign and inexplicable to a simple, good-natured English farmer. What this means for Tom is that he can never have her entirely. She lives in her own dark area, "quiet, secure, unnoticed, unnoticing," an area of memories and unsharable experiences, but most significant as the center of her inviolable carbon-self. Her separate integrity sends him, at times, into a "raging fury"; he possessively resists her withdrawal into herself. Yet as he presses for a more inclusive intimacy, he neglects the rare and valuable connection that does exist. In his demand for everything, he fails the darkness—both more mysterious and more sexual than Brangwen "blood-intimacy"—she does offer him. Intuitively, Lydia locates the heart of the problem: instead of actively pressing, he has been passively awaiting gratification: "You think you have not enough in me. But how do you know me? What do you do to make me love you?" (p. 92). As they exchange accusations, Lydia realizes why Tom cannot come to her in the achieved certainty of his manhood: he still needs her support, for he lacks fundamental confidence. In order to reinforce his being, she makes a gesture of seeming subservience: "And she put her arms round him as he stood before her, round his thighs, pressing him against her breast. And her hands on him seemed to reveal to him the mould of his own nakedness, he was passionately lovely to himself" (p. 94).

She amplifies him by showing him his own male power. This is not an artificial bolstering, but the realization of Tom's potential that both of them need. Continuing the process, Lydia stubbornly refuses to allow Tom to bow, in awe, before her femaleness. She demands that they enter the darkness as equals, that he maintain self-possession, for only the man who has himself can lose himself in something greater: "Easiest he could kiss her feet. But he was too ashamed for the actual deed, which were almost like an affront. She waited for him to meet her, not to bow before her and serve her. She wanted his active participation, not his submission. . . . And it was torture to him, that he must give himself to her actively, participate in her, that he must meet and embrace and know her, who was other than himself" (p. 95). Lydia wants the sexual merging of an entire man and an entire woman; it is not sufficient for Tom to just submerge himself in her.

Sexual consummation comes after Lydia leads Tom to his own masculinity and being. Yet the matter is complex, and success demands still another transformation. During the passion-experience, the newly established self must be relinquished as both partners, in mutual self-release, lose themselves again, this time to find themselves in the fertilizing darkness.[16] The transfiguration occurs to both of them, but the early part of the description focuses on Tom because his is the greater struggle:

> She was beyond him, the unattainable. But he let go his hold on himself, he relinquished himself, and he knew the subterranean force of his desire to come to her, to be with her, to mingle with her, losing himself to find her, to find himself in her. . . . She was there, if he could reach her. The reality of her who was just beyond absorbed him. Blind and destroyed, he pressed forward, nearer, nearer, to receive the consummation of himself, be received within the darkness which should swallow him and yield him up to himself. If he could come really within the blazing kernel of darkness, if really he could be destroyed, burnt away till he lit with her in one consummation, that were supreme, supreme. (P. 95)

This passage is typical of *The Rainbow's* style, and shows us that the teller of the tale is nearly invisible because its prose is so exceptionally intimate with the obscure reality it describes. Using repetitive rhythm and metaphorical language, the teller captures the agonizingly slow pace of emotional revelation; discovering through instinct, Tom feels his way to understanding. The inspired discipline of the teller persuades us that we are sharing Tom's wordless transformation. This experience leads Tom to the vivid insight that the satisfying, regenerating relation to the greater beyond depends on first acknowledging the beyond in the other person. This is demonstrated by a balanced entrance to the darkness, where neither partner dominates, but both are temporarily and fruitfully obliterated; equal loss leads to equal gain.

Yet problems remain. Tom is in the paradoxical position of being dependent on Lydia for independence. She bows to his weakness to give him required strength, and the contradictions inherent in the necessity are not easily resolved. Tom never does develop a precise, definite sense of self. In later years he continues to blur the distinction between himself and the people close to him: we see this not only in relation to Lydia but toward their daughter, Anna. Tom is aware of his possessive reluctance to grant his daughter's separateness, his "greedy middle-age which must stand in the way of life, like a large demon." Feeling discomfiting twinges of jealousy at his daughter's love for her cousin, Will Brangwen, Tom regrets his eternal uncertainty: "What weariness! There was no peace, however old one grew! One was never right, never decent, never master of oneself" (p. 129). The admission of irresolution indicates that on a fundamental level Tom has failed to attain self-assurance.

Such admissions increase our sense of Tom's attractive honesty and humility; moreover, Tom's acknowledgements of unsureness contribute to the force and consistency of *The Rainbow*. In this novel statement articulates the tale, where in the earlier works explicit utterances by character or narrator often contradicted the realized meaning. In *The Rainbow* all the levels of the work, statement, thought, action, and carbon-narrative, contribute to an achieved artistic unity. The various modes of presentation combine to show that Tom, for all his positive qualities, is plagued by a continuing sense of vulnerability, the haunting conviction that he is an unsubstantial man.

Tom's state-of-being receives its final form in a climactic symbolic action that vividly objectifies the character's inner struggles. The action occurs within a natural landscape and makes use of the symbolic suggestions of water. The handling of water-imagery in *The Rainbow* produces a consistent association between that element and the male tendency toward disintegration; it is both antithetic and closely linked to moon, the image for integration in woman.[17] The complexity and power of the water-image can hardly be reduced to one level of meaning (like poetry, symbols defy paraphrase). But water is used in the novel as both the emblem and the embodiment of nature's dark, primitive forces. These forces may be taken as one of the meanings of the teller's mysterious references to the "unknown" or "beyond" (nature's vitality is one of the powers beyond knowing, past cognition). Because of the destructiveness of water, its inclination to chaos, the element suggests the unknown in a dangerous manifestation. This aspect of the unknown is experienced by those who are not sufficiently individuated to keep an ultimate distinction between inner and outer darkness. Water, the engulfing element, represents the living universe as it is encountered by men who lack the self-definition to maintain themselves against it. Just as the moon reflects the woman who stands sterilely apart from the surrounding Life-Force[18] (in itself a character in the novel), so water seems indicative of both the man who fails to distinguish himself from this power and the power itself in its annihilating dimension.

Water plays a role of this kind on the night Tom is drowned by a great, sweeping flood. On that night there is an immense rainfall and Tom returns to his farm drunk, having partially extinguished his consciousness at the local pub. Descending from his cart, he walks into the storm with unthinking recklessness. His first consideration, pointing to his natural goodness, is to lead his mare into the safety of the cart-shed. But then he fails to show the same competent concern about himself. Going beyond heedlessness to self-destruction, some unconscious will-to-annihilation impels him directly into the destructive element of the overflowing pond: "He went to meet the running flood, sinking deeper and deeper. . . . He *had* to go and look where it came from, though the ground was going from under his feet. . . . He was knee-deep, and the water was pulling heavily. He stumbled, reeled sickeningly" (p. 246). To gain his bearings in the cosmic "whirl" outside him, Tom had always needed Lydia. But his wife cannot grant him permanent strength of being. Without her he is unable to withstand the unknown and the flood reifies the swimming darkness within which he needs Lydia's support. As he stumbles in the twisting whirlpools he holds "tightly" to his "gig-lamp." This exterior light (his interior light now fails him and its weakness is demonstrated) is not enough to save him: "The water was whirling, whirling, the whole black night was swooping in rings. . . . a great wonder of anguish went over him, then the blackness covered him entirely. . . . And the unconscious, drowning body was washed along in the black, swirling darkness, passively" (p. 247).

When she sees his corpse, Lydia imbues Tom with a noble separateness: "He was beyond change or knowledge, absolute, laid in line with the infinite. What had she to do with him? He was a majestic Abstraction, made visible now for a moment, inviolate, absolute" (p. 251). But these lines are partly a general statement about death, partly a reflection of Lydia's long-suffering, slightly inhuman view of the world. They should not be confused with the actual nature of the living Tom. In the fact of the black flood, he had not shown a force of separateness but a dissolution of being.[19]

3

The second generation of characters presented in *The Rainbow* exceeds the first in consciousness and creativity. But the superior capacities of Will and Anna Brangwen are misused when their relationship degenerates into a struggle of wills; their enervating conflict reduces their achievements as individuals and results in a marriage that fails its potential.

From our first meeting with Anna, we are aware that she brings a new element into the novel. She is introduced as a child with "wide, overconscious dark eyes." When she grows into an articulate young woman, Anna adds consciousness to her parents' "fecund darkness." She is verbal, wanting language to bring rational meaning to the rich emotionalism of the Brangwen house. But her parents rebuff interference with their "wordless, intense and close" way of living and communicating. "Sometimes Anna talked to her father. She tried to discuss people, she wanted to know what was meant. But her father became uneasy. He did not want to have things dragged into consciousness. . . . Mrs. Brangwen was silent, she seemed ominous. Anna could not go on with her fault-finding, her criticism, her expression of dissatisfactions. She felt even her father against her. He had a strong, dark bond with her mother, a potent intimacy that existed inarticulate and wild, following its own course, and savage if interrupted, uncovered" (p. 106).

Anna's subsequent attraction to the nonverbal Will Brangwen seems inconsistent, but constancy of character is a novelistic convention, truer to art than life. However useful and necessary this convention is, Lawrence deliberately abjured it with his carbon theory. Lawrence's character exposition, in *The Rainbow*, is based on contradictions: he is searching for a deeper unity of character than the traditional consistency of manners and attitudes. Beneath surface differences is an essence of character. Each person (this is the point wherein Lawrence's theory diverges importantly from Jung's collective unconscious)[20] has his own "radically-unchanged element." It is possible to speak of the characters in *The Rainbow* as Lawrencean archetypes, figures captured on a universal impersonal level who are yet unique individuals. Lawrence explores the *various* carbons of his characters.

In addition, working through contradictions leads to character-revelation. Anna's superficial rebelliousness is belied by her choice of a mate who resembles her parents. Not that Will fails to make his own contribution to the Brangwen tradition. He is described through bird and animal imagery: "He . . . was thin, with a very curious head, black as jet, with hair like sleek, thin fur. . . . it reminded her . . . of some animal . . . that lived in darkness . . . vividly, swift and intense" (p. 107); "His eyes were hard and bright with a fierce purpose and gladness, like a hawk's" (p. 117). These similes and related images invest Will with a penetrating male force more intense than Tom's passive virility.

Similarly, his spirituality is more consuming than Lydia's veiled, secretive religiosity. This causes an early problem between Will and Anna. His reverent participation in a church service embarrasses her: "At the very first word, his voice came strong and overriding, filling the church. . . . She was helplessly shocked into laughter" (p. 110). Her incredulous reaction to the strength of his response is an indication of how self-conscious sharpness of mind, and a tendency to mockery, diminish her depth of soul.

The essence of their conflict, however, is captured in a scene of corn harvesting. Their rhythmic, natural activity in the darkness establishes a relation to the "unknown," the animate universe that underlies all the events of *The Rainbow*.[21] But if the scene starts in teleology, it ends in ontology; the encounter with nature brings out the relative strengths of the two characters. Putting up their sheaves in the moonlit night, their work begins in mutuality: "They worked together, coming and going, in a rhythm, which carried their feet and their bodies in tune." But Will is unsatisfied with activity in independent unison. He tries persistently to join their two experiences, interweaving their beings just as he tangles and threads their respective sheaves of corn:[22] "As he came, she drew away, as he drew away, she came. Were they never to meet? Gradually a low, deep-sounding will in him vibrated to her, tried to set her in accord, tried to bring her gradually to him, to a meeting, till they should be together, till they should meet as the sheaves that swished together" (p. 123). She resists him throughout the scene, looking toward the symbol of her independence, the moon: "Why, as she came up from under the moon, would she halt and stand off from him?" Her elusiveness brings out the ominous insistence of his will: "His will drummed persistently, darkly, it drowned everything else." Finally she embraces him; he uses the kiss to try and overwhelm her individuality: "And the whole rhythm of him beat into his kisses, and still her pursued her, in his kisses, and still she was not quite overcome." The result is that *he* is overcome; he singles her out as his own, and senses her permanent dominion over him: "Something fixed in him forever. He was hers." In instinctive understanding that he removes the distinctions between them, she loosens herself from him. Aggressively dependent, he finds the way to yoke her to him permanently: "We'll get married, Anna."

Their honeymoon gives Will perfect bliss. Like a mystic encountering God, Will feels reborn, redeemed from mere diversion into the beautiful and real; he finds the turning world's still point in a woman's body: "As they lay together, complete and beyond the touch of time or change, it was as if they were at the very centre of all the slow wheeling of space and the rapid agitation of life, deep, deep inside them all, at the centre where there is utter radiance, and eternal being" (p. 145). Being more puritanical, it is harder for Will than it is for Anna to relinquish the daylight, working world; being more dependent, it is far more difficult for him to return from their soft sensuality to practical reality: "She was less hampered than he, so she came more quickly to her fullness, and was sooner ready to enjoy again a return to the outside world." Once in the darkness, Will wants to abide there. The delights of their seemingly timeless sexual union diminish his capacity to stand alone.

When Lydia failed to give Tom adequate support, his escape was destructive of no one but himself; in his frustration, Will turns to ugly, nearly violent forms of hostility.[23] Tom is passive-dependent, accepting his situation. Will is aggressive-dependent, struggling for or against what he is; the teller skillfully dissects the two men's different yet similar carbons of character. The narrator shows that the strange mixture of strength and weakness in Will twists his force. He feels "dread" and "shame" at his desperate need for her, and after Anna, exasperated, demands an end to his burdensome clinging, his soul makes an unexpected revolution from nothingness to hatred: " 'Can't you do anything?' she said, as if to a child, impatiently. 'Can't you do your wood-work?'. . . . Never had his soul felt so flayed and uncreated. . . . His hovering near her, wanting her to be with him, the futility of him, the way his hands hung, irritated her beyond bearing. She turned on him blindly and destructively, he became a mad creature, black and electric with fury. . . . He seemed a dark, almost evil thing" (p. 152). Will is a disturbing man, full of a need that turns vengeful when frustrated. The self that is so easily obliterated finds substance in a negativity based on hostility and bitter volition: he thus finds self-sufficiency and a way of denying her: "Everything had gone: he remained complete in his own tense, black will. He was now unaware of her. She did not exist. His dark, passionate soul had recoiled upon itself, and now, clinched and coiled round a centre of hatred, existed in its own power. . . . His will seemed grappled upon her" (p. 152). His self-sufficiency is deceptive, for its potency is founded on hatred of her: indirectly he continues to be defined in terms of his reactions to Anna. Anna naturally resists him, but opposing him frightens her. "There was a curiously ugly pallor, an expressionlessness in his face. She shuddered from him."

She "retreates" to her parents' farm. Will remains at their cottage, "working monotonously at the garden, blindly, like a mole." Returning, she grasps for normalcy by complimenting his work: " 'How nice you've made it,' she said, approaching tentatively down the path. But he did not heed, he did not hear. His brain was solid and dead" (p. 153). Either she will accept the terms of his overweening will, or he will malevolently negate her. Though weak, Will is paradoxically able to press relentlessly for the situation that pacifies his need. His weapon is his dependent ego's talent for hatred. The massively unyielding force of his negativity breaks her down:[24] "It was his negative insensitiveness to her that she could not bear, something clayey and ugly. His intelligence was self-absorbed. . . . Nothing could touch him—he could only absorb things into his own self" (p. 154).

Denied fusion he retreats utterly into a sub-communicative core of will; the capacity for distancing is as absolute as the desire for intimacy. He moves between total outpouring and total withdrawal, incapable of an interaction that respects the integrity of the self and the other. When he does finally regret her misery, there is no resolution; the self-abnegation he feels recapitulates the root of the problem: "He wanted to give everything to her, all his blood, his life, to the last dregs, pour everything away to her. He yearned with passionate desire to offer himself to her, utterly" (p. 155). In sheer fatigue of struggle and bruised emotions she accepts him, but: "There *was* no understanding. There could be only acquiescence and submission, and tremulous wonder of consummation."

Their religious differences closely follow their personal and sexual conflicts. Both the church and Anna's body allow Will to lose his identity into something exterior. Anna opposes Will's religious adoration because of its relation to the merging need that plagues their marriage. At the same time, Anna's antagonism to Will's belief is *her* way of being destructive. Rich spirituality is one of the strengths of his unusual character; she shows her contradictory possessiveness by trying to deny areas of experience within which he fails to need her: "She could not get out of the church the satisfaction he got. . . . In a way, she envied it him, this dark freedom and jubilation of the soul. . . . It fascinated her. Again she hated it. And again, she despised him, wanted to destroy it in him" (p. 159). She struggles against his depth as he undermines her independence.

Their minds function dissimilarly; hers is literal, his symbolic. His brain barely perceives external reality: "He was like a man whose eyes were in his chest." He perceives with his soul, and his soul is the kind that finds self-reflection everywhere. Her rational mind is a necessary ballast to Will's blurring of subject and object. For Will's undifferentiated ego the outer world is both extinction and consummation, crushing him or giving him infinite contiguity. Either way, Anna feels denied and overshadowed by the movements of his soul.

Taking his wood-panel of Adam and Eve as a sign of her diminishment, Anna attacks it: "She jeered at the Eve. . . . 'You've made Adam as big as God, and Eve like a doll' " (p. 174). This is a sharp perception. The carving does reflect Will's view of woman as a link between God, the vague greater reality, and man, a figure looking for salvation through woman. "Adam lay asleep as if suffering, and God, a dim, large figure, stooped towards him, stretching forward His unveiled hand; and Eve, a small vivid, naked female shape, was issuing like a flame towards the hand of God, from the torn side of Adam" (p. 120). Her derision inadvertently breaks his creative impulse. Challenging his (seemingly unconscious) reduction of women is harmful, since her resistance to his tyranny-of-the-weak eviscerates him. She regrets the damage done, however, and her feelings are renewed by compassion: "a new, fragile flame of love came out of the ashes of this last pain." If Anna has certain "aggressive"[25] designs on Will, she acts, basically, to protect her own integrity.

As was the case with Tom and Lydia, the strained relationship of the younger couple further deteriorates when the woman becomes pregnant. Anna's pregnancy exacerbates Will's fear of self-obliteration almost to the point of insanity: "he ended uncompleted, as yet uncreated in the darkness, and he wanted her to come and liberate him into the whole. . . . His need, and his shame of need, weighed on him like a madness" (p. 179). His characteristic reaction is to try to force her into accepting his submission. She, meanwhile, is filled with impervious optimism. Fulfilled by the embryo she carries, she reaches out to Will in her general positiveness. He cannot bear the healthy ordinariness of an emotion which places and limits his role, and resents that in Anna which exists irrespective of him.

In answer to Will's attempted compulsion Anna performs a dance of praise to a force she calls the "Lord," which seems to be an incarnation of the male principle in all its independent splendor. Her obeisance goes past Will to a greater power, and her perspective broadens when she escapes from individual insistence to an awareness of eternal process; she shifts her allegiance to "the unseen Creator who had chosen her, to whom she belonged." Indeed, the dance is aimed against Will: "She would dance his nullification." She does not dance before the self-mirroring element of moon, but in front of a fire. According to Lawrence's cosmology, there is a fairly clear relation between fire imagery and the male principle.[26] Anna's ritual-dance, then, is a ceremony of respect for that which matches and equals her: and it is not Will who is capable of effecting the balance.

After the dance scene, Will's dependency comes to a crisis. His mounting self-hatred demands a resolution to the pathological need for his wife; his only other choice is to lose his mind: "Was he impotent, or a cripple or a defective, or a fragment. . . . Why, if Anna left him even for a week, did he seem to be clinging like a madman to the edge of reality, and slipping surely, surely into the flood of unreality that would drown him? (p. 187). Incipient madness leads to the denouement of the extraordinarily intense "Anna Victrix" chapter; after forty pages of dense, repetitive prose in which the teller plunges deeply into the blind welter of hate, love, fear, and need that is Will's "radically-unchanged element," there is a sudden relaxation. Will releases his psychic grip and yields the attempted fusion: "He would insist no more, he would force her no more. . . . He would let go, relax, lapse, and what would be, should be" (p. 190). Now Will feels he has "come into his own existence," received a "separate identity." But in Will's case—and here *The Rainbow* differs from the earlier novels— Lawrence does not confer an unmerited or exaggerated substantiality on his male character. On the contrary, Will's development is tentative in the extreme ("it was a very dumb, weak, helpless self, a crawling nursling") and subtly justified. Will progresses through release, "he relaxed, something gave way in him," and what is released is the will. This leads to self-creation because the relentless obsessive application of will to an object is tantamount to a (tyrannical) dependency on that object. Constantly struggling with Anna, he is entirely involved with her; suspending his insistence he suspends—to a slight degree—his reliance on her. At last he "relaxes" into separateness, realizing that, barring death or insanity, there is no way to reduce duality to unity. He cannot compel Anna into a sharing of self or an identity of will.

His development is mitigated. Will is "free, separate and independent" enough to be a husband to his wife and a father to his new-born daughter, Ursula. But Anna is "the victor" because Will still does not grow into puissant manhood. He becomes, rather, an adjunct to Anna's womanhood and the round of biological productivity that now forms their lives. During the birth of the first of her many children, Anna feels the triumph of her femaleness: "Even the fierce, tearing pain was exhilarating. . . . She knew she was winning, she was always winning, with each onset of pain she was nearer to victory" (p. 192). For all her genuine female force, Anna's "victory" is hollow; settling entirely for the pleasures and responsibilities of the flesh, she gives up the exploration of the world beyond her individual, physical self, and is limited. Will also subserviates himself, in the body of his wife, to the female-principle of natural, physical life. Giving up ambition in the outer world, "the man's world was exterior and extraneous to his own real life with Anna," he presents no adequate counterforce to her.

The shortcomings in Anna and Will are symbolically presented in "The Cathedral" chapter. Giving external form to Will's loss-of-self urge, the huge church is a Lawrencian objective correlative.[27] The cathedral, like Anna, absorbs Will, relieving him of self-responsibility. Hinting at his equation of religious and sensual union, Will applies a feminine gender to the building; this annoys Anna who from past experience is suspicious of his ecstasies. The church's importance for Will is its resolution of diversity into unity; a perfect embodiment of singleness, the church stabilizes the fluctations of time, and cancels the individual personality, embedded in time:

> Away from time, always outside of time! Between east and west, between dawn and sunset. . . . Spanned round with the rainbow, the jewelled gloom folded music upon silence, light upon darkness, fecundity upon death.
>
> . . . .
> he gathered himself together in transit, every jet of him strained and leaped, leaped clear into the darkness above, to the fecundity and the unique mystery, to the touch, the clasp, the consummation, the climax of eternity, the apex of the arch." (p. 201–2)

Will's spiritual experiences are too vivid to be easily dismissed, for he has a large and noble comprehension of the sublime. Like Tom he is unable to be articulate in words, but he can understand, and create, articulations in stone and wood. His soul leaps upward in a Gothic cathedral, responding to its massive materialization of spiritual longing; here loss-of-self is more achievement than escape.

The satisfaction of Will's experience is qualified by Anna. She rejects his static consummation and diverges from her husband's willingness to be gathered and absorbed into a stone, closed arch: "she remembered that the open sky was no blue vault, no dark dome hung with many twinkling lamps, but a space where stars

were wheeling in freedom, with freedom above them always higher"
(p. 203). Both have loyalties to forces beyond themselves, but Will
prefers religion, which he associates with fusion, while Anna,
looking past the cathedral to "freedom," chooses the openness of
nature. (By an ironic reversal the church steeple, liberating at the
novel's opening, now represents closure.)

Within a few lines Anna minimizes the depth and dignity of her
view. Anna is so fearful of Will's absolutism that she denies the
possibility of all spiritual experience. Some carvings of "sly little
faces" on the wall provide a welcome interruption to the monolith of
the church. Revealing the narrowness of her own life-view, Anna
equates the carvings with rivalry between man and woman: " 'He
knew her, the man who carved her,' said Anna. 'I'm sure she was
his wife.'. . . . 'Hasn't he made her hideous to a degree?' . . . .
'You hate to think he put his wife in your cathedral, don't you?' she
mocked, with a tinkle of profane laughter. And she laughed with
malicious triumph. She had got free from the cathedral, and had
even destroyed the passion he had. She was glad" (p. 205). Her
remarks shatter Will's transcendent oneness by bringing domestic
strife into his pure vision.

This is an example of what F. R. Leavis accurately describes as
Anna's "destructive rationalism."[28] Going beyond destroying
Will's harmful delusions, Anna deliberately minimizes his experiential capacity. It begins to look as though Anna enjoys Will's
weakness and wants to protract his faltering unsureness. Both
characters suffer fron the extent of her mockery. Struggling with his
overweening need for soul-union, she goes too far and reduces both
his creativity and his self-realization: "His life was shifting its
centre, becoming more superficial. He had failed to become really
articulate, failed to find real expression. He had to continue in the
old form. But in spirit, he was uncreated" (p. 206). Purposely
divesting herself of all but natural concerns and crudely empirical
knowledge, she limits her own experience of life to the
reproductive-cycle: "Anna was absorbed in the child now. . . . If
her soul had found no utterance, her womb had" (p. 206).

At the end of "The Cathedral" chapter Will remains a dark,
uncreated man, who "submits" to a marriage on his wife's terms.
Under the surface, however, his former urge-toward-domination is
only quiescent. His ugly moods soon recommence. Will's darkness

leads to alternating waves of retreat and assertion. (Such reversals
are typical of Lawrence's method of character development in *The
Rainbow*.) Before long Will tries to establish supremacy again.
Anna is able to resist him, so he looks for other objects of
domination. He tries first, and unsuccessfully, to establish himself
in an ascendant position in relation to his eldest child, Ursula.
Then, beginning to drift away from home, Will forms a liaison with
a town girl from neighbouring Nottingham. The very ordinary,
lower-class girl infuses him with power. She offers him a dual
attraction: the pliant obedience of a child together with the sexuality of a woman: "The slim arm that went down so still and
motionless to the lap, it was pretty. She would be small, he would
be able almost to hold her in his two hands. . . . Her childishness
whetted him keenly. She would be helpless between his hands"
(pp. 227–28). His goal with her is a feeling of male omnipotence: a
compensation for his general feeling of being submerged in Anna's
reality.

Also important is the *impersonal* nature of Will's contact with the
girl: "He did not want to know anything about her. . . . He was
given over altogether to the sensuous knowledge of this woman, and
every moment he seemed to be touching absolute beauty" (pp.
230–31). Unaware of specific personalities, Will tests his elemental male power on the anonymous young woman. Will is revitalized
by the experience; he is reconnected to his own masculinity. Anna
corresponds to his new mood by being attracted to this formidable
and potent "stranger"; she responds fully to his new sexual force:
"She liked him better than the ordinary mute, half-effaced, half-
subdued man she usually knew him to be. . . . To his latent, cruel
smile she replied with brilliant challenge" (pp. 234–35). Their
dulling personal conflict, developed through years of marriage, is
vicariously removed by the fundamental sensuality of Will's contact with the girl. Profiting from the pleasant paradox that impersonal sexuality is best in a personal relationship, Will and Anna
rediscover one another: "They abandoned in one motion the
moral position, each was seeking gratification pure and simple. . . .
Sometimes he felt he was going mad with a sense of Absolute
Beauty, perceived by him in her through his senses. . . . This was
what their love had become, a sensuality violent and extreme as
death. They had no conscious intimacy, no tenderness of love. It

was all the lust and the infinite, maddening intoxication of the senses, a passion of death" (pp. 235–37).

As a consummately intense sexual experience that, in addition, resolves emotional alienation between the two partners, this passage seems related to Tom and Lydia's voyage into the "unknown" (pp. 94–96). Yet unlike the encounter between Tom and Lydia, Will's and Anna's sexuality is neither in touch with the beyond, nor based on an achieved balance between the partners. Rather, their sex is an adventure in the uninhibited exploration of the resources of lust. Necessary to this exploration is the eradication of shame; in *The Rainbow*, as in other works of Lawrence, the *rite de passage* past shame seems to be anal intercourse: "Shame, what was it? It was part of extreme delight. . . . The secret, shameful things are most terribly beautiful. They accepted shame, and were one with it in their most unlicensed pleasures. . . . It was a bud that blossomed into beauty and heavy, fundamental gratification" (p. 238). Will's and Anna's "infinite sensual violence" does not lead "through the doorway into the further space" of the living universe but rather to a kind of idolatry, to the worship of "supreme, immoral, Absolute Beauty, in the body of a woman."

Will's instinct for subservience keeps their sexual encounter from being equal, and this precludes the younger couple from the transfiguration experienced by Tom and Lydia. Relevantly, Lydia rejects Tom's temptation to self-minimization. But Anna receives and encourages Will's wild, humiliating desire for self-obliteration like a complacent *magna mater*: "He wanted to wallow in her, bury himself in her flesh, cover himself over with her flesh. And she, separate, with a strange, dangerous, glistening look in her eyes received all his activities upon her as if they were expected by her, and provoked him when he was quiet to more" (pp. 236–37). Will shifts from the male, pointed, Gothic arch of the church to the female, round, Norman arch of Anna's body; in both cases he is contained by the greater form and only partially created.

Yet there is a partial creation that derives from their "sensuality violent and extreme as death." In this sexuality, marked by an absence of love, the soul and the ego are ignored and only the body is recognized (hence the Nottingham girl prepared Will for the experience). But this recognition of the body, if limited, is mutual, a "voluptuousness" they enjoy "together." At a certain point their lovemaking stops being Will's ecstatic immersion in Anna and becomes something "terribly beautiful" for both of them. The point is reached when their sex becomes anal.

Anality obscurely leads the male toward some equality with the female body he perceives as awesome and enveloping. There is perhaps insufficient evidence to relate this to a fear of the *vagina dentata* (the castrating female sexual part), but in Lawrence's novels phallic power is not always a match for vaginal sexuality. Taking the female anally is one way for the male to still her dominance—the man shows his force and receives a certain beauty through shame. In *The Rainbow* the sharing of "secret shameful things" causes Anna to perceive Will's masculine strength. The vision of his body as separate and desirable leads to the sense of a single, integral self. After the male appreciates the beautiful potency of his sexuality, something in his soul crystallizes.

Finding himself through the body, however, is finding himself in her terms; physical values are Anna's—he had wanted the life of the spirit. He remains overshadowed by her life, her child-begetting and child-rearing. Hence his achievement in the outer world of ambition and action is small. Yet it is precisely the carefully gauged degree of his accomplishment that convinces. Lawrence connects the advance of the outer man to that of the inner, and he meticulously describes the "allotropic" changes and perceptions occurring within Will's hidden, unexpressed self. It is persuasive that a new self-acceptance and confidence in his "intimate life" frees Will for "public life." In relation to Will, the teller justifies the claimed progress. The character's fragile, fractional accession into being is communicated by the tale.

4

As Anna withdraws from Will into the domestic details of family life, the highly sensitive Ursula becomes the intimate of his intense inner life. His exaggerated demands and irrational, often hostile, moods shock her prematurely out of childish unawareness: "Her father was the dawn wherein her consciousness woke up." Will's object with his young daughter is to match his will against hers: to dominate the girl as he had been dominated. He wants an intimacy

through fear and he is aggressive toward her because his distur-
bances now express themselves in possessiveness. But very early
she learns to withdraw into a protective self-containment. "She was
always relapsing on her own violent will into her own separate
world of herself. This made him grind his teeth with bitterness, for
he still wanted her. But she could harden herself into her own self's
universe, impregnable" (p. 225).

Moreover, Will tries to mingle Ursula with his own inchoate
being. If we think of that which is unformed in Will as being
imaged by water, we can understand the scenes where Will leaps
into a canal with "the naked child clinging on to his shoulders."
Sinking with her beneath the formless element, it is as though he
were attempting to frighten her out of separate integrity into dark
disintegration. "The crash of the water as they went under struck
through the child's small body, with a sort of unconsciousness. But
she remained fixed. . . . the dark-dilated eyes of the child looked
at him wonderingly, darkly, wondering from the shock, yet reserved and unfathomable. . . . he would leap again with her from
the bridge, daringly, almost wickedly. . . . they fell into the water
in a heap, and fought for a few moments with death. . . . his eyes
were full of the blackness of death" (p. 225). Ursula has an
independent ego from the beginning. Will's challenges clarify her
resiliency of self, having the reverse effect of the one intended. The
immersion in the canal is one of various experiences that develop
Ursula's capacity to enter the annihilating darkness while preserv-
ing herself.

The child Ursula grows into an idealistic and large-spirited girl.
She becomes the kind of person who instinctively avoids pettiness,
and whom pettier people just as instinctively try to diminish. Yet,
in a kind of noble innocence, she expects other people to show her
own confident independence. There is a problem in her very force,
since she shows no inclination to yield to the outside world. An
adolescent with a resplendent vision of reality, she is at a loss when
people or ideas are not suffused with the expected "magic." For she
wants reality to reflect her own splendid potentialities. Thus, her
mother's "practical indifference," Anna's domestic, disordered
existence, seems limited and tawdry to Ursula: "She knew as a
child what it was to live amid storms of babies, in the heat and

swelter of fecundity. And as a child, she was against her mother, passionately against her mother, she craved for some spirituality and stateliness" (pp. 264–65).

Ursula follows her father, sharing his religious devotion, uniting with his penchant for the "ultimate." Christ provides her with an ideal she can worship, and the form the revered image takes provides an insight into Ursula's self-conception: "To her, Jesus was beautifully remote, shining in the distance, like a white moon at sunset, a crescent moon beckoning as it follows the sun, out of our ken" (p. 275). She loves the wholeness and perfection of this moon-Jesus, his untouched existence beyond the "dirty, desecrating" world.

There is no contradiction when the Jesus of her vision is also sexual and vital, for it is inclusive unity that she seeks. Her Jesus is resurrected in "body and spirit, whole and glad in the flesh, living in the flesh, loving in the flesh." Again, through the ideal-image we learn the goals and desires of the self. The connection between this Jesus and her view of the world is subtle but clear: she tolerates no wounds in the body of life, rejects the thought of flaws in her spiritual or physical being. Through religion she conceives unbounded fulfillment.

Ursula appears defined in will, ambitious in spirit, and intent on sexual experience. Force in these three areas parallels Ursula with her father. But, on the level of ego, there is an essential difference between the two characters. (I am taking ego as that which differentiates between the self and the surrounding world.) Where most of Will's considerable energies are devoted to the merger process and the rage to escape the self, Ursula asserts herself *against* that which is different from her, keeping herself apart and straining to remain unviolated.

But the matter should not be simplified. All of Lawrence's characters, male and female, go through periods when they forfeit ego-integration; Ursula is no exception and is capable of feeling like "an unfixed something-nothing, blowing about like the winds of heaven, undefined, unstated." There is no ontological certainty for Lawrence's characters: they are all prone to the alternations of self-establishment and self-disruption that form the incessant dialectic of carbon-life. Yet if there is no certainty, there are vast differences in the degree of integration that the various characters show. And Ursula is one who tends toward stability. Her independent being, strong from the beginning, develops steadily as she moves through her various "circles of experience."

Indeed her ego-strength frequently appears inflated. The exaggerated ego of woman becomes a major theme of the third section of the novel, as the inadequate ego of men is a primary concern of the first two parts. There are points where Ursula seems a monster of female egoism, a "harpy," but the novel resolves in the humbling of Ursula, in an experience that is fulfillment and chastisement at once. Her formation thus takes place in two stages: in the first she finds her self, in the second she finds something greater than the self. The perspective gained in the latter stage mitigates the egoism developed in the former. In fact, it finally becomes clear that without the egoism the greater experience would be unattainable.

But to return to the earlier drive for self-hood. Ursula's sexual-romantic relationship with Anton Skrebensky begins because she is attracted to his apparent clarity of being, derived from the confident role he plays in the larger world. The relationship with Skrebensky represents an early stage in her long process of self-definition. With him she discovers herself through sexuality, learning to be distinct in womanhood, absolutely separate and realized in bodily sensation. Between Ursula and Skrebensky the sense of self is developed through physical contacts: "It intensified and heightened their senses, they were more vivid, and powerful in their being." But something is lacking; asserting sexual force grants them self-recognition, but not intuition of the unknown:[29] "what could either of them get from such a passion but a sense of his or her own maximum self, in contradistinction to all the rest of life? Wherein was something finite and sad, for the human soul at its maximum wants a sense of the infinite" (p. 303).[30] The transforming power of the embrace fails to put them in touch with the "infinite," but does crystallize sex-distinction; asserting themselves one against the other, she feels maximally female, he completely male.[31] Ursula, especially, feels herself enhanced by the intimacy into a wondrous, sensitive femininity: "She drew away, and looked at him radiant, exquisitely, glowingly beautiful, and satisfied, but radiant as an illumined cloud." Light-imagery (as in Tom's and Lydia's relationship) is connected to the coming into being. Here the light is intense but soft; the attainment of her feminine self has left her quietly fulfilled, so she makes no demands, but wordlessly communicates her rich satisfaction. Skrebensky's reaction to her "radiance" is unexpectedly negative: "To him this was bitter. . . . He went beside her, his soul clenched, his body unsatisfied. Was she going to make this easy triumph over him?" (p. 304). Unexpectedly, her self-achievement diminishes him.

Skrebensky resents Ursula's amplification of being because his more constricted self can produce no reciprocal enlargement. His outer clarity, it rapidly becomes clear, hides an inner entropy; an abstract, generalized life, as soldier, colonialist, and servant of the state, obscures the fact that there is no discrete self within him. A conversation between them uncovers his fundamental emptiness, as it reveals her desire for a fluid, uncramped reality that limits her to no rigid role:

> "I hate houses that never go away, and people just living in the houses. It's all so stiff and stupid. I hate soldiers, they are stiff and wooden. What do you fight for, really?"
> "I would fight for the nation."
> "For all that, you aren't the nation. What would you do for yourself?"
> "I belong to the nation and must do my duty by the nation."
> "But when it didn't need your services in particular—when there *is* no fighting? What would you do then?"
> He was irritated.
> "I would do what everybody else does."
> "What?"
> "Nothing. I would be in readiness for when I was needed."
> The answer came in exasperation.
> "It seems to me," she answered, "as if you weren't anybody—as if there weren't anybody there, where you are. Are you anybody, really? You seem like nothing to me." (P. 311)

Lacking inner motivation or direction, Skrebensky seems a man without integral carbon-being. Tom and Will were dependent on the deeper level of self, but Skrebensky almost fails entirely to exist in dark separateness. This is why he is rarely presented through carbon-narrative, and why most of the latter part of the novel is narrated from Ursula's inner point-of-view. It is because Skrebensky's existence is dictated by exterior considerations that in the end he is even more unfinished than Will. The one bows too much to the female-principle; the other is a particularly hollow embodiment of the male-principle only. Fragmentary being creates fragmentary feeling: lack of a private core of affective self restricts the breadth of Skrebensky's desire: "Why did he never really want a woman, not with the whole of him: never love, never worship, only just physically want her?" (p. 316). Physicality is all he has, and all he can give her; and it is a shallow physicality, unable to match the evolution that takes place within her.

His absence of self (the outward gestures of his functioning being no substitute) helps to explain the strange violence of the two moonlit consummations Ursula and Skrebensky share. The first scene begins as Ursula has an instinctive apprehension of the unknown in the surrounding, animated night. She feels the need for intimate relation to the vivified universe: "The darkness was passionate and breathing with immense, unperceived heaving. It was waiting to receive her in flight. . . . She must leap from the known into the unknown" (pp. 317-18). Initially, Skrebensky seems to share her mood and reflect her need; they begin dancing (the scene is an outdoor wedding celebration) and enter the darkness in balance: "He took her into his arms, as if into the sure, subtle power of his will, and they became one movement, one dual movement. . . . It was his will and her will locked in a trance of motion, two wills locked in one motion, yet never fusing, never yielding one to the other." In one way, this is a highly positive description; the man and the woman are in mutual relation to one another and to the universe: "There was a wonderful rocking of the darkness, slowly, a great, slow swinging of the whole night." Yet their contact is an intimacy of wills, a struggle, not a joining.

We soon see the direction toward which his will moves. The element Ursula enters into with Skrebensky is black, overwhelming. For Skrebensky, as for Tom and Will, the universe is a dissolving force; it is an extinguishing, not a replenishing, movement that he shares with her: "but underneath [there was] only one great flood heaving slowly backwards to the verge of oblivion, slowly forward to the other verge, the heart sweeping along each time, and tightening with anguish as the limit was reached" (p. 318). Ursula turns to the "great white moon" in her self-assertive defense against the "flood," the drowning waters of "oblivion." The moon images Ursula's determination to maintain herself against the night, but the strength of her self-affirmation creates a new problem. Whereas Skrebensky nearly capitulates his being before the darkness, Ursula's assertion is too brilliant and absolute in its separateness; the moon magnifies and illuminates mere love of self. There ensues a struggle between them that represents two opposed negative forces: insufficient self and exaggerated self, her egoism of light and his nothingness of darkness. "She wanted the moon to fill in to her, she wanted more, more communion with the moon, consummation. . . . [Skrebensky] put a big, dark cloak round her, and sat holding her hand, whilst the moonlight streamed above the glowing fires. . . . But her naked self was away there beating upon the moonlight, dashing the moonlight with her breasts and her knees. . . . Oh for the coolness and entire liberty and brightness of the moon. Oh for the cold liberty to be herself, to do entirely as she liked. . . . He was the dross, people were the dross" (p. 319). In the elemental setting of moon and blackness, she finds her deepest self in a pure form, and is refined down to a separate and willful egoism. Looking to the moon for "consummation" she expresses a self-love that encloses her; her universe is an impoverished one of mere self-reflection. He, simultaneously, is a "shadow," a nought that seeks to dissolve and disappear into the darkness. Their clash is one of opposites, and her "triumph" of self-accomplishment turns ugly when she senses interference from the unfocused man who accompanies her. As he keeps trying persistently to pull her down into the darkness, she is angered into paroxysms of destruction:

> "Don't you like me to-night?" said his low voice, the voice of the shadow over her shoulder. . . . A strange rage filled her, a rage to tear things asunder. Her hands felt destructive, like metal blades of destruction. . . . she could feel his body, the weight of him, settling upon her, overcoming her life and energy, making her inert along with him.
> ....
> . . . . Looking at him, at his shadowy, unreal, wavering presence a sudden lust seized her, to lay hold of him and tear him and make him into nothing.
> ....
> . . . . He waited there beside her like a shadow which she wanted to dissipate, destroy as the moonlight destroys a darkness, annihilate, have done with.
> ....

. . . . And her soul crystallized with triumph, and his soul was dissolved with agony and annihilation. So she held him there, the victim, consumed, annihilated. She had triumphed: he was not any more. (Pp. 319–22)

The power of the scene is enormous because a tendency of Lawrence's imagination has found consummate expression within it. We have a figurative evocation of an archetypal encounter between the destructive *magna mater* and her victim. Yet, hideous as Ursula is under the moon, it would be incorrect to read the scene only as a condemnation of her. The teller's distended language presents a metaphorical annihilation that should be understood as the expression of great forces beyond the conscious personality. The full, unifying contact with nature is both a ritual initiation into religious experience and an exposure of fundamental self. The black night compels Ursula and Skrebensky into a revelation of their respective carbons of character. As a result, both her magnitude of self and his nullity are uncovered. She is so destructive at least partly because the scene is about a struggle of antagonists, a contest between something and nothing, a force and a vacuum. There can be no unification because there is no plane of similarity; either he will pull her down to his shadowed reality, or she will absorb and destroy him in her glittering light.

The ugliness of her feelings is mitigated by the trancelike quality of her state. Her underself demands an expression that her everyday self is powerless to oppose. The *involuntary* nature of the "annihilation" is of signal importance; it is instructive to compare Ursula's way of "destroying" Skrebensky to the destructiveness of a Lettie or Helena. For in *The Rainbow* the annihilation develops organically from a meeting on the carbon level and appears as the inescapable consequence of ontological imbalance. Experiencing the success of this scene, we receive some insight as to why the descriptions of negative character-traits attributed to the women of *The White Peacock, The Trespasser* and *Sons and Lovers* often seem artificial and forced: in the earlier novels the teller is searching for ways to avoid the more serious problem revealed in *The Rainbow*. Making the women frigid or castrating, the narrator deflects attention from the asymmetry of self between man and woman. The destruction based on such imbalance is not contingent on negative or positive qualities of character but is a fact of being. The issue is a lack of polarity. Ursula is an unmediated moon that leaves its orbit and becomes over-dominant because unbalanced by the check, the "sun," of a strong male.[32] Ursula's fulfillment will depend on such a counterforce to diminish her self-inflation.

With the passing of the experience, Ursula feels exaggerated guilt toward the destroyed Skrebensky. She blames herself for causing the nullity, when she actually caused only its manifestation. In reaction to the negative implications of her power, she regresses radically to a state of non-being: "Her life at this time was unformed, palpitating. . . . she *had* no self" (p. 335). While under the influence of this formlessness, Ursula develops a schoolgirl attachment to her teacher, Winifred Inger; the girl attempts to appropriate an identity through an admired model of the same sex. The two form a lesbian relationship. But held in a merely self-reflecting connection, Ursula gradually feels a cloying sense of overabundant femaleness: "a heavy, clogging sense of deadness began to gather upon her, from the other woman's contact. And sometimes she thought Winifred ugly, clayey. . . . She wanted some fine intensity, instead of this heavy cleaving of moist clay, that cleaves because it has no life of its own" (p. 344). Ursula has discovered the covert autoeroticism of bisexuality. The self-diminution with Winifred is closely related to the self-magnification under the moon: in both cases Ursula fails to go beyond herself.

Ursula introduces her Uncle Tom, a man without hope or idealism, to Winifred. His "disintegrated lifelessness of soul" is compatible with Winifred's cynical sterility. The pair of them, having relinquished belief in creation, take a perverse pleasure in destruction. Tom, a collier-manager, extends his inner dissipation into the English countryside by supporting the pervasive spread of mine-complexes and dingy colliery-towns. This section is the part of *The Rainbow* closest in theme and tone to *Women in Love*. Tom presages the later novel's Gerald Crich in his instrumentalism, his belief that a man is equivalent to his industrial function, with "[m]arriage and home . . . a little side-show." Winifred is pleased, under a surface protest, to agree with him: "It is the office, or the shop, or the business that gets the man, the woman gets the bit the shop can't digest. What is he at home, a man? He is a meaningless lump—a standing machine, a machine out of work" (p. 349).

Tom and Winifred serve as a negative example for Ursula: rejecting their belittling reductionism helps her to define herself. The mining industry Tom supports is an encroaching blight of mechanism, spreading "like a skin-disease," with the quality of "death rather than life." In reaction, Ursula develops the beginning of an organic, life-affirming view; she denies the necessity "that living human beings must be taken and adapted to all kinds of horrors. We could easily do without the pits" (p. 347). Ursula is on her way to developing an intellectual view and social sense that match her intrinsic wholeness of being. The belief in mankind places Ursula in unalterable opposition to her uncle and teacher; their "marshy-bittersweet corruption" leaves a void that is filled by the machine. Especially for Tom, theoretical instrumentalism is only a rationale for his own machine-worship: "his only happy moments, his only moments of pure freedom were when he was serving the machine. Then, and then only, when the machine caught him up, was he free from the hatred of himself" (p. 350). Tom introduces what is to become a major Lawrencian theme: the irrevocable hostility between humanisim and mechanism— as though society must choose between man and the machine. In Winifred Tom recognizes his proper partner in mechanism: "He would let the machinery carry him. . . . As for Winifred, she was . . . the same sort as himself. . . . She was his mate" (p. 352).

Retreating to her parents' home, Ursula finds herself opposed, in turn, to the "close, physical, limited life of herded domesticity" at the Marsh Farm. In the early years of the twentieth century, the inbred life of the farm seems neither satisfying nor quite responsible; social function, for Ursula, is an indispensable part of self-fulfillment. After investigation, Ursula finds that her most feasible entry into the outer world will be as a teacher. Will and Anna respond to their daughter's quest for independence with shocking hostility. The parents' scorn toward their daughter's aspirations shows an undercurrent of dissatisfaction with the narrowness of their own life-realization.

She finds employment at the local Brinsley Street School; there she encounters a functionalism at least as thorough-going as that of her Uncle Tom. The reality of the school conflicts absolutely with the "floating sentimentality" of her approach to education: "She dreamed how she would make the little, ugly children love her. She would be so *personal*. . . . She would make everything personal and vivid, she would give herself" (p. 367). Lawrence, once a schoolteacher himself,[33] describes the brutal grimness of the municipal institution with a chilling convincingness. All the warm humanity of Ursula's approach to teaching is superfluous and irrelevant in this prison-like atmosphere. Her co-teachers reject the lighthearted politeness, with its faint edge of superiority, of her manner. In all their words and actions the other teachers concentrate exclusively on teaching and, more important, controlling their pupils. When a teacher arranges for Ursula to receive a school apron, the rare act of kindly extension contains an implicit admonishment; the "black pinafore" is designed to cover, not only Ursula's clothes, but precisely those "personal" feelings she wishes to share with her students.

Ursula's attempts at humanization are, of course, easily destroyed by the school's inexorable power: "gradually she felt the invincible iron closing upon her." Such institutions are almost always more powerful than the neophytes who attempt to conquer them. Because of her liberalism her class falls behind, the students despise her, and she is the disgrace of a tightly disciplined school. Gradually her choice becomes closer: either she will have mechanistic order or she will have chaos. After a series of humiliations, she chooses mechanism. Ursula acknowledges that to be "personal" is to reach only a few of the brightest children; she now focuses "on the task, and not on the child." Ursula's experiences in the school, like so much in her life, contribute to her ontological definition. The challenge, here, arises because her young, unsure being finds it frighteningly difficult to stand against the mob hatred of a contemptuous class. At the end of her long struggle, she learns to protect her soul by retracting it; she becomes a "hard, insentient thing," a mere function: "She was to be Standard Five teacher only." The class, she realizes, will not be drawn into her terms, her culture and gentility, but has its own coarse, brutal terms which she must face. The school episode is about the clash between ego and function, and the narrator's attitude toward the clash is complex, nearly contradictory. Characters like

Tom have their egos usurped by function and this turns a person into a thing. Yet disallowing function to impinge on ego shows a lingering adolescence, a refusal to discipline the self to the challenges of the world.

The chapter remains an ideological problem in *The Rainbow* because Ursula finds no middle way between the personal and the functional. It seems that she succeeds at teaching by embracing the very mechanism she had earlier rejected. After all, she is subjecting the children of Tom's colliers to a correspondingly dehumanizing regime. On the social level, Lawrence cannot solve the problem triumphantly; the suggestion is that at this point in history, in this segment of society, mechanism is inevitable. On the personal level, however, this section records a learning experience for Ursula. Coming to the school with the expectation that it would conform to her own bright idealism is naive and egotistical. The school teaches her that realities indifferent to the self cannot be escaped; as a result of submitting herself to a larger framework Ursula goes on to an increased focusing of self and a positive stage in her growth:[34] "Her real, individual self drew together and became more coherent during these two years of teaching. . . . her wild, chaotic soul became hard and independent" (p. 407). Harshly subduing her class, though it is according to a brutal, conventional *modus operandi*, is Ursula's way to succeed in this particular "circle of experience," and prepare herself for the next, brighter sphere.

Finishing her career at the school, and before entering university, Ursula becomes briefly involved with Anthony Schofield, brother of a fellow-teacher. Schofield brings the pastoral atmosphere of Lawrence's first novel, *The White Peacock*, and his last, *Lady Chatterley's Lover*, into *The Rainbow*. Coming from a family of "caretakers, gamekeepers, farmers all in one," he is an example of that Lawrencian archetype: the fully natural man. Ursula, sensitive to pastoral beauties, is attracted to him: "Oh, I love it. What more does one want than to live in this beautiful place, and make things grow in your garden? It is like the Garden of Eden" (p. 416). But she is divorced from him by her acute consciousness: "All this so beautiful, all this so lovely! He did not see it. He was one with it. But she saw it, and was one with it. Her seeing separated them infinitely" (pp. 416–17). The teller makes no attempt to glorify

Schofield, who aside from his formidable sensuality, is a partial man with "no soul." Ursula rejects the marriage proposal he makes; her future is still obscure, but she awaits a more intricate destiny than the benighted sensual exploration Schofield offers.[35]

While attending the university Ursula does increase her understanding of the world and of herself. But the expansion, rather than coming from formal lessons (these are disillusioning—the studies are shabby and "second-hand"), is the result of a pair of nearly consecutive revelations. Her first revelation has significance for both Ursula and society at large:

> Always, always she was spitting out of her mouth the ash and grit of disillusion, of falsity. . . . That which she was, positively, was dark and unrevealed. . . . This inner circle of light in which she lived and moved, wherein the trains rushed and the factories ground out their machine produce . . . seemed like the area under an arc-lamp, wherein the moths and children played in the security of blinding light. . . . she felt the strange, foolish vanity of the camp, which said "Beyond our light and our order there is nothing" . . . ignoring always the vast darkness that wheeled round about, with half-revealed shapes lurking on the edge. (Pp. 437–38)

The passage discusses the negative consequences of Ursula's way of being, her "rejection" and "refusal" of all that is outside of her. As a result she is strong and separate, but has divorced herself from "darkness" and narrowed her sphere of existence. Darkness here has two implications: the unconscious instinctive self Ursula slights for the sake of her conscious ego, and the mysteriously vital universe that eludes her for the same reason. There is a flow from the darkness of the self to the darkness of the universe. An excess or a lack of ego destroys the desirable relation to the unknown—the capacity to merge and then emerge. The enriching darkness (opposed to Skrebensky's crushing darkness) is achievable for someone with the light of being (conscious and unconscious).

The insights are also generalized; the suggestion is made that mankind evades both dimensions of the beyond. (Part of the point is a general social avoidance of the unconscious.) Maintaining his connection between light-imagery and the ego, Lawrence takes the harsh, glaring lights of industrialism as fitting testaments to the greater social egoism.[36] And Ursula, if more aware and formed on the carbon-level than most men, must maintain adequate contact with inner and outer darkness, if she is to diminish the ego that isolates her during sexual encounters and interferes with her fulfillment.

Ursula's second revelation teaches her the indivisible unity between herself and nature in its entirety. Listening to a professor expound the mechanistic theory that life is an instance of physiochemical process, Ursula comprehends the organic interconnection of all things and the singleness of their animating force. Her vision solves, abstractly at least, the problem of her own realization: personal entelechy is dependent on the greater vitalism of the infinite. The greatest fulfillment is not of the separate self (this Ursula has achieved), but of the self in oneness with the universe:

> If [life] was a conjunction of forces, physical and chemical, what held these forces unified, and for what purpose were they unified?. . . . Was its purpose just mechanical and limited to itself? It intended to be itself. But what self? . . . She could not understand what it all was. She only knew that it was not limited mechanical energy, nor mere purpose of self-preservation and self-assertion. It was a consummation, a being infinite. Self was a oneness with the infinite. To be oneself was a supreme, gleaming triumph of infinity. (P. 441)

Skrebensky, returning from duty abroad, allows her to actualize her perceptions. Their renewed sexuality embodies the infinite: "the utter, dark kiss . . . knitted them into one fecund nucleus of the fluid darkness." Yet their sensuality is not everything to her. On a trip to the Rouen Cathedral, she distances herself from Skrebensky. Her father in her attracts Ursula to the spiritual permanence of the church: "This was now the reality; the great stone cathedral . . . which knew no transience. . . . It was majestic in its stability, its splendid absoluteness" (p. 456). Still a man of "wavering, vague" soul, who consists of "a set of habitual actions and decisions," Skrebensky falls into despair when deprived of Ursula's support; he feels relegated to the disintegrating civilization of which he is an integral part: "Now he found himself struggling amid an ashen-dry, cold world of rigidity, dead walls and mechanical traffic. . . . the lights at night were the sinister gleam of decomposition" (p. 457).

She is now woundingly negative about him and the colonialist culture he represents: "You think the Indians are simpler than us, and so you'll enjoy being near them and being a lord over them. . . . What do you govern for, but to make things there as dead and mean as they are here. . . . I'm against you, and all your old, dead things" (p. 462). Under the harsh words, her intention is finally constructive. Her invective aims at cutting away his false, outer self in order to let the vital underself emerge: "Stronger than life or death was her craving to be able to love him. . . . when all his complacency was destroyed, all his everyday self was broken, and only the stripped, rudimentary, primal man remained . . . they came together in an overwhelming passion" (p. 463). But the more she tries to immerse him in his dark, genuine self, the more his fundamental hollowness becomes clear: "After each contact, her anguished desire for him or for that which she never had from him was stronger, her love was more hopeless. After each contact his mad dependence on her was deepened, his hope of standing strong and taking her in his own strength was weakened. He felt himself a mere attribute of her" (p. 463). She tries to remove his ersatz surface-self so that the elemental man in him might meet the elemental woman in her; but the more she strips him down, the more she finds nothingness.

He now proposes marriage to her. Unwilling to place their union in the social context she so vehemently rejects, Ursula firmly refuses him. He begins to weep, not like a hurt man, but like a defective machine deprived of its power-source: "His head made a queer motion, the chin jerked back against the throat, the curious crowing, hiccuping sound came . . . his face twisted like insanity, and he was crying, crying blind and twisted as if something were broken which kept him in control" (p. 467). Skrebensky's grotesque disintegration contrasts with the crude power of the cab-driver who takes them back to their hotel-room. The driver disturbs Ursula with his look "of a quick, strong, wary animal that had them within its knowledge, almost within its power" (pp. 468–69). Looking back to her vision of the "wild beasts," and ahead to the scene with the wild horses, the driver betokens the male force Skrebensky lacks.

Ursula's longing for a compelling force, potent enough to balance and moderate her own power, begins the second moonlit love-making scene. Skrebensky is not capable of embodying the oppositional strength necessary to her fulfillment: "The salt, bitter passion of the sea, its indifference to the earth, its swinging, definite motion, its strength, its attack, and its salt burning . . . tantalized her with vast suggestions of fulfilment. . . . Skrebensky['s] soul could not contain her in its waves of strength, nor his breast compel her in burning, salty passion" (p. 478). As she moves toward the wild, separate element of the sea, the moon rises above her. The moon has a dually negative effect: as it unveils the "secret" of Skrebensky's lack-of-self, it pulls Ursula into overamplification. Unrestrained by a counterforce, Ursula fails to be transfigured by nature, and transforms nature into an extension of self; the ego-reflecting white moon blanches the sand and the sea. Ursula's unification with her surroundings includes no joining with the desired opposed, compelling force but is a movement toward the forces reflecting the self.

> There was a great whiteness confronting her, the moon was incandescent as a round furnace door, out of which came the high blast of moonlight, over the seaward half of the world, a dazzling, terrifying glare of white light. They shrank back for a moment into the shadow, uttering a cry. He felt his chest laid bare, where the secret was heavily hidden. He felt himself fusing down to nothingness, like a bead that rapidly disappears in an incandescent flame. . . . And she went forward, plunging into it. . . . She . . . seemed to melt into the glare, toward the moon. The sands were as ground silver, the sea moved in solid brightness, coming toward them. . . . She gave her breast to the moon, her belly to the flashing, heaving water. He stood behind her, a shadow ever dissolving." (P. 479)

She grips him in a frenzied expression of rapacious female sexuality. She becomes a monstrous "harpy" to him, partly because of her genuinely ugly overassertiveness, but also because of Skrebensky's inability to exhibit potency on the carbon level. Yet she also longs for "fulfillment" through the "salt, bitter passion of the sea," a hint that if Skrebensky were able to embody the counter-element of water, Ursula would go beyond herself toward him. But his emptiness is exposed; both Ursula and the stark primality of the natural setting challenge him to an "ordeal of proof"—a test of his manhood as well as his very being, for the passage deals *inter alia* with an inequality of sexual strength:

> Then there in the great flare of light, she clinched hold of him, hard, as if suddenly she had the strength of destruction, she fastened her arms

round him and tightened him in her grip, whilst her mouth sought his in a hard, rending, ever-increasing kiss, till his body was powerless in her grip, his heart melted in fear from the fierce, beaked, harpy's kiss. . . . He felt as if the ordeal of proof was upon him. . . . The fight, the struggle for consummation was terrible. It lasted till it was agony to his soul, till he succumbed, till he gave way as if dead, and lay with his face buried, partly in her hair, partly in the sand, motionless. . . . he only wanted to be buried in the godly darkness, only that, and no more. (P. 480)

The scene is something of a repetition of the previous encounter, only more extreme, more final. Again, neither character should be blamed for the essential truths-of-being revealed under the moon. The scene does not so much impute the source of the failure as ascertain that the combination of a defined female and a null male leads to carnage. Ursula and Skrebensky are both dehumanized by this last experience and brought to the extreme negative limits of themselves. She becomes, in a pitiable parody of cold, isolated femininity, a metallic, illumined statute: "he watched . . . the unaltering, rigid face like metal in the moonlight, the fixed unseeing eyes in which slowly the water gathered . . . and ran trickling, a tear with its burden of moonlight" (pp. 480–81). He is reduced to the lowest level of matter, an inchoate bit of flotsam: "his brain grew dark and he was unconscious with weariness. Then he curled in the deepest darkness he could find, under the sea-grass, and lay there without consciousness" (p. 481).

Once again, Ursula is horrified by her capacity for destruction. She reacts by denying her deeper self and regressing to the security of social, conventional life. With abject contrition she begs Skrebensky to permit her submission to him: "I cannot tell you the remorse I feel for my wicked, perverse behavior. . . . instead of thankfully, on my knees, taking what God had given, I must have the moon in my keeping. . . . I swear to you to be a dutiful wife, and to serve you in all things" (p. 485). Ursula has undergone such reversions before; they occur when her appalled surface-self retreats from her elemental being.

Fortunately for her own integrity (and that of a great novel) Ursula is forced, with profoundly beneficial effect, to confront the fundamental element she tries to evade. A herd of wild horses she meets in a field suggests (like much of Lawrence's animal-imagery) the immense powers of nature. In earlier incarnations, for example when figured by the sea, such forces have failed to subdue Ursula's ego. Lacking the subduing force, she never finds her "transfiguration," and we conclude that transfiguring experience cannot result from the joining of an individual and the universe. If the individual is weak, like Skrebensky and many of Lawrence's male characters, he is absorbed by nature; if the individual is strong, like Ursula and many of Lawrence's female characters, she imbues nature with herself. Three components are necessary for real fulfillment: a full apprehension of nature in its magnitude, and the male and female principles in their complete expressions. The latter two balance and maintain one another, above nullity but below egoism, in mutual awareness and realization. The herd of horses have a dual symbolic significance: *they embody both the dark water of inhuman nature and the fiery potency of the male principle*. The insistent use of fire-imagery to describe them affirms that the horses symbolize precisely the compelling, polarizing maleness Ursula needs:[37] "Their great haunches were smoothed and darkened with rain. But the darkness and wetness of rain could not put out the hard, urgent, massive fire that was locked in those flanks. . . . She was aware of the great flash of hoofs, a bluish, iridescent flash surrounding a hollow of darkness" (p. 488).

Encountering the fire and rain of the horses Ursula is nearly "dissolved into water," as Skrebensky was disintegrated by the moon and the night. But in the end she does not dissolve: the same fierce hands that had wanted to destroy Skrebensky save her from the horses: "Her body was weak but her hands were hard as steel." Her hands pull her up into an "oak-tree" and then over a "high hedge" so that she can pass to the "high-road and the ordered world of man" (p. 489). The force of being that had earlier looked so cruel now saves her from the horses' annihilating stampede. Alongside Skrebensky she had seemed monstrous, but in conjunction with the horses her strength redeems her. Her capacity to confront the dark night and primitive maleness of the horses grants Ursula her long-awaited transfiguration. In a reversal of Will's more ordinary upward-moving mysticism, the encounter with wild blackness takes Ursula beneath normal experience to some fundamental truth: "she sat there, spent, time and the flux of change passed away from her . . . everything rolled by in transience, leaving her there . . . unalterable and passive, sunk to the bottom of all change. . . . She seemed destined to find the bottom of all things to-day: the bottom of all things" (pp. 490–91). Ursula endures when she is forced into the heart of darkness, but her arrogance and egoism are destroyed.

The trauma of the episode causes a transitional illness. In the course of the sickness all the "falsity" of Skrebensky and his world falls away from her. The "old, decaying, fibrous husk" of her withers, allowing the "naked, clear kernel" of new, pure self to emerge. The final effect of her battering by the horses is manifestly positive. Because she herself is so strong, her encounter with the horses has the result of tying her to the unknown without drowning her in its power. Thus her vision of the rainbow at the end of the novel is painstakingly earned.[38] In Ursula's case (and the arch of Tom and Lydia signifies less), the rainbow represents the connection between her consummated individual self, painfully developed through so many experiences, and the unknown realm with which she is now in intimate contact: "It was the unknown, the unexplored, the undiscovered upon whose shore she had landed, alone, after crossing the void, the darkness" (p. 494).

Yet Ursula's fulfillment is strangely, inhumanly abstract. She is not balanced by a male, but by an incarnation of the male principle: it is almost as though the teller were admitting his inability to create a living man to match her. But it should be added that at the end of the novel she awaits a man who shares her connection to the beyond: "The man should come from the Infinite and she should hail him. . . . She was glad that this lay within the scope of that vaster power in which she rested at last. The man would come out of Eternity to which she herself belonged" (p. 494). Clearly this is a reference to Rupert Birkin, the man who ostensibly equals Ursula in *Women in Love*. But whether Lawrence really produces a man to rival her power in that novel, remains to be seen.

Notes to Chapter 4

1. Frieda Lawrence, *Not I, But the Wind* . . . (New York: Viking Press, 1934), p. 57. I would want to add that the tone here is Frieda's, not Lawrence's. Where Lawrence struggled intensely with this apprehension, Frieda sounds too absolute, too glibly confident. Yet the evidence of the novels suggests that her insight is finally accurate.

2. The term "unconscious" only has relevance to *The Rainbow* if we employ it in the Lawrencian, not the Freudian, sense. The Freudian unconscious (that Lawrence hated—and sadly reduced—considering it a mass of "repulsive little horrors"), has little relation to the substratum of self Lawrence examines in the novel. Rather, the "carbon" of *The Rainbow* is connected to the Lawrencian unconscious, "the root of all our consciousness and being." Lawrence fully discusses his concept of the unconscious, its nature and function in his two polemical essays, reprinted in "*Psychoanalysis and the Unconscious*" and "*Fantasia of the Unconscious*," introduction by Philip Rieff (New York: Viking Press, 1960). (Above quotations from pp. 5, 28.)

3. The letter was written to Lawrence's publisher, Edward Garnett. Its best-known remarks were made in response to a comment by the futurist writer, Marinetti, that the "heat of a piece of wood or iron is in fact more passionate, for us, than the laughter or tears of a woman." Lawrence's reaction to this was to say, *inter alia*:

> I don't so much care about what the woman *feels*—in the ordinary usage of the word. That presumes an *ego* to feel with. I only care about what the woman *is*—what she IS—inhumanly, physiologically, materially—according to the use of the word: but for me, what she *is* as a phenomenon (or as representing some greater, inhuman will), instead of what she feels according to the human conception. . . . You mustn't look in my novel for the old stable ego—of the character. There is another *ego*, according to whose action the individual is unrecognisable, and passes through, as it were, allotropic states which it needs a deeper sense than any we've been used to exercise, to discover are states of the same single radically unchanged element. (Like as diamond and coal are the same pure single element of carbon. The ordinary novel would trace the history of the diamond—but I say, 'Diamond, what! This is carbon.' And my diamond might be coal or soot, and my theme is carbon.)

The Collected Letters of D. H. Lawrence, ed. Harry T. Moore (London: William Heinemann, 1962), 1:281–82.

4. Ibid., p. 281.

5. Robert Sale discusses Lawrence's handling of time in *The Rainbow*, which Sale considers the fundamental component of the novel's original style, in "The Narrative Technique of *The Rainbow*," *Modern Fiction Studies* 5, no. 1 (Spring 1959): 29–38.

6. *The Rainbow* (1915; reprint ed., Harmondsworth, Middlesex: Penguin Books, 1949), p. 63.

7. In *The Rainbow* Lawrence reworks, with greater control of direction and sureness of purpose, many of the themes of his first three novels: the first section reexamines the pastoral concerns of *The White Peacock*; the second section returns to the ecstasy and merger motifs of *The Trespasser*, and the third section contains many of the *Bildungsroman* elements of *Sons and Lovers*.

8. Most critics read these lines as *mimesis*. Julian Moynahan, for example, notes that the "powerfully rhythmic phrasing of the description seems designed to re-create in language an equivalent of the condition itself." *The Deed of Life: The Novels and Tales of D. H. Lawrence* (Princeton, N.Y.: Princeton University Press, 1963), pp. 51–52. Keith Sagar expresses nearly the identical view; "The rhythm flowing from nature into the blood of the Brangwens corresponds to the pulsing rhythm of Lawrence's prose." *The Art of D. H. Lawrence* (Cambridge: Cambridge University Press, 1966), p. 45. For a different application of the two terms, *mimesis* and *methexis*, see Wylie Sypher, *Loss of the Self in Modern Literature and Art* (New York: Random House, 1962), p. 129.

9. For related views on the condition of the Brangwen men, see Baruch Hochman,

Another Ego: The Changing View of Self and Society in the Work of D. H. Lawrence (Columbia, S.C.: University of South Carolina Press, 1970), p. 36; and Robert Burns, "The Novel as Metaphysical Statement: Lawrence's *The Rainbow*," *Southern Review* 4, no. 2 (1970): 141.

10. I borrow these terms from H. M. Daleski, who argues that in Lawrence "duality is viewed as . . . all-pervading," and that the "male-female opposition is not merely an instance of a dual reality but its underlying principle." In the course of his study Daleski abstracts and lists the various qualities Lawrence considers as either "Male" or "Female." Among the listings found under the "Female" heading are "Stability," "Nature," and "Movement towards the Origin," while "Activity," "Knowledge," and "Movement toward Discovery" are "Male" attributes. ("Being" is associated with the female principle.) *The Forked Flame* (Evanston, Ill.: Northwestern University Press, 1965), pp. 20, 30–31.

11. It may be worth noting that this successful encounter comes just after Tom's mother's death. I believe the point is relevant, but hesitate to overstress it because the text gives comparatively little basis for viewing Tom's difficulties in the light of an Oedipal problem. One critic who does so, John E. Stoll, extrapolates unjustifiably from *Sons and Lovers* to make comments like: "Paul's and Tom's identical ages, twenty-three, seem to reveal their related significance for Lawrence. The portrait of Tom begins where that of Paul ends, and Tom's relation to women includes the author's view of the abnormalities associated with Paul." *The Novels of D. H. Lawrence: A Search for Integration* (Columbia, Mo.: University of Missouri Press, 1971), p. 111.

12. F. R. Leavis' statement about the importance of the love-relationship in *The Rainbow* is precisely accurate in relation to Tom, but only very generally applicable to Lydia: "Either lover is for the other a 'door'; an opening into the 'unknown,' by which the horizon, the space of life, is immensely expanded, and unaccepted limits that had seemed final are 'transgressed.' " *D. H. Lawrence: Novelist* (1955; reprint ed., New York: Clarion, 1969), p. 115. Leavis fails to distinguish between the types and the degrees of dependency Tom and Lydia have on one another.

13. In "The Study of Thomas Hardy," a work nearly simultaneous with *The Rainbow*, Lawrence writes: "Let a man walk alone on the face of the earth, and he feels himself like a loose speck blown at random. Let him have a woman to whom he belongs, and he will feel as though he had a wall to back up against. . . . No man can endure the sense of space, of chaos, on four sides of himself." *Phoenix: The Posthumous Papers of D. H. Lawrence*, ed. Edward D. McDonald (New York: Viking Press, 1936), p. 446.

14. The association between moon-imagery and the ego-integrity of women has been elaborated elsewhere in this study, and need not be labored here. For further confirmation of the connection the reader is directed to my note Seventeen, and the moonlit lovemaking scenes between Ursula Brangwen and Anton Skrebensky later in the novel.

15. The superior self-certainty that Lydia manifests has been detected by very few critics. One exception is Stephen Miko who says: "[Lydia's] strange, still smile seems to indicate a kind of inner surety. . . . It is often referred to in descriptions of her, descriptions which tend to emphasize her mysterious qualities and her unquestioning acceptance of all that causes Tom anxiety." *Toward "Women in Love": The Emergence of a Lawrencian Aesthetic* (New Haven, Conn.: Yale University Press, 1971), p. 129.

16. Mark Spilka overequates the respective realizations that take place in Tom and Lydia during the consummation-scene: "In the sexual consummation . . . they discover and affirm each other's independent being; then each goes his own way again, transfigured, separate,

yet firmly bound together as the other's gateway to life." *The Love Ethic of D. H. Lawrence* (Bloomington, Ind.: Indiana University Press, 1955), pp. 96–97. It is true that both partners are transfigured into an all-important relation with the beyond; but it is in Tom alone that a necessary creation-of-self takes place before the transformation can occur. H. M. Daleski's discussion of this scene utilizes the concept that loss of self leads to finding the self in something greater: "paradoxically, and the phraseology is suggestive of a mystical illumina- tion, the moment he 'loses' himself, the moment he overcomes his fear and willingly allows the intact self to be 'destroyed', he 'finds himself in her.' " *The Forked Flame: A Study of D. H. Lawrence* (Evanston, Ill.: Northwestern University Press, 1965), p. 88. Daleski and I differ in our views of the reason for Tom's initial avoidance of the full, equal union with Lydia. Daleski believes that, previous to the transfiguration, Tom's problem is his denial of Lydia's "otherness," and his desire to merely use her as a means "to subdue the unknown to the known—in the flesh. . . . When he finally 'relinquishes himself,' he lets go of a self that is accustomed to seeking its own expansion through her." *The Forked Flame*, pp. 87–88. In my reading of Tom and Lydia, he, rather than denying Lydia's being, has no firm belief in his own, and the obstacle to balanced, regenerating unification is his desire to obliterate himself in her.

17. In "Fantasia of the Unconscious," Lawrence describes the moon in terms of individuation: "The moon is the centre of our terrestrial individuality in the cosmos. She is the declaration of our existence in separateness. . . . She it is who sullenly stands with her back to us, and refuses to meet and mingle. She it is who burns white with the intense friction of her withdrawal into separation, that cold, proud white fire of furious, almost malignant apartness, the struggle into fierce, frictional separateness." Pp. 191–92. (The negative tone of the excerpt is relevant to the over abundance of "moon-like" separateness in Ursula.)

18. Mark Spilka finds intellectual kinship between Lawrence's living universe and "Wordsworth's religious flux, Nietzsche's Dionysian force [and] Bergson's *élan vital*." Spilka also notes the influence on Lawrence of "*mana*, the *theos* concept" of the ancient Greeks, which infused the entire universe with God. *The Love Ethic of D. H. Lawrence*, p. 14.

19. I can understand the reasoning behind Stoll's interpretation of Tom's drowning, although—as often—the critic weakens his case by being too exclusively Freudian: "Trapped within the narrowing circle of his bondage to Lydia, he disintegrates, merges with her foreign darkness, and loses his own identity. Tom's failure to separate himself . . . ends with his regression to the womb." Womb-regression is perhaps suggested by Tom's drowning, but it is not its entire meaning. *Search for Integration*, p. 114. Arnold Kettle, arguing from his Marxist standpoint, sees Tom's death in socioeconomic terms: the coming of industrialism literally kills the yeoman-farmer as it symbolically destroys his class: "The coming of the canal (serving the new collieries) . . . kills Tom Brangwen." *An Introduction to the English Novel* (1951; reprint ed., New York: Harper and Row, 1968), p. 294.

20. As is well known, Jung considered the collective unconscious "universal." Carl G. Jung, *The Integration of the Personality*, trans. Stanley M. Dell (New York: Farrar & Rinehart, 1939), p. 52. Lawrence also believed in an unknown source of the personality, but took an entirely different view of its nature: "By the unconscious we wish to indicate that essential unique nature of every individual creature." "*Psychoanalysis and the Uncon- scious*." p. 15.

21. Moynahan considers Will's and Anna's sheavegathering a "ritual scene:" one of the various incidents in the novel that "dramatize, frequently in solemn ceremonial gesture and

in a ceremonious prose, the ultimate relation of the 'essential' man or woman—usually it is a woman—to what Lawrence calls the 'unknown.' . . . The artistic strategy of the sheavegathering scene involves the use of incremental repetition in combination with vivid imagery to suggest that Will and Anna enact in their sensual pursuit of and retreat from one another the larger rhythms of the 'living cosmos.' " *The Deed of Life*, pp. 63, 65. Moynahan's comments are illuminating, but this is only part of the scene's interest.

22. Daleski points out this highly revealing detail, *The Forked Flame*, p. 96.

23. Colin Clarke refuses to discredit Will for either his dependence or destructiveness: "Will doesn't, or shouldn't, lose marks for his inability to stand alone. . . . The potency and the capacity for degradation—the fear of the night and the splendid dark sensuality—belong to a single individual, and what is being deviously suggested is that the potency can't be had *without* the degradation." *River of Dissolution: D. H. Lawrence and English Romanticism* (London: Routledge & Kegan Paul, 1969), p. 49. Clarke here generally fits Will into the pattern of corruption and disintegration that Clarke considers the neglected positive in Lawrence's work. Clarke himself is so intent on seeing the benefits in dissolution that he fails to make some elementary discriminations in regard to Will's character.

24. T. H. Adamowski describes Will's hostile denial of Anna's being as "ontological homicide." "*The Rainbow* and 'Otherness,' " *The D. H. Lawrence Review* 7, no. 1 (Spring 1974): 68.

25. Harry T. Moore calls Anna "the more aggressive partner" in the relationship. *The Life and Works of D. H. Lawrence* (New York: Twayne, 1951), p. 137. Though he is more qualified in his appraisal, F. R. Leavis essentially agrees with Moore's judgment. *D. H. Lawrence: Novelist*, p. 123.

26. Lawrence describes the gender of fire in an important but little-known essay: "Aphrodite born of the waters, and Apollo the sun-god, these give some indication of the sex distinction. . . . if we must imagine the most perfect clue to eternal waters, we think of woman, and of man as the most perfect premise of fire." "The Two Principles," in *The Symbolic Meaning: The Uncollected Versions of "Studies in Classic American Literature*," ed. Armin Arnold (New York: Viking Press, 1960), p. 169. The connection between woman and water is understandable, for the relation of woman to man is equivalent to the relation of nature to man: both have the effect of overwhelming him, and both can thus be identified with the water that literally drowns Tom. We can thus comprehend the linkage Lawrence makes, in "Fantasia of the Unconscious," between moon and water: "The moon is not water. But it is the soul of water, the invisible clue to all the waters." P. 187.

27. S. L. Goldberg dislikes the very precision of the cathedral sequence: "beneath its subtlety, the writing seems rather too sure about its final destination, rather unresponsible to other possible attitudes." But then Goldberg, an intelligent but somewhat contradictory critic, also faults *The Rainbow* for just the opposite reason, complaining of Lawrence's "romantic assumptions, this impatience and vagueness, that reach their culmination in the last pages of the book." "*The Rainbow:* Fiddle-Bow and Sand," *Essays in Criticism* 11, no. 4 (October 1961): 432.

28. Leavis, *D. H. Lawrence: Novelist*, p. 12.

29. Leavis seems correct to me when he says: "Love between man and woman in the three generations of *The Rainbow* is most successful in the first." Leavis also indicates the basis for the success: "It is in the establishment of a sure relation with the 'beyond' that the creativeness of a valid marriage has its inclusive manifestation." *D. H. Lawrence: Novelist*, pp. 119, 117.

30. Mark Spilka uses these lines to make some harsh, though finally justified, inductions

about Ursula: "So it is the self, cut off from the rest of life, which Ursula tries to affirm . . . really an assertion of triumph over the rest of life, rather than conjunction with it." *The Love Ethic of D. H. Lawrence*, p. 112.

31. According to Lawrence, sexual contact intensifies and purifies the sex-difference between men and women: "In Love, in the act of love, that which is mixed in me becomes pure, that which is female in me is given to the female, that which is male in her draws into me, I am complete, I am pure male, she is pure female." "Study of Thomas Hardy," *Phoenix*, p. 468.

32. Moon and sun are among Lawrence's preferred symbols for the female and male principles. (See, for example, "Fantasia of the Unconscious," p. 187). Daleski invokes this symbolism when he says, "[Skrebensky] is called on to produce a 'man-being' to match the 'woman-being' of Ursula, a sun to rival her moon." Daleski also remarks, pertinently, that the moonlit scene "is a brilliant example of the 'carbon' of character in action." *The Forked Flame*, p. 112.

33. Lawrence was a teacher at the Davidson Road School, Croydon, South London, from October 12, 1908, until March 19, 1912. Harry T. Moore, *The Intelligent Heart: The Story of D. H. Lawrence* (New York: Farrar, Straus and Young, 1954), pp. 73, 111.

34. Therefore Hough's contention that "the school-teaching episode" is not in "the main thematic line" must be rejected. *The Dark Sun*, p. 68.

35. Moynahan makes related observations about the bargeman Ursula meets just after first discovering Skrebensky's hollowness (*The Rainbow*, pp. 311–16): "He is oriented in physical experience, unhaunted by the conventions and abstractions of modern culture, satisfied to inhabit his own body. . . . To Ursula he is a reminder that fulfillment lies elsewhere than in a life with Anton. She cannot go live on a barge—she is too well-educated, too intellectually self-aware for this pastoral reversion—but she must find a way of including in her future the value which the bargeman represents." *The Deed of Life*, p. 61.

36. Ursula's attitude toward the modern, electrically-illumined town is utterly, even arrogantly, negative: "The stupid, artificial, exaggerated town, fuming its lights. It does not exist really. It rests upon the unlimited darkness, like a gleam of coloured oil on dark water, but what is it?—nothing, just nothing." *The Rainbow*, p. 447. This contrasts strikingly with the end of *Sons and Lovers* where Paul Morel walks toward the town's lights in a not entirely convincing gesture of salvation. The difference indicates the clarification of Lawrence's view of industrialism, as well as a general strengthening of the depth and consistency of his thought and symbolism.

37. Most critics, relating the horses to elemental forces, have descried but one of the two major implications of the wild herd. In rather banal language Mary Freeman connects the horses to the power of nature: "Here is the vast nonhuman world, heedless of mankind and its antics, but strong and inescapable, and, above all, wonderful." *D. H. Lawrence: A Basic Study of His Ideas* (Gainesville, Fla.: University of Florida Press, 1955), p. 47. Moynahan considers the horses an analogue for an inner, rather than an outer, immense, anarchic drive: "they symbolize the power of the life of instinct, the life which underlies the upper layers of the self, underlies the accretions of moral and psychological conditioning that hide the deep, turbulent impulses of 'flesh' and 'blood' in every individual." *The Deed of Life*, p. 67. Anais Nin adds an original twist: "The horses are symbols of maternity and the sexual experience of marriage. . . . and purely physical existence." *D. H. Lawrence: An Unprofessional Study* (1932; reprint ed., Denver, Colo.: Swallow, 1964), p. 31. This would equate escaping from the horses with escaping from an Anna-like life with Skrebensky.

Few critics connect the horses to male power, yet Lawrence himself made such a correlation: "a man has a persistent passionate fear-dream about horses. He suddenly finds himself among great, physical horses, which may suddenly go wild. Their great bodies surge madly round him, they rear above him, threatening to destroy him. At any minute he may be trampled down. . . . the horse-dream refers to some arrest in the deepest sensual activity in the male. The horse is presented as an object of terror, which means that to the man's automatic dream-soul, which loves automatism, the great sensual male activity is the greatest menace." "Fantasia of the Unconscious," in "Psychoanalysis and the Unconscious" and "*Fantasia of the Unconscious*" p. 199. Mark Spilka relates the horses to "powerful male sensuality" and notes the dream, albeit in an undeveloped footnote. However, he makes an somewhat misplaced connection between the horses and Skrebensky: "Ursula's vision of malignant horses can be traced back, ultimately, to her basic fear of powerful male sensuality. . . . we know that Ursula has battled and destroyed that [sensual] activity, not in herself, of course, but in Skrebensky." *The Love Ethic of D. H. Lawrence*, p. 120. Quite to the contrary, accepting the "automatism" of a social, devitalized marriage with Skrebensky would be *renouncing* "powerful male sensuality"; the wild horses violently prevent the renunciation.

38. In one of his essays Lawrence describes the formation of the rainbow as "that which comes when night clashes on day, the rainbow . . . which leaps out of the breaking of light upon darkness, of darkness upon light, absolute beyond day or night; the rainbow, the iridescence which is darkness at once and light, the two-in-one; the crown that binds them both." "The Crown," *Phoenix II: Uncollected, Unpublished and Other Prose Works by D. H. Lawrence*, ed. Warren Roberts and Harry T. Moore (New York; Viking Press, 1968), p. 373.

5

The Teller Reasserted: Exercisings of the Will in *Women in Love*

"You'd have to have it your own way, wouldn't you?" [Ursula] teased. "You could never take it on trust."

[Birkin] changed, laughed softly, and turned and took her in his arms, in the middle of the road.

"Yes," he said softly.[1]

1

The covenant between man and God, whose traditional sign shines so hopefully at the end of *The Rainbow*, is shattered in *Women in Love*. The mood of the latter novel is harsh and pessimistic, nearly despairing, with humanity written off as "dry rotten" and "full of bitter, corrupt ash." The final impression *Women in Love* makes is of a bleak apocalypse, a world ending in cynicism and freezing; this is partly because it presents hopelessness with superb force, while its hope is full of qualification and lacks conviction. The teller analyzes the destructive relationship of Gerald Crich and Gudrun Brangwen with a savage certainty of perception, but brings less realization to his portrait of the marriage between Rupert Birkin and Ursula Brangwen.[2] The reason for the discrepancy is that whereas tale and teller unite in the depiction of Gerald and Gudrun, the description of Birkin and Ursula is self-contradictory, a dramatic illustration of tale/teller division in Lawrence's fiction.

The corrosive death struggle between Gerald and Gudrun is

admirably articulated. Symbol, action, dialogue, and—most impressively—the alterations of the hidden underself, the carbon of character, all advance this tale of master and slave reversals, of the will to power answering the will to be overpowered. The power-alternations between Gerald and Gudrun seem evenly distributed, with each character taking his turn at ascendancy.[3] But a close examination reveals that the mind-dominated Gudrun has a cold integrity of self and cruel survival-capacity, making her a far stronger figure than the will-driven Gerald. Gudrun's final indifference protects her, giving her a frigid intactness, while Gerald's pressing needs make him vulnerable, a sacrifice to the violent winds blowing through *Women in Love*. Gudrun's being is perverse, but Gerald's is disintegrative. Between the two of them, he is the one condemned; all his manipulations of power are but attempts to counter his underlying weakness. In their demonic way Gerald and Gudrun present the fundamental Lawrencian tale: the interaction between an ontologically strong woman and a less individuated man. (Their entanglement remains Lawrence's most vivid example of the destructive potentialities of such a relation.)

Where Ursula and Birkin are concerned, the teller distorts the respective strengths-of-being the two characters show as the tale reveals an ontological imbalance between them. Ursula incarnates a pure, mysterious wholeness of being: she is suffused with "a golden light" that indicates self-integrity. Birkin, in contrast, is implicated in the social and individual corrosion that causes a degradation of being. The tale shows Ursula providing the solution to this degradation; Birkin has a chance of swimming clear of the "river of dissolution" that threatens to flood their doomed society by aligning himself with her. The conception of Ursula as antidote to dissolution is worked out carefully in sustained character-development and realized symbolic incidents. Yet the teller seems to avoid this inherent conclusion, this natural proclivity of his novel. *Women in Love* works against itself, and the contradiction is revealed by a contrived, overinsistent tone, when Ursula submits her healthy soul and will to the more corrupted Birkin. Describing this submission, the teller attributes redemptive properties to the same force of corruption that is throughout depicted as destructive. And this contradiction is at the heart of the tale/teller problem in *Women in Love*: for while the negative implications of corruption are fully dramatized by the tale, its positive powers are only asserted by the teller. The narrator is required to make the assertion in his effort to justify the unequal consummation-scene that climaxes the novel. There the teller unthrones the *magna mater*, putting Birkin in a superior position while claiming to show equality. It is a dual tension, opening gaps between both tale and teller and tale and the reader's knowledge of experience. Hence the willed subjugation of Ursula to Brikin leads to discrepancies that mar this otherwise very great work.[4]

2

The central technical accomplishment of *Women in Love*, like that of *The Rainbow*, is the apprehension of the carbon of character. But where *The Rainbow* is based on a myth of carbon, the technique of *Women in Love* is that of carbon-symbolism. In the earlier novel Lawrence analyzes the way in which the fundamental experiences of life—birth, marriage, sex, and death—register on the obscurely emotional, instinctive self; *The Rainbow* is a recapitulation of the life-cycle as it is perceived on the carbon level. In *Women in Love* the teller replaces these general renderings of carbon-states with sharp, specific images of inner being; he hypostatizes the carbon-self, giving it various, concrete forms. This gives *Women in Love* a febrile vividness lacking in its predecessor. (On the other hand, Lawrence's extended exposition of his characters' underselves—tedious as it sometimes becomes—gives *The Rainbow* a sustained depth unmatched elsewhere in his fiction.)

More consistently than Ursula and Birkin, Gudrun and Gerald are described and developed through the effective device of carbon-symbolism. An early example of an image that serves as an objective correlative for a psychic essence of being is evoked by Gudrun; she is observing the light that seems to gleam about the handsome industrialist, Gerald Crich: "There was something northern about him that magnetized her. In his clear northern flesh and his fair hair was a glisten like sunshine refracted through crystals of ice. And he looked so new, unbroached, pure as an arctic thing. . . . 'Am I *really* singled out for him in some way, is there really some pale gold, arctic light that envelops only us two?' " (pp. 15–16).

Gudrun and Gerald are united in frigid incandescence, but not only they are "enveloped" by the pale light. We learn from a later interior monologue of Birkin's that such light represents a kind of psychic disintegration. The monologue, stimulated by the memory of an African statue, grimly prophesies the "universal dissolution" of mankind, asserting that the process will take two forms: African and Arctic:

Thousands of years ago . . . in these Africans . . . the desire for creation and productive happiness must have lapsed, leaving the single impulse for knowledge in one sort, mindless progressive knowledge through the senses, knowledge arrested and ending in the senses. . . . There is a long way we can travel, after the death break: after that point when the soul in intense suffering breaks, breaks away from its organic hold. . . . We fall from the connexion with life and hope, we lapse from pure integral being, from creation and liberty, and we fall into the long, long African process of purely sensual understanding, knowledge in the mystery of dissolution. . . . It would be done differently by the white race. The white races, having the Arctic north behind them, the vast abstraction of ice and snow, would fulfil a mystery of ice-destructive knowledge, snow-abstract annihilation. (Pp. 285–86)

In the "African" way the personality is disrupted: the "outspoken mind" which looks to ideas and values is abandoned and so is the chance for creative self-expansion. Incapable of enlargement, the organism turns to reduction, depleting itself by feeding on its own frictional sensations; the self becomes a closed envelope, experiencing only itself and, because trapped in the corporeal body, finally having nothing to experience but its own decomposition. Hence it lives according to "knowledge in disintegration and dissolution, knowledge such as the beetles have, which live purely within the world of corruption and cold dissolution" (pp. 285–86). The "white races" of the Arctic way partake of the same principle of dissolution. Here too the self is enclosed, receives its satisfactions within the enclosure, and is diminishing by the limitation. But this more complex process occurs against the backdrop of a "vast abstraction." The point seems to be that Western man, with his intellect-based culture, is held within his self-conscious mind; he therefore experiences his body through a self-observing consciousness that holds sensation at one remove. (The Arctic and African processes are closely related, but not identical.)[5] The way of "ice-destructive knowledge, snow-abstract annihilation" is the way of a mind that makes coldly abstract ideas and images out of experience, yet is incapable of going beyond the experience of the corruptible self. It thus ends with a frigid apprehension of disintegration. In both the African and Arctic ways, the organism loses contact with the pleasure that comes from the creative, reproductive functions of organic life, and seeks the subtler sensations found in "knowledge in dissolution and disintegration." (Hence Birkin reasons that the phallus is not the source of the deeper "sensual realities," and implies that the anus holds the most mysterious and profound "sensual understanding.") The African or Arctic process is one of corruption because it only conceives the dying curve of the organic cycle, and has lost all response to the engendering, growing, or blossoming aspects of organic life.

Gudrun's image (I ask the reader's indulgence for my digression) links Gerald and herself to the qualities connected to the Arctic way. (The image, as should be obvious, describes a distortion at the level of the carbon-of-character.) As presented in the novel, both characters' lives involve a cold savoring of dissolution, and most critics have seen them as equally participant in a frigid attenuation of self.[6] Yet there is an essential distinction between Gudrun's and Gerald's ways of being. Gudrun experiences through a fanciful mind that keeps reality remote and frees her for a frostily indifferent view of life. Gerald participates in a different version of the Arctic way: he concentrates on sensation controlled in the self and imposed on others by a dominating will.[7] The difference between living according to the manipulating mind or the dominating will is this: the will needs responding objects on which to exert itself, while the mind can content itself with its own perceptions and creations. This distinction explains Gerald's greater dependency in the relationship and accounts for his final defeat in the destructive struggle between the two characters.

Gudrun's vitality-denying life-of-the-mind is familiar, recalling many earlier (and subsequent) Lawrencian women. Prefigured by the "negative" Lettie, the Lettie-as-Eve in *The White Peacock*, Gudrun's true predecessor is Helena, the fanciful heroine of *The Trespasser*. Gudrun consistently alters the world in her transforming imagination, because, like Helena, she fears physical reality. An artist, Gudrun disarms the surrounding world by rendering it into a simplified creation of her own making; she mentally places people, organizing and clarifying their importance for her until each is "like a character in a book, or a subject in a picture, or a marionette in a theatre. . . . She knew them, they were finished, sealed and stamped and finished with, for her. There was none that had anything unknown, unresolved" (p. 15). Gudrun, as her sister Ursula notes, has a penchant for the minuscule: "she must always work small things, that one can put between one's hands, birds and tiny animals. She likes to look through the wrong end of the opera-glasses, and see the world that way" (p. 42). In her art, as in her mind, Gudrun prefers the small things that fit neatly into her ordering imagination. When reality nevertheless stubbornly intrudes on her, as when some colliers' wives call derisively after the well-dressed young woman, her fancy becomes murderous: "She would have liked them all annihilated, cleared away, so that the world was left clear for her."

Gudrun feels a perplexing attraction-repulsion toward her native mining-country: "Why had she wanted to submit herself to it, did she still want to submit herself to it, the insufferable torture of these ugly, meaningless people, this defaced countryside? She felt like a beetle toiling in the dust" (pp. 11–12). The scarab or dung-beetle is associated with waste matter and hence with the "corruption and cold dissolution" that signifies the slow reduction of organic life to death; the beetle is a sign of the ultimate debasement of material life. In a kind of carbon-permutation, Gudrun becomes a "beetle" temporarily. Immersing herself in the "gritty" defacement of industrial corruption, she becomes a beetlelike forager in technological wastes. The masochistic submersion in ugliness satisfies, in some perverse way, Gudrun's craving for mind-stimulation. Yet Gudrun withdraws from the actuality of the blighted landscape. Self-protectively, she tries to mitigate the inherent force of the mining-scene by turning it into a creation of fancy. Taking something genuinely demonic, she reduces it to the make-believe demonism of her imagination: "It is like a country in an underworld. . . . it's marvellous, it's really marvellous. . . . The people are all ghouls, and everything is ghostly. Everything is a ghoulish replica of the real world" (p. 12).

Exposing herself to frightening phenomena, she finds excitement and develops resistance. She is drawn to Gerald Crich because the

Nordic brutality of his presence suggests a twisted stimulation: "His gleaming beauty . . . did not blind her to the significant, sinister stillness in his bearing, the lurking danger of his unsubdued temper. . . . she really felt this strange and overwhelming sensation on his account, this knowledge of him in her essence, this powerful apprehension of him" (pp. 15–16). This masochism should not be confused with self-destructiveness; the violence Gudrun perceives in Gerald promises macabre additions to the spectrum of her experience.

Violence is Gerald's central, typifying characteristic. Through Gerald, Lawrence develops a daring view of industrialism as the product of the aggressive psyches of disordered men. In Gerald's hands, technology is a gigantic apparatus for punishing external nature. His punitive instrument is the *machine*, which serves to effect his will on a universe he regards as an eternal antagonist. The relevant question Gudrun asks about Gerald, "where does his *go* go to," finds its answer in Gerald's struggle to engage and subdue his environment. His is the energy of will, the energy that imposes itself; and he applies "the latest appliances" in order to overcome nature:[8] "There were two opposites, his will and the resistant Matter of the earth. And between these he could establish the very expression of his will, the incarnation of his power, a great and perfect machine, a system, an activity of pure order, pure mechanical repetition, repetition *ad infinitum*, hence eternal and infinite" (p. 256). Gerald uses the machine to blight the green earth, to bow nature in mechanical service. The persistent automatic-motion Gerald worships, moreover, is a concretization of his own driving will to power. The machine is a primary carbon-symbol for the wealthy young industrialist, master of the midland collieries and overseer of the corruption Gudrun finds so perversely magnetic. The cold light she descries in him is, at least on one level, the harsh glare of burnished metal.

In his social views, Gerald is an instrumentalist: he equates a man's importance with his function, his role within the great progressing machine-society: "the idea was, that every man was fit for his own little bit of a task—let him do that, and then please himself. . . . Only work, the business of production, held men together. . . . Apart from work they were isolated, free to do as they liked" (p. 114). Denying the social significance of the private self mechanically bifurcates the human personality. In Gerald himself, the public and private selves mirror each other with cruel precision. The unity in these two parts of him shatter his theories about the detachability of the working self from the sexual self. Gerald's own experiences suggest that the instrumentalization of the social man is part of the dehumanization of the whole man.

Gerald's relationship to Minette,[9] a dissipated model and member of the degenerate café society Gerald meets through Birkin, shows the destructive similarity in his professional and personal lives. Minette's appeal for Gerald recalls Will's attraction to the Nottingham working-girl in *The Rainbow:* Gerald is drawn toward an abusable woman who gives him the illusion of omnipotence: "He felt an awful, enjoyable power over her. . . . For she was a victim. . . . He would be able to destroy her utterly in the strength of his discharge" (p. 71). But the slavish foulness about Minette contributes an aura lacking in the relationship in *The Rainbow;* she brings in the true note of corruption, and here is the common element between Gerald's ways of working and loving. In his work, Gerald receives satisfaction from the effective application of a subduing will that spreads corruption. In his lovemaking, he receives pleasure by immersing himself in corruption in order to dominate it: he thus finds his sensations, not through the body, nor the mind, but through the will: "Her inchoate look of a violated slave, whose fulfillment lies in her further and further violation, made his nerves quiver with acutely desirable sensation. After all, his was the only will, she was the passive substance of his will" (p. 88). In social functioning or sex Gerald abuses whatever is under his volitional power.

Minette herself, like the rest of the Pompadour Cafe group, is involved in sensual dissolution. Birkin describes Minette's liaison with another member of the group, Halliday, as an African connection, "a return along the Flux of Corruption, to the original rudimentary conditions of being" (p. 432). Minette incarnates African corruption as she indicates the nature of Gerald's sensuality. Because he knows that Minette has shared his own way of sex, Gerald recoils from her: "he must go away from her, there must be pure separation between them."

Similarly, the primitive statue he observes in Halliday's flat is a symbol for evaded aspects of himself. Birkin, who frequently assumes the role of Gerald's intellectual mentor, explains the significance of the carving: " 'it is an awful pitch of culture, of a definite sort.' 'What culture?' Gerald asked, in opposition. He hated the sheer barbaric thing. 'Pure culture in sensation, culture in the physical consciousness, really ultimate *physical* consciousness, mindless, utterly sensual' " (p. 87). Gerald himself is one step away from this level of reduction. But the statue, whose significance for Gerald parallels the beetle's relationship to Gudrun, is a reminder that the "Flux of Corruption" pervades and taints those who enter it. Receiving sensual corruption into the mind or will, the receiver becomes corrupted. Gerald does not live for pure "physical consciousness," but he is devoted to his own kind of will-based "culture in sensation." His resentment of Minette and the statue indicate his self-deception, his refusal to understand that the sensuality of corruption draws him inevitably into the knowledge of disintegration.

We can both equate and distinguish between Gudrun's and Gerald's ways of dissolution. Gerald actively creates sensation-through-corruption, while Gudrun is passively excited by the same process. But both are stimulated by the forces that reduce organic life. Gerald and Gudrun share an ability negatively to affect nature itself, to project and extend their perversions *into* the circumambient universe instead of (in the familiar, positive Lawrencian pattern) being healed *by* it. A series of vivid animal-scenes communicate Gudrun and Gerald's mutual, viciously effective, need to disrupt the organic dignity of living things.

In the first of these scenes Gerald bullies his "red Arab mare" into enduring the chaotic passage of a seemingly endless train:

> He bit himself down on the mare like a keen edge biting home, and *forced* her round. . . . he held on her unrelaxed with an almost mechanical relentlessness, keen as a sword pressing into her. . . . the eternal trucks were rumbling on, very slowly, treading one after the other. . . . The connecting chains were grinding and squeaking as the tension varied, the mare pawed and struck away mechanically now, her terror fulfilled in her, for now the man encompassed her; her paws were blind and pathetic as she beat in the air, the man closed round her, and brought her down, almost as if she were part of his own physique. (Pp. 123-24)

Here is the typical product of Gerald's energy—the transformation

of the organic into the mechanical. Her spasmodic pawings reveal
how the mare's integrity has been usurped.[10] Gerald terrorizes the
animal until it is unable to function from its own centers of being:
he subordinates the horse to the locomotive, forcing the creature to
emulate the machine. At the same time, the animal becomes an
extension of Gerald's own rigid automatism. A man more often
controlled by his will than able to control it, Gerald is in this sense
as "mechanical" as the creature he subdues. Gerald's bearing
down on the mare is charged, also, with sexual implications; "the
bright spurs . . . pressing relentlessly" join with the sexual
suggestiveness of the train itself to imply a sadistic violation. This
implicitly sexual violence brings Gudrun, who observes the incident together with Ursula, to the point of swooning: "The world
reeled and passed into nothingness for Gudrun, she could not know
any more." But she soon regains herself: "When she recovered, her
soul was calm and cold, without feeling." Even Gerald's brutality,
though it briefly fills her mind with overwhelming sensations, fails
lastingly to affect her cold control.

A scene where Gudrun teases a herd of bullocks reverses
Gerald's brutalization of his mare.[11] The beasts frighten Ursula,
but Gudrun dances insinuatingly close to the animals, expressing
her fearless independence before them. She is excited by the
animals' physical force, which she acknowledges. But her movement puts *her* in control: she stuns and confuses the bullocks,
subordinating their lurking power to her imagination by turning
them into manipulated figures in her dance-fantasy:

> Gudrun, with her arms outspread and her face uplifted, went in a
> strange palpitating dance towards the cattle . . . her breasts lifted and
> shaken towards the cattle, her throat exposed as in some voluptuous
> ecstasy towards them. . . . the cattle . . . ducked their heads a little in
> sudden contraction from her, watching all the time as if hypnotized,
> their bare horns branching in the clear light, as the white figure of the
> women ebbed upon them, in the slow, hypnotizing convulsion of the
> dance. She could feel them just in front of her, it was as if she had the
> electric pulse from their breasts running into her hands. Soon she
> would touch them, actually touch them. . . . Oh, they were brave little
> beasts. (P. 187)

When Gerald appears, calling out to break the animals' mesmeric
spell, Gudrun scatters them in a final gesture that leads to their

diminishment: "she lifted her arms and rushed sheer upon the long-horned bullocks . . . they ceased pawing the ground, and gave way, snorting with terror . . . galloping off into the evening, becoming tiny in the distance, and still not stopping" (pp. 189–90).

The ensuing struggle between Gerald and Gudrun, ostensibly concerning the bullocks, is really about the extent of Gerald's potency of will. The cattle, which belong to Gerald, are a metonymy for his maleness. He insists on their formidability, bringing out Gudrun's defiance. Though she had admired Gerald's dominance from a distance, Gudrun invokes her own stories of violence when the industrialist becomes palpably overbearing:

> "You think I'm afraid of you and your cattle, don't you?" she asked.
> His eyes narrowed dangerously. There was a faint domineering smile on his face. . . .
> She was watching him all the time with her dark, dilated, inchoate eyes. She leaned forward and swung round her arm, catching him a light blow on the face with the back of her hand. . . .
> And she felt in her soul an unconquerable desire for deep violence against him. . . . She wanted to do as she did, she was not going to be afraid. . . .
> He recoiled from the slight blow on his face. . . . For some seconds he could not speak, his lungs were so suffused with blood, his heart stretched almost to bursting with a great gush of ungovernable emotion. It was as if some reservoir of black emotion had burst within him, and swamped him.
> "You have struck the first blow," he said at last, forcing the words from his lungs, in a voice so soft and low, it sounded like a dream within her. . . .
> "And I shall strike the last," she retorted involuntarily, with confident assurance. He was silent, he did not contradict her. (Pp. 190–91)

Both characters are overwhelmed by the dark, demonic feelings they inspire in each other, but there is a marked distinction. Gudrun, intoxicated with violence as she is, acts effectively. She strikes a blow just heavy enough to warn Gerald that he is forbidden to interfere with her. Gerald is too overcome by uncomprehended emotions to respond easily. Gudrun is calculating within the unstated hatred that submerges them, whereas Gerald is "swamped" (revealing word) by it. At a crucial point in the encounter he is without self-governance (a man who would be foolish if he were not so dehumanized), while she seems consciously diabolical.

Gerald is similarly "swamped" by his emotions in a chapter, "Water-Party," that sees him literally sink beneath the surface of Willey Water, the Crich family's private pond. Water is clearly associated with death and disintegration in *Women in Love* (compare Birkin's disquisition on the "dark river of dissolution"). Gerald therefore experiences both literal submersion and submersion in his uncontrolled emotional self: the dark masses of water reflect and extend his own "ungovernable" waves of feeling. A series of chapters advance the relationship of Gerald and water, revealing that he lacks the integrity of ego to defy that annihilating element. In "Diver," first of all, he shows a superior mastery over Willey pond, enjoying a splendid isolation amid the "grey, uncreated water" he feels as his true element.[12] But already in "Sketch-Book" the matter is complicated, for there Gerald's clumsy wilfulness costs him his dignity, preventing him from sharing Gudrun's remoteness from the muddy pond. In "Water-Party," Gerald senses that the cold depths suggest his inescapable fate: "it's curious how much room there seems, a whole universe under there; and as cold as hell, you're as helpless as if your head was cut off. . . . when you are down there, it is so cold, actually, and so endless, so different really from what it is on top, so endless—you wonder how it is so many are alive, why we're up here" (p. 206). And "Snowed Up" describes the culmination of Gerald's relationship to water, the element which adumbrates his inner chaos, and to which he grows increasingly close until, finally, he dissolves in the frozen waters of the snowy Alps. In a subtle way, Gerald's very rigidity consigns him to watery disintegration: the suggestion is that the man who holds himself together most rigorously is the man most likely, in the end, to come apart.

The scene involving Bismarck, the Crich family's great, white rabbit, is a blood-rite, a pact in destruction made by Gudrun and Gerald. The rabbit itself, in its blind, unthinking savagery, symbolizes the souls of the two human beings in this scene: here Gudrun, Gerald, and Bismarck are all *one:* " 'God be praised we aren't rabbits,' she said in a high, shrill voice. The smile intensified on his face. 'Not rabbits?' he said, looking at her fixedly.

Slowly her face relaxed into a smile of obscene recognition" (p. 273). Gerald's mauling of the beast, and the bloody scratches it scores on the arms of both Gerald and Gudrun, create a grotesque version of Birkin's *Blutbrüderschaft:* the swearing of eternal loyalty between man and man becomes a swearing of eternal viciousness and violence between man and woman. Gudrun's and Gerald's understanding has a metaphysical aspect. Gerald swoons before a mystical essence of evil, a demonic version of the life-giving "Beyond" of *The Rainbow:* "The long, shallow red rip seemed torn across his own brain, tearing the surface of his ultimate consciousness, letting through the for ever unconscious, unthinkable red ether of the beyond, the obscene beyond" (p. 273).

In all three of the major animal-scenes Gudrun gives, at some point, a cry like a seagull's caw (pp. 125, 186, 270). The narrator also uses the seagull's scream to typify Ursula in one of the moon-scenes describing her annihilation of Anton Skrebensky. The aural-visual image is eerily successful, with an effectiveness that defies explication. But it is clear that the figure shows woman at her most horrible: a heartless, voracious creature. The seagull is a scavenger that lives off the battered leavings of the sea, and the sea is the element that reduces men of insufficient self. The equating of Gudrun and the seagull is one of many indications that Gudrun will outlive Gerald, that despite their "mutual hellish recognition," theirs is a hell in which the woman survives the man. Indeed, at points Lawrence makes explicit that underneath it is Gudrun who has the vanquishing force: "Gudrun looked at Gerald with strange, darkened eyes, strained with underworld knowledge, almost supplicating, like those of a creature which is at his mercy, yet which is his ultimate victor" (p. 272).

A chapter called "Death and Love" develops the difference between Gudrun's and Gerald's ways of being. The chapter describes two closely related subjects: the death of Gerald's father, Thomas Crich, and the subsequent intensification of Gerald's relationship with Gudrun. From his ideologically confused but utterly resolute father, Gerald learns to live by the principle of the unrelenting will. Initially, even death seems to have no influence on the two strongly-resolved men: "And the father's will never relaxed or yielded to death. . . . In the same way, the will of the son never yielded" (p. 363). But, eventually, Thomas Crich's dying graphically reveals the limitations of human power. Watching his father's pitiful helplessness erodes Gerald's belief in the omnipotence of mortal volition—but the new awareness costs him his own rigid self-integration: "as the fight went on, and all that he had been and was continued to be destroyed, so that life was a hollow shell all round him, roaring and clattering like the sound of the sea . . . he knew he would have to find reinforcements, otherwise he would collapse inwards upon the great dark void which circled at the centre of his soul" (p. 363).

Losing his father, Gerald feels the "fearful space of death" within himself. Confronting the emptiness previously hidden by his deceptive self-assurance, Gerald now turns, with all the pathos of Will's fumbling need for Anna, to Gudrun:

> Something must come with him into the hollow void of death in his soul, fill it up, and so equalize the pressure within to the pressure without. . . . In this extremity his instinct led him to Gudrun. . . . He would follow her to the studio, to be near her. . . . He would . . . aimlessly pick[ing] up the implements, the lumps of clay . . . looking at them without perceiving them. And she felt him following her, dogging her heels like a doom. (Pp. 363–64)

As a result of his redoubled need, Gerald draws Gudrun to him in their first physical embrace. The contact has an assuaging effect as she becomes the "reinforcement" of being he requires: "he seemed to be gathering her into himself . . . drinking in the suffusion of her physical being, avidly."

Gerald is capable of the suspension of ego the teller refers to when he describes "melting" or "flowing" or "passing out" into the "darkness" (the "darkness" is the area beyond self-consciousness). But Gerald's self-loss consists of the absorption of one ego by another—it is a merger based on weakness; he takes Gudrun into himself, imbibing her as a means of restoring his enfeebled being: "His arms were fast around her, he seemed to be gathering her into himself, her warmth, her softness, her adorable weight, drinking in the suffusion of her physical being, avidly. He lifted her, and seemed to pour her into himself, like wine into a cup" (p. 373).

As for Gudrun, her ability to "swoon" and "pass away," "exquisite" while it briefly lasts, soon yields to her assertive, circumscribing ego.[13] Coming back to consciousness Gudrun turns self-forgetting physical intimacy into an aggressive mind-intimacy. She gathers Gerald, through the tactile sense, into a mind that disintegrates all the mystery he brings from the darkness:

> There seemed a faint, white light emitted from him, a white aura, as if he were a visitor from the unseen. She reached up, like Eve reaching to the apples on the tree of knowledge, and she kissed him. . . . This was the glistening forbidden apple, this face of a man. . . . She wanted to touch him and touch him and touch him till she had him all in her hands, till she had strained him into her knowledge. Ah, if she could have the precious *knowledge* of him. (P. 374)

Eve is an apposite image for Gudrun. There is a parallel here between Lawrencian and Christian thought; in both world views original sin is the desire to know the unknowable: to transgress the prohibition against forbidden knowledge. For the Judaeo-Christian tradition the "unknowable" is the total moral wisdom implied by the knowledge of good and evil. Such knowledge is commensurate with God's omniscience, but it leads man to self-consciousness, shame, and guilt. Eve's desire *to know*, in its *hubris*, destroys the innocent, oblivious sensuality she shared with Adam, and brings, in its stead, the burden of self-awareness. For Lawrence the "unknowable" is the partner in the love-relationship.[14] Intellectually apprehending another ego is intruding on a separate self that should remain inviolate and mysterious. Moreover, such knowledge destroys the possibility of redemptive self-forgetting.

The teller shows that Gudrun and Gerald want to imbibe and absorb one another. Gerald tries to take Gudrun into his very being and find protection against the void. Gudrun, the Eve-figure, attempts to take Gerald into her mind, to ingest him cognitively. Yet the two characters should not be equated. He is the weaker, for he looks to her for life itself; she is the uglier, for she feeds off him like carrion, picking at his body for stimulating knowledge that feeds her mind. Using imagery that recalls Ursula, the narrator describes Gudrun as a vulturelike creature of destruction: "How much more of him was there to know? Ah, much, much, many days' harvesting for her large, yet perfectly subtle and intelligent hands upon the field of his living, radio-active body. . . . her hands, like birds, [w]ould feed upon the fields of his mystical plastic form" (p. 375). There is cruel irony, then, in Gerald's looking to Gudrun for support. He comes to her in all his pressing ontological need—but instead of being completed, he is to be devoured.

Gerald, however, is a willing victim, preferring a see-saw of annihilation to isolation. When Gudrun fails to appear for three days, he is overcome by an urgent drive for union with her. In a daze of "somnambulistic automatism"[15] he stumbles toward her home. Yet there is an unconscious deliberateness in the movement, indicative of the connection between dependency and bullying. Because Gerald is incapable of being without her, Gudrun is unable to resist him. This is a dominating dependency to which Gudrun must submit: "She knew there was something fatal in the situation, and she must accept it" (p. 387).

The passages describing their first sexual consummation are vivid almost to the point of unbearability:[16]

> And she, she was the great bath of life, he worshipped her. Mother and substance of all life she was. And he, child and man, received of her and was made whole. . . . the miraculous, soft effluence of her breast suffused over him, over his seared, damaged brain, like a healing lymph, like a soft, soothing flow of life itself, perfect as if he were bathed in the womb again.
>
> . . . .
>
> He buried his small, hard head between her breasts and pressed her breasts against him with his hands. And she with quivering hands pressed his head against her, as he lay suffused out, and she lay fully conscious. The lovely creative warmth flooded through him like a sleep of fecundity within the womb. Ah, if only she would grant him the flow of this living effluence, he would be restored, he would be complete again. . . . Like a child at the breast he cleaved intensely to her. . . . He was glad and grateful like a delirium, as he felt his own wholeness come over him again, as he felt the full, unutterable sleep coming over him, the sleep of complete exhaustion and restoration. (Pp. 389–90)

In two of the novel's most resonant and disturbing carbon-symbols, Lawrence presents Gerald as both a foetus and an infant. (We remember the African statue he hates reminds Gerald of a "foetus"—p. 82.) A powerful need to revert to the womb exists within him alongside an equally insistent desire for mother-son unison-in-dependence that is surely Oedipal in its origin. The dual image unites in a complex depiction of a fragmentary ego, a partial man. Thus Lawrence provides a context for the problem of Gerald's deficiency of being (the context is amplified by the suggestive, if unelaborated, tensions between Gerald and his mother, Christiana Crich). Moreover, the womb-imagery, with its evocation of the amniotic fluid, subtly refers to Gerald's complex relationship to water. The attraction to water includes a desire for womblike security that is not only regressive but destructive, since what is life for the embryo is death for the man. (In general, Gerald's infantilism is the underside of his aggression. His brutality may thus express frustration at severance from an earlier union; indeed, brutality is a way of *forcing* merger.) But here unconsciousness replaces violence to ease Gerald's pain, for it allows him a simulacrum of the full, assuaging fusion.[17] Beneath the subterfuge of his aggression, he longs for this comforting maternal flood and the dissolution of identity. Yet this unconsciousness, so paradisal for the moment, looks ahead to his death. Gerald's mind, tortured by the pain of separation, and a self-smothering need for fusion, eventually moves toward its own extinction.

The infant-foetus image is a brilliant example of the carbon-symbol technique that reveals parts of being below the perceivable personality. The technical success of the Gerald/Gudrun sections of the novel is based on this technique (as *The Rainbow* depends on the carbon-myth for its power). It is a notable demonstration that when Lawrence is technically successful he describes the struggles between a man of weak ego and a woman of superior ego-strength; it is arguable that Lawrence's style breaks down—as in *The White Peacock, The Trespasser, The Lost Girl* and *The Plumed Serpent*—when he tries to insist on ontological parity, or on male supremacy, in the man-woman relationship. This supports the conclusion that imbalance characterizes Lawrence's fundamental apprehension of males and females, and that a narrative describing this imbalance in action is the authentic tale he has to tell.[18]

The brilliant description of Gerald's regressive core-of-being is matched by an equally acute rendering of Gudrun's carbon-self:

> She was exhausted, wearied. Yet she must continue in this state of violent active superconsciousness. She was conscious of everything—her childhood, her girlhood, all the forgotten incidents, all the un-realized influences and all the happenings she had not under-stood. . . . It was as if she drew a glittering rope of knowledge out of

the sea of darkness, drew and drew and drew it out of the fathomless depths of the past, and still it did not come to an end, there was no end to it, she must haul and haul at the rope of glittering consciousness, pull it out phosphorescent from the endless depths of the unconsciousness, till she was weary, aching, exhausted, and fit to break, and yet she had not done. (P. 391)

Gudrun suffers intensely from her tyrannical mind that exacts the penance of overconsciousness. Her darkness-excluding ego, imprisoning her within a relentless self-awareness, causes Gudrun's separation from peace, from union, from "lapsing out." Though irrevocably single, she is severely limited, living according to an overactive brain that is eternally tortured by memory and victimized by time. The "glittering rope of knowledge" functions as the moon does in the Ursula/Skrebensky consummation scenes: a bitter refulgence, it is a sign of the woman's egoistical isolation.

The lovemaking sequence in "Death and Love" forcefully demonstrates the distinction between Gerald's unfinished self on the one hand, and Gudrun's distorted being on the other. This distinction is inherent in the respective faculties they live by. The will is a dependent faculty of the personality (the central point bears repeating) because it always needs immediate, direct objects on which to exercise itself. Whether venting his rage on the exterior world, or turning desperately to a woman for protection (paradoxically, self-diminishment in womb-like embrace is his defense against complete disintegration), Gerald is emotionally, sometimes passionately, reliant upon something external and *other*. Gudrun, functioning through her abstracting mind, is integral and isolate. Though she suffers from her self-enclosing mind, she is also defended by it, and saved from the humiliating compulsions that strip Gerald of his self-possession. Gerald's interfering will impels him toward the outside world and constantly tears at the boundaries of his self. But living within her consciousness leads Gudrun to a full, frigid independence from other people—though not from the endless "automatic" activity of her mind.

This frigidity is complexly developed and symbolized in two late chapters of the novel, "Continental" and "Snowed Up." Snow provides the setting for the late sections of *Women in Love* and is the last of the novel's major carbon-symbols. But the image does more than indicate that a loveless, abstract quest for sensation has reduced Gudrun and Gerald in a snowy dissolution. The problem with such a reading is that it sees Gerald and Gudrun as equal partners in "ice-destructive knowledge, snow-abstract annihilation."[19] Yet an accurate description of the final stages of their relationship is: Gudrun's lust for "ice-destructive knowledge" causes Gerald's "snow-abstract annihilation." He dies and she lives as she is transformed into a sinister force that destroys him. Her cold-bloodedness becomes so chilling and complete that her soul is fairly imaged by the surrounding snow. Gerald's being, if cold and dehumanized, cannot be identified with the snow in the end: observing the last acts of the two characters, it seems more adequate to say that he is sacrificed to the frozen element within her. For Gerald begins to show positive emotions and become something more than a man of dark rage and will. But Gudrun deliberately goads him, wanting him to remain ungoverned and negative, preventing their connection from taking a creative form and developing wholeness: " 'Won't you say you'll love me always?' she coaxed. . . . 'I will love you always,' he repeated, in real agony, forcing the words out. . . . 'Try to love me a little more, and to want me a little less,' she said, in a half contemptuous, half coaxing tone. The darkness seemed to be swaying in waves across his mind, great waves of darkness plunging across the mind. It seemed to him he was degraded at the very quick, made of no account" (p. 498). Gerald's acknowledged vulnerability, so incongruous in their relationship based on malice, causes his "agony"; and it is her jeering that reduces him to a chaos he no longer wants. Moments like this one help generate the sympathy that many readers feel toward Gerald.[20]

Understanding the relationship of Gerald to the snow, then, is hardly a simple matter; indeed the connection between character and symbol is extremely subtle. Making no pretence at a full elucidation of the startling effects Lawrence achieves through his snow-symbolism, I would point out first that the snow represents a phase in the development of Lawrence's water-imagery. As a literal medium of engulfment, water becomes symbolic of the outer world that threatens to figuratively engulf men of unformed ego. In addition the engulfing element indicates the *nature* of the man engulfed; the watery element only drowns a watery man, who lacks solid form. Tom Brangwen is swept away in a flood that represents the death-wish in his unsure being. The brilliant touch of turning the water to snow refers to the mechanistic coldness of Gerald: the frigidity Gerald achieves at his worst is something foreign to Tom. But we have seen that Gerald is not merely mechanistic. The snow tells us at least as much about Gudrun as it does about Gerald. Gerald has a tendency to regress to infantile, dependent states, and his engulfment suggests a reversion to the security of the womb. The snow thus becomes a cruelly ironic but suitable image for Gudrun, the wintry woman Gerald has paradoxically chosen as the object of his reversion.

It is not surprising that high in the Alps Gudrun views a "great cul-de-sac of snow and mountain peaks" that fills her with "strange rapture"; the white enclosure has an enveloping, containing quality: "the cradle of snow ran on to the eternal closing-in. . . . This was the centre, the knot, the navel of the world" (p. 450). The dazzled ecstasy Gudrun feels toward the cul-de-sac is aroused because the snow-womb is felt as a contiguous extension of herself. When the snow allows Gudrun a rare moment of self-transcendence, the mystical union places her: Gudrun is revealed as an instance of the principle of universal cold: "If she could but come there, alone, and pass into the infolded navel of eternal snow and of uprising, immortal peaks of snow and rock, she would be a oneness with all, she would be herself the eternal, infinite silence, the sleeping, timeless, frozen centre of the All" (p. 461). Her loss of self is based on discovering an element identical with the self.

Like Gerald, Gudrun is not a one-dimensional character. Her coldness is not preordained, but chosen. Capable of intense, emotional moments, she works to extirpate them. She wills to freeze and numb herself because she sees feeling as the beginning of self-destruction. The wish to prostrate herself in self-abasement before Gerald reveals her fear and her whirlpool-emotions that suck in the self: "She was aware of his frightening, impending figure standing close behind her, she was aware of his hard, strong, unyielding chest, close upon her back. And she felt she could not bear it any more, in a few minutes she would fall down at his feet, grovelling at his feet, and letting him destroy her" (p. 467). The depiction of Gerald's strength demonstrates one reason for Gudrun's frigid egoism, for it shows the immense threat she perceives in his masculinity. She thus finds any momentary loss of control potentially devastating, and must constantly protect herself against her urge for self-prostration before Gerald's power. But above all the problem is in herself. Feeling for her is like a motor that starts a sadomasochistic whirligig, a power struggle she *must* win to survive. The solution is not to feel (Gerald's less effective solution is to vanquish). A thoroughgoing ironic cynicism is her defense against loss of control; the strategy allows her to maintain her cool supremacy and to conquer her masochistic impulses.

Mockery is the mode of Loerke, the German artist Gudrun and Gerald meet during their holiday. Loerke, a pure embodiment of Arctic reduction, is at once protective and stimulating; he denies the natural feelings which, in Gudrun's case, endanger strength, while affirming the mental processes that reinforce her cold integration. Gudrun transfers her favor from Gerald, the master of the machine, to Loerke, the artist of the machine, because of Loerke's disdainfully profound "knowledge in the mystery of dissolution." Gerald spreads disintegration out of uncomprehended drives, but Loerke has an objective understanding of mechanical reduction. Aloof, dispassionate contemplation of cold reducing-down is the most diabolical form of Arctic-being. This is the perverse pleasure Gudrun and Loerke—*not* Gudrun and Gerald—share. Loerke's art interprets the mechanical work, the mechanical play, that he sees as the essence of the contemporary world: "What is man doing when he is at a fair . . . ? He is fulfilling the counterpart of labour—the machine works him instead of he the machine. He enjoys the mechanical motion of his own body" (p. 477).

Moreover, he lives this unversal principle within his own being. He is himself both mechanical and corruptive; the one develops from the other, for mechanical functioning ends by signifying the corruption of soul and body. Loerke savors the dismemberment of his own ego, the inner corrosion that occurs when the self is frozen shut and unable to love or participate in organic life. Without the growth that comes from creatively natural life, or the hope that derives from belief in a greater ideal, what remains for Loerke is to immerse himself in disintegration, "to explore the sewers [like] the wizard rat that swims ahead." Gudrun, fatigued by Gerald's constant tearing at the borders of the self, desires the processes that take place in the closed envelope of the ego. She accepts the gradual erosion that is inevitable once the ego closes off replenishment and growth from the outside.[21] (Gerald's problem is the reverse, lacking independent integrity his being is exposed to the universe he needs for self-completion; where she is too closed, he is too opened.) Turning now to Loerke, whose mastery of dissolution is supreme, Gudrun devotes herself to "sensation within the ego, the obscene religious mystery of ultimate reduction, the mystic frictional activities of diabolic reducing down, disintegrating the vital organic body of life" (p. 508).

Yet there is a paradox here that critics of *Women in Love* have not noticed. Loerke seduces Gudrun, in fact, with the promise of stability. "[Loerke] was single and, by abstraction from the rest, absolute in himself." The lust for disintegration has an integrating effect. The dismemberment toward which they inexorably move is in the distant future; within the novel, Gudrun and Loerke find a ghastly *modus vivendi*. If they sometimes experience "inorganic misery," they still do not share Gerald's chaos and doom. It is Gerald, with his trace of human vulnerability and organic feeling, who is destroyed by the death-flow. Unconfused concentration on breaking-down is a way of existence, though it is living for dying.

Gerald increasingly irritates Gudrun as his strenuous will and his insistent, laborious energy interfere with her: "She was weary, oh so weary of Gerald's gripped intensity of physical motion." Gerald intrudes on the exhilarating freedom Gudrun and Loerke find by "rising above" the tedious world, "the dreariness of actuality, the monotony of contingencies." Theirs is a superiority of indifference, a sardonic intactness that comes from conceiving life as pure game. Their play pretends that action has no consequence and exults in cynicism. Without belief in life's positive meaning, there is only disintegration and that is best enjoyed when flavored with mockery. What remains for them is cynical jokes and nihilistic fancies, to play as the world approaches its end. The snow is the ideal backdrop for their inhuman gaiety.

In the climactic, final scene between the three characters, Gerald's rigid jealousy suddenly ruins Gudrun and Loerke's "perfect . . . silvery isolation and interplay." Loerke's *savoir faire*, with its combination of derision and whimsy, continues despite Gerald's determined intrusion on the careless scene; the little artist's contemptuous gallantry drives Gerald to violence. But the blows he gives the smaller, weaker man are paltry compared to the "great downward stroke" Gudrun delivers to Gerald's face and chest. (This is, allegorically, his execution, that "last" blow referred to in "Water-Party.") Gerald responds insanely, seizing Gudrun by the throat; this is an act of the dependent will *in extremis*; murder, in Gerald's case, is the most vicious, yet most pathetic, admission of the need to have a profound effect on an object. Through the strangling, Gerald shatters Gudrun's remoteness, and forces from her, at last, a total, passionate reaction: "The struggling was her reciprocal lustful passion in this embrace, the more violent it became, the greater the frenzy of delight, till the zenith was reached, the crisis, the struggle was overborne, her movement became softer, appeased" (p. 531).

Yet he soon abandons the attack, because Gerald is less murderer than self-destroyer. His murderous and suicidal impulses are both rooted in an insubstantiality of self. Choking Gudrun is a bizarre way to achieve fusion, but he finds a deeper, more satisfying merger by dissolving into the "hollow basin of snow." Gerald fades unconsciously into the snowbanks, losing all life-direction: "He drifted, as on a wind, veered, and went drifting away." When he drifts into nothingness, releasing his grasp on being, as when he attempts murder, driven helplessly to destroy Gudrun's more integral being, Gerald is admitting the defeat of the self.

Disappearing into the snow-basin, Gerald creates a pantomime of his relationship with Gudrun. He literally recapitulates what he has long been undergoing metaphorically: union-in-frigidity, self-reduction in an enclosure that rejects and freezes him. There was always a paradox in Gerald's bringing his merger-need to so chilling a receiver as Gudrun. Why should Gerald look for his intermingling to a woman that rejects him, unless his urge to be saved hides a stronger urge to be destroyed. High in the glacial mountains he resolves the contradiction when he moves toward his death. Gerald dies under a "small bright moon," a "painful brilliant thing" that contributes to the fatigued confusion of his last moments. The image interweaves the death with the larger pattern of Lawrence's symbolic events, for moon suggests Gudrun's unified, malevolently separate ego, and snow its punishing counterpart, the fate that is left to Gerald when he depends on a woman who evades him.[22]

Gerald's death brings together his longing for fusion and his self-destructive impulses: indeed the one is included in the other. Instilling one identity into another is finally impossible, but the desired dissolution of self can be achieved in death. And by immersing himself in the perfect metaphor for her, Gerald simulates the longed-for symbiosis with Gudrun. Blinded by the moonlight he cannot "escape," Gerald moves toward the "hollow basin" of snow; there he stumbles toward a frozen peace in an icy womb.

3

Most critics of *Women in Love* regard the relationship between Ursula and Birkin in one of two ways. The traditional approach to the novel sees Ursula and Birkin as representing a "positive" alternative to Gerald's and Gudrun's corruption.[23] This view, nearly normative in the earlier Lawrence criticism, almost invariably takes its support from Birkin's ideological *statements* affirming wholeness and integrity of self. The following conception, which succeeds Birkin's long rumination on the African and Arctic ways, is an important example:

> There was another way, the way of freedom. There was the paradisal entry into pure, single being, the individual soul taking precedence over love and desire for union, stronger than any pangs of emotion, a lovely state of free proud singleness, which accepted the obligation of the permanent connexion with others, and with the other, submits to the yoke and leash of love, but never forfeits its own proud individual singleness, even while it loves and yields. (P. 287)

Elsewhere, Birkin calls this idea "star-equilibrium"; it conceives the ideal man-woman relationship as a perfect balance, where integrity of self and profound connection are equally maintained. From Birkin's statements about "singleness of self" and "star-equilibrium," some of Lawrence's most significant and persuasive critics have concluded that Ursula and Birkin represent integration, just as Gudrun and Gerald represent disintegration. But there is a problem with this view. As an abstraction, "star-equilibrium" appears entirely cogent and meaningful. Wholeness of being is the logical affirmative value for the novel, as balanced wholeness strikes the perfect contrast to the relationship of Gudrun and Gerald. But to verify whether Birkin and Ursula exemplify integration, we must separate what Birkin says from the novel's tale. Once we do so we realize that in action Birkin *struggles* to achieve wholeness of being, and in conception he does find the way to avoid dissolution. But it is not certain that the idea and the actuality are ever united in dramatic realization. This problem goes beyond Birkin to the teller and the author. Lawrence is working with the entirely convincing idea that disintegration is related to unequal relationships, that neither women who absorb nor men who are absorbed can love in balance. Yet, as we shall see, the Lawrencian narrator cannot seem to balance the scales without weakening his art and substituting a Great Father for the *magna mater*.

A more recent approach sees Ursula and Birkin experiencing, in a particularly liberating fashion, the *necessary* dissolution that involves all the characters of the novel. Critics holding this view insist that any division between integration and disintegration in *Women in Love* is entirely too moralistic and simple.[24] For these critics, dissolution, as an intrinsic part of living processes, is equally intrinsic to Lawrence's vitalism. They argue, moreover, that in *Women in Love* ego-dissolution is imperative and desirable, because the insular ego closes man off from significant experiences, from the impersonal darkness in himself and in the universe; it is thus essential "to smash the false integrity of the ego in order to make possible the true integrity of the blood."[25] The view that places dissolution at the center of Lawrence's value-system includes among its evidence another strain in Birkin's ideology— his statements asserting the centrality of corruption: " 'It is your reality' . . . he said; 'that dark river of dissolution. You see it roll in us . . . the black river of corruption. And our flowers are of this . . . all our reality, nowadays. . . . Dissolution rolls on, just as production does,' he said. 'It is a progressive process—and it ends in universal nothing—the end of the world, if you like' " (pp. 192–93). This approach is serious, enlarging our understanding of the novel by informing us that dissolution is a central motif, which cannot be excluded from a circle of purity Ursula and Birkin inhabit. Yet critics who argue for the pervasiveness of dissolution err when they make corruption a goal and end in itself—for it can legitimately be understood only as a means toward balanced wholeness. The valid point that *is* suggested by the more recent view is that wholeness of being cannot be achieved without acknowledgment of the dark forces of moral and physical corruption which work against it. The pro-dissolution critics, in another instance of weakening a good case by exaggerating its implications, go too far when they annihilate any hint of moral distinction between the novel's two central couples, since the tale confirms that such a distinction profoundly exists.

Both approaches simplify the role of dissolution in the Ursula-Birkin relationship.[26] The processes of corruption play a subordinate part in the larger story of man's struggle for equality with woman. The overall tale of *Women in Love* concerns the *magna mater*, her perverse triumph in the Gerald-Gudrun involvement, and a purported resolution in the balanced relationship between Ursula and Birkin. Birkin is offered, by the narrator, as a man who is a match, in strength-of-self, for his woman.

My contention is that this balancing of the scales is willed and desired but not accomplished. It is created by two separate voices in the novel: that of Birkin, a *commentator* who brings in a structure of ideology, and that of the narrator, who endorses Birkin's asseverations. There are two chapters that present an equilibrium between man and woman: the preliminary, comic "Mino" and the serious, climactic "Excurse." Both chapters are problematically self-contradictory because Birkin (or the narrator) describes equality based on the mutual transcendence of the ego, while statement and event keep sliding over into male-domination. We feel that both the commentator and the narrator believe in balance explicitly and male-domination implicitly. The tension produced by the conflict results in strained rhetoric that gives the two chapters a forced, contrived quality. Neither the offered polarity nor the hidden male ascendancy is transformed into realized art; the two approaches to the Birkin-Ursula relationship are expressions of the teller, and do not succeed in becoming part of the tale.

The tale is carried by different chapters that treat Ursula and Birkin, "Moony" and "Flitting," among others, and these present the more familiar pattern of a male who feels himself weaker than the woman with whom he is involved. The motif of dissolution comes into this larger theme in a complex way. Birkin is shown as more affected by the surrounding social disintegration than Ursula is. The forced reversal where male superiority is covertly upheld entails the overvaluation of the corruption associated with the male.

But let us turn now to the evidences of the novel itself. Birkin, the most complex character in the book, exists between the principles of creation and corruption (critics generally ignore his connection to the one or the other). We meet Birkin as he is extricating himself from an affair with Hermione Roddice, a woman profoundly immersed in the Arctic way. His withdrawal from Hermione expresses his search for a healthier way of being, but his history with her reveals he has been involved in the life that emphasizes the mind at the expense of the body. (On our first view of him we learn: "He went with a slight trail of one foot, which only came from self-consciousness," p. 21.) Now, however, he vociferously attacks Hermione and her manner of existence; above all, it is her self-observing lack of spontaneity that inspires his violent hostility: "You [are] the most deliberate thing that ever walked or crawled . . . you want to have everything in your own volition, your deliberate voluntary consciousness. You want it all in that loathsome little skull of yours, that ought to be cracked like a nut. . . . what you want is pornography—looking at yourself in mirrors, watching your naked animal actions in mirrors, so that you can have it all in your consciousness, make it all mental" (p. 46). Having shown unequivocal antagonism to stimulation-through-the-mind, he affirms its antithesis: a dark and mindless life-of-the-senses. He now wants "sensuality" and "nothing else" because: "It is a fulfilment—the great dark knowledge you can't have in your head—the dark involuntary being. It is death to one's self—but it is the coming into being of another. . . . In the blood . . . when the mind and the known world is drowned in darkness—everything must go—there must be the deluge. Then you find yourself in a palpable body of darkness, a demon—" (pp. 46–47). This darkness sounds similar to the ego-transcending, redemptive darkness we know from other works of Lawrence; and yet it should not be forgotten that in *Women in Love* the unconscious life of the body is one of the two ways of corruption, the element of the beetles. The African way, the knowledge-in-dissolution Birkin describes in "Moony," is also purely "sensual" knowledge.[27] The dark life of the blood described in "Class-Room" and the African way are perhaps not identical. But no clear distinction between the two is made in *Women in Love*. (They are both based on "sensuality.") Recoiling from Hermione Birkin affirms a way of being that is, at the very least, closely related to sensual dissolution. Despite all his assertions, Birkin might be exchanging one means of disintegration for another.

Birkin's ambivalent relationship to the African way continues when he expresses his strong interest in Halliday's primitive statue. " 'It conveys a complete truth,' said Birkin. "It contains the whole truth of that state, whatever you feel about it. . . . Pure culture in sensation, culture in the physical consciousness, really ultimate *physical* consciousness, *mindless*, utterly sensual. It is so sensual as to be final, supreme' " (p. 87). Birkin is tentative about the statue, qualifying his description; a subtle thinker, he generally allows for ambiguity in his statements. But he is never ambiguous about the Arctic self-consciousness that wins his disgust. And he is deeply intrigued by the tribal carving, with its "weight of sensation," its sheer physicality. He has spoken convincingly about the need to live from "another centre" than the self-watching mind, but is that "centre," after all, the reality incarnated by the statue? If, as might be argued, Birkin acknowledges the statue only to subsume and transcend its meaning, then it would be necessary for the tale to convincingly demonstrate the value to which he moves—and this does not occur.

Yet Birkin is extraordinarily self-conscious, qualifying and eternally re-qualifying his ideas. Part of his extreme antagonism to Hermione arises because he has shared her tedious, endless mental processes. In reaction to this Arctic existence, he is fascinated by purely sensual experience, undiluted by consciousness. Thus, when he copies a drawing of a Chinese goose, Birkin tries to involve himself utterly in its sensory way-of-being. A discussion with Hermione about the drawing becomes, in effect, a contest between the African and Arctic ways: "She *must* know. It was a dreadful tyranny, an obsession in her, to know all he knew. For some time he was silent, hating to answer her. Then, compelled, he began: 'I know what centres they live from—what they perceive and feel—the hot, stinging centrality of a goose in the flux of cold water and mud—the curious bitter stinging heat of a goose's blood, entering their own blood like an innoculation of corruptive fire—fire of the cold-burning mud—the lotus mystery.' . . . he caught her, as it were, beneath all her defences. . . . She suffered the ghastliness of dissolution, broken and gone in a horrible corruption" (p. 99). On one level, Hermione and Birkin recapitulate the struggle between "mental-consciousness" and "blood-consciousness," with Birkin fighting for the fully vitalized life-of-the-body and Hermione upholding the enervated, minimizing life-of-the-mind.[28] Yet the "blood" is "corruptive" and exclusively somatic existence includes the principle of dissolution. So that two concurrent revelations take place in this scene. Hermione feels "destroyed" because Birkin tears away her protective mental-consciousness. Turning away from the mind he describes a consciousness that exists exclusively in the senses, making Hermione face sensuality and corruption by forcing her to confront the physical reality she holds at a distance.

But Birkin is also intuiting an existence in "cold water and mud" that bears a close resemblance to the "world of corruption and cold dissolution" that describes the African way. He does not necessarily approve of this state, but his profound insight into the goose's being demonstrates that his attention is increasingly fixed on purely bodily experience, and there is no convincing evidence that he gets off the African-Arctic treadmill. Birkin uses the goose effectively and tellingly against Hermione, but its "corruptive" blood-consciousness is no satisfactory alternative to her mind-locked manner of perception. And it seems that Birkin substitutes corruption-through-the-senses for the corruption-through-the-mind he justifiably rejects.

The goose is Birkin's weapon against Hermione and her entire civilization of knowledge. She, with neat reciprocity, also uses an *objet d'art* against him. Later in the chapter, she takes a "blue, beautiful ball of lapis lazuli," and strikes Birkin on the head—protesting, through this finished artifact, against the instinctivism Birkin now embodies for her. Hermione strikes in the name of her threatened culture, of bogus spirituality and sham artiness, of contrived feeling and sex-in-the-head, of all the things that Birkin opposes with his savage, accurate attacks. But above all Hermione's hitting Birkin is a brutal act of the will. She is violent to the man who rejects and denies her. Not only does Hermione share

Gudrun's tormenting "superconsciousness," but, like Gerald, she compensates for inadequate being with a malicious will. She deceives herself into thinking the deficiency is the fault of someone else and can be remedied by his destruction: "Her whole mind was a chaos, darkness breaking in upon it, and herself struggling to gain control with her will, as a swimmer struggles with the swirling water. . . . She must break down the wall—she must break him down before her, the awful obstruction of him who obstructed her life to the last" (pp. 116–17).

Submersion into non-being (the water-imagery is significant in this regard) is a very real danger for Hermione. Her means of self-maintenance—and this is the sure sign of psychic disturbance—is her interfering will. Because a will of this kind substitutes for a healthy being, subversion of its supremacy implies a complete disintegration of the self. And Birkin, who attacks her mind, resists her will, and highlights her lack of self-sufficiency, constitues a major threat that elicits an explosive assertion.

But subtler applications of power over other creatures can also be used to redress a fragmentary being. It is in relation to an animal that we see a more oblique example of Hermione's oppressive volition. A minor but revealing incident shows Hermione tormenting the creature in an act of quietly malicious bullying—and this is significant for *Women in Love* has its moral coherence in an opposition to the reduction, oppression or deprivation of one being by another. The bullying is performed by Hermione on Birkin's male cat. This is the same "Mino" whose innate right to coerce and intimidate a female cat Birkin defends, with tortured logic, at another point in the novel. Now Mino is coerced in turn as he is frustrated by Hermione:

> She lifted the cat's head with her long, slow, white fingers, not letting him drink, holding him in her power. . . . The cat reached forward again and put his fine white paw on the edge of the saucer. Hermione lifted it down with delicate slowness. This deliberate, delicate carefulness of movement reminded Ursula of Gudrun. . . . And [Hermione] kept her finger on the softly planted paws of the cat, and her voice had the same whimsical, humorous note of bullying (Pp. 337–38)

All this is infinitely more delicate than Gerald's treatment of his mare, but Hermione, too, interrupts an animal's normal functioning. Each character debilitates in his own way: Gerald tears at his animal, while Hermione toys with hers. Indeed, in each case the intruded-upon creature is forced to emulate the intruder. Gerald fractures his horse's organic unity-of-being, while Hermione creates a deliberate space, an elaborately refined distance, between the cat and the satisfaction of his appetites.

In the scene where Hermione strikes Birkin, she loses her hauteur in a desperate reaching for control. Birkin's reaction to Hermione's blow is to escape her and the culture she represents, a culture that encourages destructiveness by eviscerating natural instincts and distorting human life. Wandering toward a "wild valleyside," he immerses himself in an unthinking, entirely sensuous contact with nature. Importantly, he is nearly unconscious during the experience: "He was aware that he could not regain his consciousness, that he was moving in a sort of darkness." He thereby embraces the verdure around him without interruption from self-consciousness:

> He took off his clothes, and sat down naked among the primroses, his legs, his knees, his arms right up to the arm-pits, lying down and letting them touch his belly, his breasts. It was such a fine, cool, subtle touch all over him, he seemed to saturate himself with their contact.
> ....
> Nothing else would do, nothing else would satisfy, except this coolness and subtlety of vegetation travelling into one's blood. (Pp. 119–20)

Like his empathetic entry into the goose's perceptions, this is an experience that dispenses with the mediating presence of the self-conscious mind. But we should not overidentify the two actions. Sympathetically sharing the "bitter stinging heat of a goose's blood . . . like . . . corruptive fire," is something very different from being filled by the "coolness and subtlety of vegetation travelling into one's blood." In the second immersion, Birkin throws himself into an element that is organic and flowering, and evidences a capacity to escape dissolution and join the positive expressions of life. Birkin is therefore not limited to the principle of corruption and should not be classified with characters who are, like Loerke, Hermione, Gerald, or Gudrun.

Birkin has gone beyond these other characters in his range of experience: he is manifestly able to escape the self-awareness that impoverishes life, for he can act according to spontaneous impulse, and put himself in touch with areas of being beneath consciousness. The two experiences, indeed, display his freedom from both the domination of the mind and the imprisonment of the ego. Yet he has still not achieved the organic integrity of self that contrasts with Gudrun's and Gerald's "disintegration and dissolution." "[F]ree proud singleness" is conceived in opposition to "sensual knowledge," it is attained when the "individual soul" achieves absolute wholeness and independence of being, in conjunction with a faithful, committed relationship preventing the partners from being limited to the sensations of the closed self. (It is significant that when he desires this "way of freedom" he feels an irresistible compulsion to go to Ursula.) The incidents we have been examining have one fundamental common characteristic—they are experiences in the "blood"—Birkin continues to limit himself to his senses and enclose himself within the sensual body. Whatever Birkin may *say* about himself and his ideals, figuratively significant actions and encounters establish that his state of being is ambivalent: he is unarguably struggling against Arctic-consciousness, but the values he is putting in its place are disturbingly close to sense-enslavement. While not altogether damned, neither is he saved.

Among the *dramatis personae* in *Women in Love*, only Ursula appears a wholly integrated character who is untouched by dissolution. This integrity is exemplified by her relation to nature and natural creatures. Such relations have ontological import. Gerald, for example, violates nature in an attempt to mold it to his own contorted being. Contrarily, Ursula, being whole herself, has no need to control or reduce the exterior world. (This distinguishes her, as well, from Gudrun and Hermione; fearing and despising nature, they maintain a brittle governance over it through the mind and will.) Interfering volition, the intrusion on another being, arises from some lack in the being of the intruder. This is foreign to Ursula, but intrinsic to Gerald, and hence their intense clash when Gerald bullies his horse before the railroad crossing. As Ursula watches the domineering act, she is brought to a frenzied antagonism: " 'And she's bleeding! She's bleeding!' cried Ursula, frantic with opposition and hatred of Gerald. She alone understood him perfectly, in pure opposition" (p. 124). Horses, for Lawrence, are animals of immense life-energy, of creative, vital physical being.[29] Ursula feels the affront to the horse's independent spontaneity so deeply because she has a correspondent living wholeness of her own. Gudrun and Gerald lack sympathy for the animal, since they cannot comprehend its intrinsic, profound life-of-the-body. Unable to value the animal's separateness, they use the horse and receive satisfaction from distorting its energy. Ursula's empathy for an organic creature, the "living thing" she defends so emphatically, is the logical result of her being independent and whole herself, a manifestation of her spiritual depth.

As she struggles with the magnate who mechanizes nature, so she opposes the artist who interprets nature mechanically; and again, the focal point of the conflict is a "living creature." Looking at a statue Loerke has done of a horse, Ursula rejects the figure as "stock and stupid and brutal"; Loerke, in return, derides the naiveté of her criticism: "that horse is a certain *form*, part of a whole form. . . . It is not a picture of a friendly horse to which you give a lump of sugar" (p. 483). Theirs is an aesthetic argument, a clash between formalist and vitalist world-views, with Loerke disdainfully denying the relation between life and art, and Ursula insisting on the inextricable connection. Loerke's dialectics are clever, but Ursula's words have the ring of simple truth when she says: "As for your world of art and your world of reality . . . you have to separate the two, because you can't bear to know what you are. . . . The world of art is only the truth about the real world, that's all" (p. 485). This statement stands because of a fundamental point: that art is of the artist and the artist lives in the world, so that it is impossible for him to make a statement that is not about himself and his relation to life. (The aesthete's search for "pure" form may be a statement about the *wish* to escape from life, but there can be no actual escape.) Invariably, the artist's being and beliefs are exposed in his work. Showing that Loerke himself is revealed in his "stiff, hide-bound brutal" statue, Ursula merely reiterates what he himself had claimed earlier:[30] that he is an interpreter, and devotee, of industry. So intent is he on this function, in fact, that he attributes mechanical characteristics to an organic, sensitive animal. Loerke recapitulates, in his way, Gerald's reduction of the horse. Ursula's understanding of the horse's organic being, and her recoil from any attempt to diminish that being, point up her own participation in the living, healthy body of life. (It may be remembered that she philosophically apprehends her place in a vitalist, organic universe in *The Rainbow*, during her university experience.)

Ursula's creative integration distinguishes her from the corrosion that subsumes the novel's other characters. The difference between Ursula and Gudrun, for example, is disclosed through a pair of dramatically contrasting carbon-symbols:

> What [Gudrun] could see was mud, soft, oozy, watery mud, and from its festering chill, waterplants rose up, thick and cool and fleshy. . . . she could feel their turgid fleshy structure as in a sensuous vision, she *knew* how they rose out of the mud, she *knew* how they thrust out from themselves. . . .
>
> Ursula was watching the butterflies, of which there were dozens near the water, little blue ones suddenly snapping out of nothingness into a jewel-life, a large black-and-red one standing upon a flower and breathing with his soft wings, intoxicatingly, breathing pure, ethereal sunshine; two white ones wrestling in the low air; there was a halo round them; ah, when they came tumbling nearer they were orange-tips, and it was the orange that had made the halo. Ursula rose and drifted away, unconscious like the butterflies. (P. 132)

Gudrun's is the familiar Arctic experience; she takes the corrupt productions of the mud, these *fleurs du mal*, into herself, experiencing their overripe turgidity vicariously. She always remains conscious, her mind observing her senses. Ursula, clearly, is paralleled with the butterflies, and they are presented as pure, spontaneous creations.[31] Aside from the highly affirmative tone with which the butterflies are described, Birkin places them for us in a later speech. Discussing mankind as a regrettable evolutionary error, "like the ichthyosauri," he rates butterflies far higher in the creation-hierarchy: "look at elder-flowers and bluebells—they are a sign that pure creation takes place—even the butterfly. But humanity never gets beyond the caterpillar stage" (p. 143). The aura of warm light that pervades the passage differentiates Ursula from women connected to the cold light of the moon. This milder radiance—used frequently to typify Ursula—indicates a strong female ego, but without the usual destructive qualities.[32] Ursula is also not self-entrapped. She can lose herself, not in Gerald's self-dissolving way, but in identification with other beings. Achieving a sympathetic, "unconscious" relation with creatures

that suggest the beauty of organic life, Ursula associates herself
with growth and realization, the positive elements in the natural
cycle. Birkin has a similar experience among the primroses; but
Birkin's connection to the creative force is partial, while Ursula is
entirely identified with this affirmative principle.

This also means that Ursula is one-sided in her apprehension of
nature, for the butterflies will go back to the mud and Ursula is
oblivious of the corruption that is inevitable in natural life. Ursula
is strangely, naively unaware of the processes of disintegration that
are so strikingly prevalent in *Women in Love*. All her emphasis and
interest, the very movement of her soul, is toward organic integration. She is at the other extreme from her sister, who is obsessively
concerned with the mud of dissolution.

Birkin might be seen to have the desirable balance: he acknowledges the corruption no living creature can escape, but is not
identified with the progressive movement of decay. Ursula, according to this line of reasoning, needs Birkin to put her in touch
with the principle of degeneration—to help her to take note of
dissolution in order to be free of it. This element does exist within
their highly complex relationship; Birkin sometimes plays a grimly
necessary enlightening role with Ursula, ironically informing her,
when she describes herself as "a rose of happiness," that men are,
inevitably, partly *fleurs du mal* as well.

But where she needs his subtle and intelligent grasp of reality,
he needs her believing and whole faith in life. She requires his
knowledge, but he relies on her being. For Birkin, as we have
noted, has more than his share of corruption; the same Birkin who
can strike precisely the right note, granting degeneration its
inescapable due, also stands in real danger of going the way of
death. Therefore he needs Ursula to give him positivity and hope
through her wholeness of being. Ursula's "pure, ethereal" integrity
of self is richly communicated by the light-imagery that surrounds
her throughout the novel. Birkin finds Ursula's "golden light" of
selfhood immensely compelling: "He saw her face strangely enkindled, as if suffused from within by a powerful sweet fire. His soul
was arrested in wonder. She was enkindled in her own living fire.
Arrested in wonder and in pure, perfect attraction, he moved
towards her. She sat like a strange queen, almost supernatural in
her glowing smiling richness" (pp. 144–45).

Birkin's reactions to Ursula's "sweet fire" are varied and complex, and of signal importance to an understanding of his relationship with her. The "attraction" which leaves Ursula unviolated gradually develops into Birkin's attempts to dominate Ursula's "golden light" and subordinate her luminous being to his darker self. Birkin's subtle applications of the will are a response to his being dependent on Ursula for redemption, his sense that she reclaims and intensifies the intact, valuable part of him. Such a recognition forms the background to the centrally important love-scene (unaccountably ignored by critics) described in "Flitting." Birkin's thoughts are the medium through which the passage is presented, but in this case the comments conform to the revelations of the figurative imagery. Indeed, his perceptions of Ursula cannot be categorized as abstract commentary, for they proceed through the same imagery of light and soft radiance that consistently characterizes her. Birkin's thoughts are based on the carbon-symbol that objectively places Ursula for us. His view of her in "Flitting" culminates the idea presented elsewhere: that he can only reach the bright state of creation that is life in conjunction with her; she is the source of self that restores him. In addition to the light that pervades the passage, Birkin conceives of Ursula in terms of floral imagery. For Lawrence, as we know, flowering in plants is equivalent to the full achievement of self in people:[33] "she was new and frail like a flower just unfolded, a flower so new, so tender, so made perfect by inner light, that he could not bear to look at her, he must hide her against himself, cover his eyes against her. She had the perfect candour of creation, something translucent and simple, like a radiant, shining flower that moment unfolded in primal blessedness. She was so new, so wonder-clear, so undimmed" (p. 416). Then, relatedly, the image that has become the emblem for Ursula is evoked: "the immanence of her beauty . . . was not form, or weight, or colour, but something like a strange, golden light." Thinking about himself, Birkin acknowledges that he is tainted, sullied by his involvement with the dissolute society of Breadalby and the Pompadour Café:

> And he was so old, so steeped in heavy memories. Her soul was new, undefined and glimmering with the unseen. And his soul was dark and gloomy, it had only one grain of living hope, like a grain of mustard seed. But this one living grain in him matched the perfect youth in her. . . . But the passion of gratitude with which he received her into

his soul, the extreme, unthinkable gladness of knowing himself living and fit to unite with her, he, who was so nearly dead, who was so near to being gone with the rest of his race down the slope of mechanical death, could never be understood by her. (Pp. 416–17)

The passage precisely describes the nature of the contact leading Ursula and Birkin to a full and mutual consummation. Birkin, who has been seriously affected by the surrounding forces of degeneration, has not gone completely "down the slope of mechanical death." There is an uncorrupted part of him, a "seed" of wholeness. But this "grain" of healthy being depends entirely on Ursula's organic integrity to come to its fruition. He reaches salvation through the "primal blessedness" of a meeting with her, accepting that he is the more destroyed partner and going to her with his need. Then he discovers and enlarges that which is intact within him: "This marriage with her [was] his resurrection and his life." After he is delivered and enhanced by her, they can move together toward a realm of experience that is beyond either of them. In the proximity of her wholeness he establishes a unity-of-being of his own. They fuse as equals, merging and leaving the isolation and conflict of the separate ego behind: "In the new, superfine bliss, a peace superseding knowledge, there was no I and you, there was only the third, unrealized wonder, the wonder of existing not as oneself, but in a consummation of my being and of her being in a new one, a new, paradisal unit regained from the duality. . . . I have ceased to be, and you have ceased to be: we are both caught up and transcended into a new oneness where everything is silent, because there is nothing to answer, all is perfect and at one. Speech travels between the separate parts. But in the perfect One there is perfect silence of bliss" (p. 417). To be sure, to achieve this transfiguration they need each other. She is "childish," untutored and callow without him; needing words and explanations, she would not know intuitively how to meet him in a quietly profound union. Nevertheless, the merger that transcends the self has its deepest, most ultimate root, in the woman's wholeness of self.

Considering that Ursula's "radiant" self-integrity is something Birkin lacks and desires, it is both surprising and understandable that he should sometimes attempt to control the woman on whom he is dependent. Surprising, for we wonder how the less-integrated character can establish dominance; understandable, for such an attempt may be made out of the resentment at an intrinsic inequality. The first suggestion that Birkin is capable of exerting his own oppressive volition is discernible when he indirectly defends Gerald's domineering will. The defense is made early in the novel, as several of its characters discuss the incident where Gerald maltreats his mare. As the discussion develops, Ursula finds herself arguing against Gerald, Hermione, *and* Birkin. Gerald and Hermione, as might be expected, insist that the brutalization of the animal was appropriate; according to their view of life, one either asserts a position of power or is overpowered. But it is less expected that Birkin should confirm their opinions:

> "Oh, I hated you so much the other day, Mr. Crich."
> "What for?" said Gerald, wincing slightly away.
> "For treating your horse so badly. Oh, I hated you so much!"
> . . . .
> "She is a living creature, why should she stand anything, just because you choose to make her? She has as much right to her own being, as you have to yours."
> "There I disagree," said Gerald. "I consider that mare is there for my use. Not because I bought her, but because that is the natural order. It is more natural for a man to take a horse and use it as he likes, than for him to go down on his knees to it, begging it to do as it wishes, and to fulfil its own marvellous nature."
> Ursula was just breaking out, when Hermione lifted her face and began, in her musing sing-song:
> "I do think—I do really think we must have the *courage* to use the lower animal life for our own needs. I do think there is something wrong, when we look on every living creature as if it were ourselves. I do feel, that it is false to project our own feelings on every animate creature. It is a lack of discrimination, a lack of criticism."
> "Quite," said Birkin sharply. "Nothing is so detestable as the maudlin attributing of human feelings and consciousness to animals."
> "Yes," said Hermione wearily, "We must really take a position. Either we are going to use the animals, or they will use us."
> "That's a fact," said Gerald. "A horse has got a will like a man, though it has no *mind*, strictly. And if your will isn't master, then the horse is master of you. And this is a thing I can't help. I can't help being master of the horse!" (Pp. 154–55)

Though what they say is not altogether wrong, and Ursula is too absolute in her insistence on the inviolable integrity of all creatures at all times, Hermione and Gerald's statements suit symbolic action to reveal the two characters' belief in bullying, the physical expression of a dominating will. Aside from what is disclosed in regard to this moral question, Hermione is also guilty of confusing the issue. She accuses Ursula of failing fully to maintain the distinction between herself and the animal; her assumption is that Ursula can have strong feelings about another creature only if she identifies with it. And yet Ursula's compassion and indignation are based on an opposed conception: she calls for the recognition of the animal's separate being. [34] The ones who refuse to acknowledge the idependent integrity of other creatures are Hermione and Gerald. This is what makes Birkin's remark problematical; the timing and tone of his statement suggest annoyance at Ursula's position and corroborate Hermione's misrepresentation of the other woman's ideas. Indirectly, his rejection of what he takes to be Ursula's "maudlin" attitude may be interpreted as a defense of the other characters' harsher views.

In relation to Gerald Birkin's defense soon becomes less indirect. Birkin puts himself on the wrong side of the central bifurcating division in the novel, that between being and will, [35] when he goes on to a sophisticated justification of Gerald's bullying: since horses are torn between competing desires for submission and freedom, Gerald's violence resolved a conflict within the mare herself: "Every horse, strictly, has two wills. With one will, it wants to put itself in the human power completely—and with the other, it wants to be free, wild" (p. 156). The concept of a submissive will is foreign to Ursula, however. When she challenges the notion, Birkin answers, startlingly, by asserting the superiority of the urge for surrender: "It's the last, perhaps highest, love-impulse: resign your will to the higher being." This point becomes more troubling when Birkin applies it explicitly to women: "And woman is the same as horses: two wills act in opposition inside her. With one will, she wants to subject herself utterly. With the other she wants to bolt, and pitch her rider to perdition." But it is the first will, according to Birkin, which is "highest." Despite Birkin's assertions, Ursula recognizes only the instinct for freedom: " 'Then I'm a bolter,' said Ursula, with a burst of laughter." Birkin affirms Gerald's will with subtlety: he does not justify the other man explicitly, but by asserting the desirability of female submission, he implicitly sanctions male domination.

In "Mino" Birkin expresses his admiration for the dominant male more elaborately and fully. Birkin does not fail to suggest, after having established this admirableness, that as a male he must assume the privileged position in his relationship with Ursula. The process through which he comes to such conclusions is singularly valuable as a disclosure of the tale/teller problem in *Women in Love*. For "Mino" brings together, in close, revealing juxtaposition, Birkin's ideological statements, the dramatized action of the tale, and the narrative voice that contradicts the realized events.

Early in the chapter, before the appearance of the eponymous cat, Birkin engages in a lengthy discourse before the skeptical Ursula. The theory he develops posits a mutual entrance into unexplored areas of the self, there to make an undetermined, unpredictable connection, based on a courageous immersion in the unknown: " 'There is,' he said, in a voice of pure abstraction, 'a final me which is stark and impersonal and beyond responsibility. So there is a final you. And it is there I would want to meet you—not in the emotional, loving plane—but there beyond, where there is no speech and no terms of agreement. There we are two stark, unknown beings, two utterly strange creatures, I would want to approach you, and you me. And there could be no obligation, because there is no standard for action there, because no understanding has been reaped from that plane. . . . I deliver *myself* over to the unknown, in coming to you, I am without reserves or defences, stripped entirely, into the unknown' " (pp. 162–63). On this deepest plane the self is discovered at the root, and possessed utterly; thus pure singleness can be combined with profound relation, and an unpredominating balance established: "What I want is a strange conjunction with you . . . not meeting and mingling . . . but an equilibrium, a pure balance of two single beings:—as the stars balance each other" (p. 164).

At this point in his disquisition there occurs an incident between Mino and a female cat:

> A crouching, fluffy, brownish-grey cat was stealing up the side of the fence. The Mino walked statelily up to her with manly nonchalance. She crouched before him and pressed herself on the ground in humility, a fluffy soft outcast. . . . So she crept . . . crouching in a wonderful, soft, self-obliterating manner, and moving like a shadow.
>
> He, going statelily on his slim legs, walked after her, then suddenly, for pure excess, he gave her a light cuff with his paw on the side of her face. She ran off a few steps, like a blown leaf along the ground, then

crouched unobtrusively, in submissive, wild patience. . . . She began to quicken her pace, in a moment she would be gone like a dream, when the young grey lord sprang before her and gave her a light handsome cuff. She subsided at once, submissively.

The Mino turned his face in pure superiority to his master, and slowly closed his eyes, standing in statuesque young perfection. . . . Then again, like a shadow, she slid towards the kitchen.

In a lovely springing leap, like a wind, the Mino was upon her, and had boxed her twice, very definitely, with a white, delicate fist. She sank and slid back, unquestioning. He walked after her, and cuffed her once or twice, leisurely, with sudden little blows of his magic white paws. (Pp. 165–66)

What occurs in these lines is of considerable importance to our understanding of the tale/teller problem in the novel. The prose is strained, indicative of the presence of something false and forced. The strain results from the special pleading that infuses the passage. A profusion of positive epithets are attributed to Mino, but they are unearned, inappropriate to a description of one animal tormenting another. The result is bathos. The teller tries but fails to make the "self-obliterating," "shadowy," female innately inferior, and the "lordly" male her natural master, entitled to brutally enforce a leadership that is his by some mysterious fiat. Between what is truly shown (an act of bullying), and what the teller wishes to show (the necessary disciplining of the "promiscuous" female by the "stabilizing" male), is a discrepancy typical of the tale/teller conflict as it is manifested in Lawrence's work. The revealed action is contradicted precisely when the authorial voice labors to attach intrinsic superiority to the male. At the same time, typically, a teller-problem leads to a tale-problem. Because the event is pulled in contrary directions, no tale, no achieved imaginary fact, is created.

Birkin's analysis of the event intensifies the misrepresentation to which it is subjected. When Ursula expresses her anger at Mino's behavior, Birkin tries to match the incident to his theories about "mystic" connections. But the parallel, instead of increasing our approval of Mino, reduces our belief in Birkin's notions. Examining Birkin's words carefully, we realize that the connection he envisions with Ursula is not a mutual entry into an area beyond self-awareness. His approach to man-woman relationships, that "star-equilibrium" or "freedom together" he later talks about, is gradually exposed as the woman's freedom to subjugate herself to the man.[36]

"Mino," said Ursula, "I don't like you. You are a bully like all males."

"No," said Birkin, "he is justified. He is not a bully. He is only insisting to the poor stray that she shall acknowledge him as a sort of fate, her own fate: because you can see she is fluffy and promiscuous as the wind. I am with him entirely. He wants superfine stability". . . .

"I quite agree with you, Miciotto," said Birkin to the cat. "Keep your male dignity, and your higher understanding". . . .

"Oh, it makes me so cross, the assumption of male superiority! And it is such a lie! One wouldn't mind if there were any justification for it". . . .

"It is just like Gerald Crich with his horse—a lust for bullying—a real *Wille zur Macht*—so base, so petty."

"I agree that the *Wille zur Macht* is a base and petty thing. But with the Mino, it is the desire to bring this female cat into a pure stable equilibrium, a transcendent and abiding *rapport* with the single male. Whereas without him, as you see, she is a mere stray, a fluffy sporadic bit of chaos."

"Ah—! Sophistries! It's the old Adam."

"Oh yes. Adam kept Eve in the indestructible paradise, when he kept her single with himself, like a star in its orbit."

"Yes—yes—" cried Ursula, pointing her finger at him. "There you are—a star in its orbit! A satellite—a satellite of Mars—that's what she is to be! There—there—you've given yourself away!" (Pp. 166–67)

Birkin's statements, here, clarify his earlier preachings; a specific event causes the theoretics of balance to give way to an actuality of domination. Birkin's casuistry, throughout "Mino," is based on his wanting to have things both ways: to empathize with Mino's superiority as he denies that domination is relevant to the issue. The assumption on which Birkin proceeds, his way of unifying the cat's bullying and the concept of "star-equilibrium," is that the male has some intrinsic capacity for deep rapport that the female lacks because of her instinct for "chaos." But it is precisely the attribution of some innate substantiality to the male that strains Birkin's logic and the narrator's prose. We feel the hollowness of the mere *claim* for the greater amplitude of male being, and reject such an assessment.

Nor, again, should the importance of the above event be dismissed because it merely concerns a pair of domestic animals. Birkin clearly understands the incident with the cats as a paradigm from which Ursula must learn. The implication is that she is in need of his stabilizing leadership. Suffering from an inherent flightiness, Ursula must learn that the ultimate desideratum is permanent, "mystic" conjunction. She must also understand that Birkin has, for obscure reasons, entrance into the desired state, and would be justified, if necessary, in compelling her to bow to this "higher" good.

The encounter between the two cats, and Birkin's analysis of the occurrence, amount to an elaborate rationale for male dominance. Yet Birkin continues to solemnly asseverate his belief in "mystic balance and integrity—like a star balanced with another star." As Ursula rightly points out, the starry analogies are themselves suspect. For while it is true that Birkin never uses the word "satellite," he nevertheless posits an original precedence of male over female when he states: "Adam kept Eve in the indestructible paradise, when he kept her single with himself, like a star in its orbit." Male superiority is woven into the fabric of his theories, but Birkin evades this fundamental implication of his own statements. He is thereby false to Ursula and, possibly, to himself. Though Birkin's theories, in "Mino," seem irreproachable, since he is asking for a relationship at the level of the underself, it is a contradiction in terms for such a relationship to be demanded by the conscious will. Still, *Women in Love* is never a simple novel, and it should be recognized that many of the objections to what Birkin says are made by Ursula. But her giving the other side of the case still does not prevent it from being craftily slanted against her. Having Ursula point out *selected* reservations about Birkin's arguments is a complex rhetorical strategy; it has the effect of anticipating and stilling the reader's objections without truly answering them.[37]

In "Mino" the omniscient narrator has a subversive purpose up his sleeve that works against the narrative. In "Moony" there is unity between tale and teller as the narrator returns to his most powerful technique: dramatized action with rich metaphorical implications. The opening paragraphs of "Moony" describe Ursula's psychological state and recall a theme developed in *The Rainbow*: the negative ramifications of a strong female ego. Ursula suffers the egoistical loneliness of feeling only herself, among all things, to be actual: "She herself was real, and only herself—just like a rock in a wash of flood-water. The rest was all nothingness. She was hard and indifferent, isolated in herself" (p. 275). One side of Ursula's resilient life-force is a spurning of all connection to the world, a derisive, hard separateness: "her heart was closed in this hidden, unconscious strain of contemptuous ridicule. . . . the strange brightness of her presence, a marvellous radiance of intrinsic vitality, was a luminousness of supreme repudiation, nothing but repudiation" (p. 276). Independence is connected to rejection.

The moon symbolizes Ursula's mood. This is evidenced as she moves through a dark moonlit landscape, trying to escape both the "deadly smile" of the "white planet" and her own isolating state: "she wished for something else out of the night, she wanted another night, not this moon-brilliant hardness. She could feel her soul crying out in her, lamenting desolately." The "moon-brilliant hardness" refers to the "repudiation" that is intrinsic to her self-sufficiency.

Ursula, unobserved herself, notices that Birkin is nearby. Looking at the reflection of the moon in Willey Water, he throws dead flowers on the pond, as if in mock offering to some blighting power therein. In an aggrieved tone, he makes a strange invocation: "Cybele—curse her! The accursed *Syria Dea*! Does one begrudge it her! What else is there—?" The pagan goddesses Birkin mentions have cruelly debilitating powers, emasculating the males who worship them (certain priests of Cybele demonstrated their loyalty through "ecstatic self-castration").[38] Birkin then makes a frenzied assault on the moon-pervaded water by flinging a series of stones into it, the result is an extended, kinetic image of dazzling brilliance:

> the moon had exploded on the water, and was flying asunder in flakes of white and dangerous fire. Rapidly, like white birds, the fires all broken rose across the pond, fleeing in clamorous confusion, battling with the flock of dark waves that were forcing their way in. . . . But at the centre, the heart of all, was still a vivid, incandescent quivering of a white moon not quite destroyed, a white body of fire writhing and striving and not even now broken open, not yet violated. . . . Then, almost immediately, came the second shot. The moon leapt up white and burst through the air. Darts of bright light shot asunder, darkness swept over the centre. There was no moon, only a battlefield of broken

lights and shadows, running close together. . . . The white fragments pulsed up and down . . . like the petals of a rose that a wind has blown far and wide. . . . Like a madness, he must go on. He got large stones, and threw them, one after the other, at the white-burning centre of the moon, till there was nothing but a rocking of hollow noise, and a pond surged up, no moon any more, only a few broken flakes tangled and glittering. . . . Though . . . in the darkness was a tumult of ebbing flakes of light, a cluster dancing secretly in a round, twining and coming steadily together. They were gathering a heart again, they were coming once more into being. Gradually the fragments caught together reunited, heaving, rocking, dancing, falling back as in panic, but working their way home again persistently . . . flickering nearer, a little closer to the mark, the cluster growing mysteriously larger and brighter, as gleam after gleam fell in with the whole, until a ragged rose, a distorted, frayed moon was shaking upon the waters again, reasserted, renewed, trying to recover from its convulsion . . . to be whole and composed, at peace. (Pp. 278–80)

Birkin's action should be seen as his aggression against a destructive female-principle.[39] We understand the incident more thoroughly by regarding its imagery in the larger context of Lawrence's moon and water symbolism. The usual pattern shows the independent woman whose cold unity of being is imaged by the moon as having destructive supremacy over the less-integrated man whose tendency to come apart is figured by water.

Discovering the reason for the moon's centrality in Lawrence's symbolism takes us into the realm of speculation (although the role of tradition should not be underestimated). But its primary significance is most clearly expressed in the garden-scene of *Sons and Lovers*. There the unborn Paul Morel participates in a union between Gertrude Morel and the restorative, suffusing moonlight. An association is made between woman, moon, and some feeling of primal merger: the foetus is subsumed by the greater forces. The self-reductive feelings Lawrencian males have before the moon plays upon the same archetypal association. Moon is an image for the *magna mater*, indicative of Oedipalism in the larger sense of the boy's identity being submerged in the mother. The burden Lawrence's "moon-struck" males carry is dual: longing for a return to the earlier union, they also fear renewed absorption. Their ambiguous feelings toward refusion are at the heart of the problems they endure.

Birkin's assault strikingly attempts to *reverse* the usual pattern;

by dispersing the female-ego into the pond, he tries to drown the vanquishing *magna mater*, for once, in the waters of dissolution. His intent is to break the dreadful integrity that oppresses him. Yet the laws of material reality foredoom his attempt. Birkin's action must be seen as a drama with a foregone conclusion, a hopeless endeavor to change an irreversible situation. Birkin cannot ultimately scatter the moon; it regathers, "growing mysteriously larger and brighter," recovering gradually from the attack. The forcible diminution of female being that occurs elsewhere in the novel is not achieved in a passage based on symbolic action. The female cannot be disintegrated symbolically, just as she does not disintegrate actually.

Aside from its general emblematic significance, the moon refers to Ursula specifically. A direct connection is made at the point where the reflection is most shattered by Birkin's stones: just when there is "no moon any more," because its image is entirely fragmented and drowned in the pond, Ursula feels "dazed, her mind . . . all gone . . . fallen to the ground and . . . spilled out, like water on the earth." Accordingly, we may conclude that she feels reintegrated as she watches the glittering flakes "coming steadily together."

At the same time the incident reveals Birkin by revealing his obsession. The usurping "madness" driving him to attack the moon exposes the depth of his resentment against what it signifies. His is a wild assault on the image of the force that dominates him. But the persistent re-formation of the ravaged moon suggests the hold the enveloping female has on Birkin's mind; his violence only temporarily deflects the moon's dominion.

After stoning the moon Birkin turns to Ursula in acknowledgement of his need for her. He expresses the idea that the two of them must move together into the fluid darkness of a less personal, less determined way of life.[40] But a closer look at their interaction shows that Birkin, rather than asking for a mutual escape from the ego, is merely demanding that Ursula submit her ego to his. Still engaged in a struggle with female-being, he now changes the terms of the engagement radically. He continued to conceive of women through light-imagery, but no longer blindingly white the light is now "golden." Birkin has a different approach toward this benevolent light, this attractive aspect of Ursula's integrity. Where he had earlier tried to *destroy* the female ego, he now attempts to *appropriate* it. Having learned he cannot disperse the fearful power the female-image has over him, he tries to dominate it. He thus asks Ursula to transfer her glowing wholeness to him: " 'There is a golden light in you, which I wish you would give me. . . . I want you to give me—to give your spirit to me—that golden light which is you—which you don't know—give it me.'. . . It was a great effort to him to maintain this conversation, and to press for the thing he wanted from her, the surrender of her spirit" (p. 281).

Ursula plays a dual and contrasting role for Birkin. Through her he can reach peace and self-achievement; simultaneously she is associated in his imagination with the incapacitating Great Mother. He needs the mild radiance of the individual, Ursula, to regenerate him from the damage done by the *magna mater* (also, on one level, Ursula). She is destroyer and healer at once. The paradox is explicable in light of the following pattern: a man weakened by an overinvolving relationship with the first woman in his life, later looks to another woman to heal the breach. But coming to the other woman for deliverance, the man repeats the dependent relationship which initially violated his integrity: the escape turns into a repetition. The idea accounts for Birkin's twofold view to Ursula, yet is ventured cautiously, because we never learn about Birkin's background. (His history, indeed, is carefully evaded.) But we do know that the figure of the Great Mother who bears and loves and buries man is a central image in Birkin's mind:

> it seemed to him, woman was always so horrible and clutching, she had such a lust for possession, a greed of self-importance in love. She wanted to have, to own, to control, to be dominant. Everything must be referred back to her, to Woman, the Great Mother of everything. . . . It filled him with almost insane fury, this calm assumption of the Magna Mater, that all was hers, because she had borne it. . . . And Ursula, Ursula was the same. . . . he knew the unthinkable overweening assumption of primacy in her. She was unconscious of it herself. . . . It was intolerable, this possession at the hands of woman. Always a man must be considered as the broken-off fragment of a woman, and the sex was the aching scar of the laceration. (Pp. 224–25)

Such perceptions are most revealing of the perceiver: it is Birkin who feels like a "broken-off fragment." Ursula takes on the properties of the *magna mater* in relation to him.[41] The *magna mater* is a Romantic, demonic image tenuously related to actual women. Moreover, Birkin's view of sex as "the aching scar of the laceration" helps clarify the passage where he rejects Ursula's physical passion. His feeling of partiality puts him at a disadvantage in the act of love. Hence he minimizes Ursula by stilling her sexuality. He finds it necessary to prevent the full expression of her womanhood:

> To be content in bliss, without desire or insistence anywhere, this was heaven: to be together in happy stillness. For a long time she nestled to him, and he kissed her softly, her hair, her face, her ears, gently, softly, like dew falling. But this warm breath on her ears disturbed her again, kindled the old destructive fires. She cleaved to him, and he could feel his blood changing like quicksilver. "But we'll be still, shall we?" he said. "Yes," she said, as if submissively. . . . And then, out of a full throat, she crooned: "Kiss me! Kiss me!" And she cleaved close to him. He kissed her many times. But he too had his idea and his will. He wanted only gentle communion, no other, no passion now. So that soon she drew away, put on her hat and went home. (Pp. 284–85)

The problem here is that their quiet entrance into "gentle communion," their purported going beyond desire and will, is Birkin's desire and will. He wants to control Ursula's "destructive fires," the aggressive sexuality which threatens him. He imposes his own vision in the course of doing so. This is not to deny that a part of Ursula is threatening. She cannot be altogether distinguished from the Ursula of *The Rainbow*; in *Women in Love* too she can exhibit (albeit rarely) the alternating repudiation and possessiveness which mark Lawrence's destructive women: there is a negative element to her force.

Altogether, Birkin feels that Ursula has the stronger ego and therefore keeps urging their mutual escape from the ego. But there is a serious difficulty with the idea because the inequality between Ursula and Birkin exists on the carbon-level of personality as well as on the plane of ego: this is the conclusion drawn from the moon-stoning scene. Though not acknowledged as such, Birkin's theories amount to a method for defeating the fundamental imbalance between Ursula and himself.

In "Excurse" Birkin goes a step further and tries to invert the imbalance. This chapter is pervaded by the two fallacies which most consistently disclose the interfering teller in *Women in Love:*

willed reversal, where the supremacy of the male is forced upon the female, and claimed polarity, within which the domination is counterpointed by an abstract description of equality. The rhetoric of balanced transcendence becomes highly sophisticated in "Excurse," for the transcendence Birkin envisions is startling and original. Developing his concept of a dichotomized self (divided between the individual surface personality and the essential being that partakes of fundamental life-and-death processes), he concludes that reaching the deeper underself requires full acknowledgment of corporeal decay. The route to fundamental being is through the organ of corruption, the death-path: anal contact brings complete self-recognition. Receiving pleasure from the death-suggesting orifice is a triumphant understanding of man's whole nature: "There were depths of passion when one became impersonal and indifferent, unemotional. Whereas Ursula was still at the emotional personal level—always so abominably personal. . . . He had taken her at the roots of her darkness and shame—like a demon, laughing over the fountain of mystic corruption which was one of the sources of her being, laughing, shrugging, accepting, accepting finally. As for her, when would she so much go beyond herself as to accept him at the quick of death?" (p. 343). Where recoil from the processes of bodily corruption causes misanthropy in a writer like Swift, the same functions are an affirmation for Lawrence. Going a step further than denying shame and self-rejection, Lawrence sees bodily processes as a part of vital, universal life cycles; in this sense, anal intercourse is a discovery of essential, "impersonal" levels of being. The case for the positive effects of corruption is finally extremely strong. Indeed, the novel contains a theoretical structure that successfully neutralizes the *magna mater*. It suggests that her strength-of-self is insignificant below the ego at the level of dark corruptive process, so at that level both partners discover a new way of being and loving.

However serious and interesting these ideas are in themselves, in the context of *Women in Love* they lead to several problems. First, the teller uses the same concepts simultaneously for damnation and salvation, for disintegration and integration.[42] If, as is vividly demonstrated throughout, corruption denotes self-dissolution, the fall from organic, creative being, how can corruption supply, at the same time, the means for attaining such being?

Hitherto, the point had been that man is damned if his soul is turned toward corruption, with no belief in creative wholeness or love to take him beyond his own decay. Now Birkin (who is soon to be reaffirmed by the teller) attests that man finds his freedom by focusing on corruption. Indeed, the contradiction is sharper still. We might be willing to accept that full self-discovery can subsume anal corruption, but the problem is the cool ignoring of everything in the novel which points the other way. Dissolution functions as its own antithesis and antidote in *Women in Love,* and the linguistic and conceptual strain is immense, pushing ambiguity to the point of chaos, for never in the novel is an adequate distinction made between redemptive and destructive corruption.

Later in "Excurse" the teller confirms Birkin's affirmation of corruption. When the compelling abstract theory gives way to novelistic practice we have, again, strained rhetoric, prose going in two different directions: explicitly calling for balance, it implicitly sanctions male domination, and the self-contradiction results in a scene that does not, quite, convince. A potentially beautiful solution to the *magna mater*'s dominion is bedeviled by the total identification of redemptive corruption with Birkin; Ursula cannot be delivered from herself without delivering herself over to him. Therefore, during the chapter's consummation scene we are not shown a *mutual* movement toward either dissolution or transcendence. On the contrary, the processes of decomposition raised to quasi-religious status are Birkin's means for dominating Ursula. The scene shows us an Ursula *bowing* to Birkin, releasing to him her "golden light" (now "soft and yielded"), submitting, in essence, her organic being to the corruption suddenly granted positive properties:

And she was drawn to him strangely, as in a spell. Kneeling on the hearth-rug before him, she put her arms round his loins, and put her face against his thighs. Riches! Riches! She was overwhelmed with a sense of a heavenful of riches. . . .

Unconsciously, with her sensitive finger-tips, she was tracing the back of his thighs, following some mysterious life-flow there. . . . It was here she discovered him one of the sons of God such as were in the beginning of the world, not a man, something other, something more.

. . . . this was neither love nor passion. It was the daughters of men coming back to the sons of God, the strange inhuman sons of God who are in the beginning.

Her face was now one dazzle of released, golden light, as she looked up at him and laid her hands full on his thighs, behind, as he stood before her. . . .

She closed her hands over the full, rounded body of his loins, as he stooped over her, she seemed to touch the quick of the mystery of darkness that was bodily him. She seemed to faint beneath, and he seemed to faint, stooping over her. It was a perfect passing away for both of them, and at the same time the most intolerable accession into being, the marvellous fullness of immediate gratification, overwhelming, outflooding from the source of the deepest life-force, the darkest, deepest, strangest life-source of the human body, at the back and base of the loins.

After a lapse of stillness, after the rivers of strange dark fluid richness had passed over her, flooding, carrying away her mind . . . leaving her an essential new being, she was left quite free, she was free in complete ease, her complete self. . . . He stood before her, glimmering, so awfully real, that her heart almost stopped beating. He stood there in his strange, whole body, that had its marvellous fountains, like the bodies of the sons of God who were in the beginning. There were strange fountains of his body, more mysterious and potent than any she had imagined or known, more satisfying, ah, finally, mystically-physically satisfying. She had thought there was no source deeper than the phallic source. And now, behold, from the smitten rock of the man's body, from the strange marvellous flanks and thighs, deeper, further in mystery than the phallic source, came the floods of ineffable darkness and ineffable riches. (Pp. 352–54)

Lawrence is often amazingly skillful at re-creating states wherein the self is escaped in intense, erotic experience, but his talent for such re-creation does not, finally, serve him here. The scene is far from being bad, it is filled with Lawrence's special genius, but it has a forced quality, an unconvincing yoking of self-escape and subordination. The real difficulty is that Ursula's *final* discovery is not the unknown in herself or the universe but the godlike quality of Birkin. Perhaps for this reason the experience of being overwhelmed is insecurely captured. By contrast, the consummation between Tom and Lydia in *The Rainbow* (pp. 94–95) successfully presents a restoring self-transcendence, a losing the self in darkness to find a finer, more complete being. In the earlier scene, significantly, the man finds something awesome in the woman; she is the vessel of darkness in which he dies to be born again, through which he enters the "beyond," and the encounter is moving and accomplished.

Reversing the relationship, presenting the male as the vessel of redeeming darkness, Lawrence's powers are far less confident: here the teller speaks and no finished tale is achieved. Willed inversion of the usual pattern underlies the problems of the passage and causes the repetition and over-insistence that critics have frequently observed.[43] The uncertainty of articulation suggests that the conception described does not grow out of the deepest sources of Lawrence's belief or understanding or intuition. The other fallacy I have described, that of false polarity, is also present here and adds to the confusions of the section: in the by now familiar pattern, the teller simultaneously affirms and denies male superiority. Thus, the claimed "perfect passing away for both of them," this purportedly mutual "intolerable accession into being," is contradicted, first of all, by the contrasting positions from which the accession takes place.[44] With Ursula below on her knees, and Birkin above, the literal male ascendency can hardly avoid having metaphorical suggestions. More importantly, Lawrence's diction and tone give us something very different from equality: they depict an Ursula freed and released by her communion with Birkin's dark sources of being. The Biblical language about the "sons of God" and "daughters of men," besides being the source of some hollow prose, contains an element of male superiority since it is only the man who is deific.

Moreover, it is precisely the corruption within him which is the source of his godliness. The "dark riches" of his lower body suggest both the blood of his unconscious being and his excretory processes.[45] Though Birkin is not associated with corruption only, it is to the man's river of dissolution that Ursula submits. Having discovered the Africa in himself, Birkin feels godlike, and Ursula bows to the dark god. Yet the tale informs us that the African way is one of the two paths to the disintegration of the self.

Like the passages from "Mino," the quoted excerpt fails because of its contrived attempt to attach intrinsic awesomeness to male being. Hard as Lawrence labors at this premise, he fails to convince us of it. Indeed, in the course of trying to substantiate the inherently superior depth and stability of maleness, Lawrence over-extends himself. The strange comparison of Birkin to an "Egyptian Pharoah," coming slightly later in the chapter, instances the exaggerated lengths to which the teller goes in order to establish the supremacy of the male. There, Birkin's "Egyptian" qualities make him precisely analogous to Mino; for they bestow an intimacy with darkness which gives Birkin a suprarational mastery over Ursula's "fate," and makes him her natural master:

> she had a full mystic knowledge of his suave loins of darkness, dark-clad and suave, and in this knowledge there was some of the inevitability and the beauty of fate, fate which one asks for, which one accepts in full. He sat still like an Egyptian Pharoah, driving the car. He felt as if he were seated in immemorial potency, like the great carven statues of real Egypt. . . . He knew what it was to have the strange and magical current of force in his back and loins. . . . And from this source he had a pure and magic control, magical, mystical, a force in darkness, like electricity. (P. 358)

The passages I have quoted and discussed above, however, do not represent the triumphant consummation of Ursula's and Birkin's relationship. That climactic union comes at the end of "Excurse":

> She had her desire of him, she touched, she received the maximum of unspeakable communication in touch, dark, subtle, positively silent, a magnificent gift and give again, a perfect acceptance and yielding, a mystery, the mystery of that which can never be known, vital, sensual reality that can never be transmuted into mind content, but remains outside, living body of darkness and silence and subtlety, the mystic body of reality. He had his desire fulfilled. For she was to him what he was to her, the immemorial magnificence of mystic, palpable, real otherness. (P. 361)

This seems to me very disappointing, far more so than the "dark riches" passage. In this description the theoretical element in the novel, Birkin's ideology, reaches its fruition. But the narrator of the novel, in his desire to show that Ursula's bowing to Birkin brings them both into the darkness within and in each other, appears to have lost touch with his characters. There is no feeling here that we are sharing the experience of Ursula and Birkin, but only the clear sense of a teller bringing his tale to a balanced, conclusive finale.

In my last point I wish to return to the more significant, earlier scene at the inn. A major function of this consummation is to unthrone Ursula in her role as *magna mater*. Previous to the experience, Birkin feels his usual fierce resentment toward this aspect of her: "it was nauseous and horrible. . . . Ursula was the perfect Womb, the bath of birth, to which all men must come!" Driving toward the inn, Birkin feels rejuvenated by an unspecified new source and freed from the tyranny of the female: "the life flowed through him as from some new fountain, he was as if born out of the cramp of a womb" (p. 351). During the fateful encounter in the inn's parlor a new basis or root of being is posited: the womb of the dominating female is replaced by the "loins" of the dominating male. Birkin, as we know from "Moony" and elsewhere in the novel, is dominated by a woman: not so much by the woman he is actually with as by the woman the moon symbolizes, the oppressive maternal image to which he is ontologically bound. (In Birkin, as in Gerald, psychological disturbance precedes his involvement in a general social dissolution.) The scene in "Excurse" attempts to reverse this incompleteness, this obligation to the female, by bowing the *magna mater* to an enclosure, a containing organ, of the male. Specifically, the anus is substituted for the uterus as the controlling center, the arbiter of submission and domination. Thus inverting their positions, the teller reaches the height of his effort to give Birkin preeminence and supremacy in his relationship with Ursula. But this inversion is forced, causing the stylistic strain noted in the quoted passage.[46] The failure of art reveals the effort as a gesture of the author's conscious will, a strategy of the interfering teller; on the level of rendered art *Women in Love* presents an opposed story, telling of the irrefragable primacy of women and the fearful effects of that primacy on the minds of men.

Notes to Chapter 5

1. D. H. Lawrence, *Women in Love* (1921; reprint ed., Harmondsworth, Middlesex: Penguin Books, 1960), p. 209.

2. Dr. Leavis is one critic who insists that the meaning and nature of Ursula's and Birkin's relationship is artistically realized: "the position for which Birkin contends in his wooing of Ursula does emerge from the 'tale' vindicated, in the sense that the norm he proposes for the relations of man and woman in marriage has been made, by the varied resources of Lawrence's art, sufficiently clear, and, in its intelligibility, sufficiently cogent, to compel us to a serious pondering." *D. H. Lawrence: Novelist* (1955; reprint ed., New York: Clarion Books, 1969), p. 176. Many subsequent commentators, however, have disagreed with Leavis' view. W. W. Robson, for example, judges Lawrence's presentation of Gerald's and Gudrun's relationship to be far superior to his description of Ursula and Birkin: "If the

whole book had a convincingness equal to what we find in the treatment of the Gerald theme, it could be judged an assured artistic success. . . . Dr. Leavis would have us believe that the Birkin-Ursula relationship sets up a standard—or at least moves towards a standard—from which the Gerald-Gudrun experience is a deviation. But do we feel this in reading the novel? Surely what we feel in reading the novel is that Birkin too is a sick and tortured man, who does not (except at a few ideal moments which give rise to some of the worst writing in the book) achieve with Ursula the kind of fulfilment which he has made his *raison d'être*. "D. H. Lawrence and *Women in Love*," in *The Pelican Guide to English Literature*, ed. Boris Ford (Harmondsworth, Middlesex: Penguin Books, 1961), 7: 297, 299. Eliseo Vivas comes to a conclusion similar to Robson's, and notes the division between intention and performance that exists in the Ursula-Birkin relationship: "There is no question that Lawrence's intention coincides with that of the novel as regards Gerald and Gudrun; their relationship is destructive, catastrophic. But the relationship between Birkin and Ursula can hardly be said to be an exemplar, to be a "norm" by which to interpret the full disastrous meaning of the other." *D. H. Lawrence: The Failure and the Triumph of Art* (Bloomington, Ind.: Indiana University Press, 1960), p. 266.

3. Critics have generally failed to recognize that Gudrun is the stronger character throughout. H. M. Daleski for example, while more sensitive to the difference than most, considers the relationship between the pair to consist of a series of balanced submission/domination reversals: "Gudrun oscillates between a desire for victimization and for dominance. . . . Gerald's will to dominate has as a disturbing counterpart a child-like tendency to be utterly dependent on Gudrun. . . . Gerald's 'selfishness', however, also has its paradoxical counterpart: a deep desire for a surrender of self. . . . Gudrun, too, though she is more naturally self-sufficient than Gerald, succumbs on occasion to the desire for containment." Although noting Gudrun's greater self-sufficiency, Daleski does not proceed to what seems to me the necessary conclusion—that Gerald's weaker being foredooms him, making the end result of the conflict between Gerald and Gudrun inevitable. *The Forked Flame: A Study of D. H. Lawrence* (Evanston, Ill.: Northwestern University Press, 1965), pp. 158–59.

4. This subjugation has been noted by Kate Millett. But her splenetic distortions disqualify points which could, if handled more objectively, have some basis. Hence, it is utterly false to say that "Birkin is full of opinions and ideas and holds forth all through the book while Ursula puts docile leading questions to him." *Sexual Politics* (Garden City, N.Y.: Doubleday, 1969), p. 264. Ursula is not "docile" at all, but bitterly and sometimes crushingly defiant (see *Women in Love*, p. 346). Millett simplifies the matter absurdly—and this is typical of her procedure.

5. In his definition of the Arctic and African ways, Robert L. Chamberlain is correct to stress that the processes are interlinked phases of one larger devolutionary movement. But he simplifies when he makes the two processes synonymous and interchangeable; they are, in fact, clearly and manifestly distinct: "The African and Nordic progressions are modes of the same process. . . . The two halves of the great cultural contrast which gives the novel its most brilliant effects are more than complementary at the level of the individual; they are identical, each by implication encompassing the other. What matters is the break, the rift—not whether the break first manifests itself in a mind sense-enslaved or in a sensuality mind-enslaved." "Pussum, Minette, and the Africo-Nordic Symbol in Lawrence's *Women in Love*," *PMLA* 78 (September 1963): 416.

6. Mark Spilka's belief that Gudrun and Gerald are equally implicated in "Northern

ice-destructiveness" is, in the last analysis, overly general. *The Love Ethic of D. H. Lawrence* (Bloomington, Ind.: Indiana University Press, 1955), p. 140.

7. Leavis's discussion of Gerald's will-driven automatism, and its relation to industrial society, is impressively comprehensive, and, up to a certain point, definitive. *D. H. Lawrence: Novelist*, pp. 152–70. But Leavis makes no distinction between mind-dominated and will-dominated ways of being automatic, probably because Lawrence himself described "mental-consciousness" as the product of the combined will and mind. See "Psychoanalysis and the Unconscious," in *"Psychoanalysis and the Unconscious" and "Fantasia of the Unconscious,"* introduction by Philip Rieff (1921, 1922; reprint ed., New York: Viking Press, 1960), pp. 47–49. Yet Lawrence's essays, however suggestive, cannot take precedence over his fiction, and within *Women in Love* there is a difference between Gerald, whose mechanical intelligence serves an aggressive will, and Gudrun, whose demanding will is subordinate to her objectifying mind.

8. Leavis' statement that "where Gerald's 'go' goes to ultimately is self-destruction" is surely correct; but on its way to this final destination the function of the will is the one I describe. *D. H. Lawrence: Novelist*, p. 156.

9. As a feminine or diminutive version of "Mino," the name of Birkin's domineering, much-admired tomcat, the girl's very name suggests her submissive role. It is perhaps also indicative of the girl's ministering function that "minette" is a politely bawdy term for fellation. See, for example, the anonymous work of Victorian pornography, *My Secret Life*, introduction by G. Legman (New York: Grove Press, 1966), pp. 306–7.

10. Daleski notes that Gerald reduces "the spontaneous struggle of the mare to a 'mechanical' pawing of the air." *The Forked Flame*, p. 153.

11. The word "bullock" is interestingly ambiguous. Aside from simply meaning a young bull, bullock refers to a castrated bull, and this is in keeping with Lawrence's symbolic use of the animals. Daniel Ort further refines the point, noting that a bullock is sterile, but not impotent. This, Ort goes on to say, is applicable to Gerald, who is sexually capable, but whose love is "mechanical," not fertile. *Explicator* 27, no. 5 (January 1969): item 38.

12. Angelo P. Bertocci makes this point: "Gerald [is] presented in some sort as a master of the watery element." "Symbolism in *Women in Love*," in *A D. H. Lawrence Miscellany*, ed. Harry T. Moore (Carbondale, Ill.: Southern Illinois University Press, 1959), p. 88. Bertocci's article contains a fine discussion of the novel's water-symbolism.

13. Being limited to the conscious, enclosed self makes Gudrun irredeemably corrupt. According to "The Crown" (a major essay that has the same relation to *Women in Love* that "Study of Thomas Hardy" has to *The Rainbow*—in both cases the essay puts in expository form ideas that are central and germane to the novel), those who remain trapped within the ego, who do not break or transcend the walls of the self, are relegated to the processes of dissolution: "Only when we fall into egoism do we lose all chance of blossoming, and then the flux of corruption is the breath of our existence. . . . So there goes on reduction after reduction within the shell. And we, who find our utmost gratification in this process of reduction, this flux of corruption, this retrogression of death, we will preserve with might and main the glassy envelope, the insect rind, the tight-shut shell of the cabbage, the withered, null walls of the womb. For by virtue of this null envelope alone do we proceed uninterrupted in this process of gratifying reduction. And this is utter evil, this secret, silent worship of the null envelope that preserves us intact for our gratification with the flux of corruption." *Phoenix II: Uncollected, Unpublished and Other Prose Works by D. H. Lawrence*, ed. Warren Roberts and Harry T. Moore (London: William Heinemann, 1968), pp. 393–94. Gudrun's

ego, then, which remains enclosed in its integument, is horrible in its very strength; but Gerald, if less ego-imprisoned than she, is too unformed and disturbed a man to be saved; Gerald, in his violence, struggles between egoism and a self-disintegration that can only end in death. Yet there is, for Lawrence, a redemptive form of self-dissolution; the relationship between egoism and corruption is handled very complexly in "The Crown," and later in the essay Lawrence seems to contradict himself: "And corruption, like growth, is only divine when it is pure, when all is given up to it. . . . Corruption will at last break down for the deadened forms, and release us into the infinity. But the static ego, with its will-to-persist, neutralizes both life and death. . . . We may give ourselves utterly to destruction. Then our conscious forms are destroyed along with us, and something new must arise. But we may not have corruption within ourselves as sensationalism, our skin and outer form intact." *Phoenix II*, pp. 403–4. Lawrence resolves the contradiction by distinguishing between negative corruption, occurring within the ego, and positive corruption, which breaks down the ego. Many critics base their interpretations of *Women in Love* on this notion of positive corruption, believing that Birkin leads Ursula through corruption to a level of being beyond the ego, beyond the old, "deadened forms" (see my note 24). But it is my contention that the distinction between the two kinds of corruption is never clarified and developed within the novel. Thus, in "Excurse," in the novel's consummation-scene, we do not witness a breaking free of confinements (ego and womb); what we see, actually, is Birkin subordinating Ursula to a new confine, the male body that incarnates his ego and his corruption.

14. In his essay on Poe, Lawrence vividly expresses his hostility to relationships based on mind-knowledge: "to try to *know* any living being is to try to suck the life out of that being. Above all things, with the woman one loves. Every sacred instinct teaches one that one must leave her unknown. You must know your woman darkly, in the blood. To try to *know* her mentally is to try to kill her. Beware, oh woman, of the man who wants to *find out what you are*. And, oh men, beware a thousand times more of the woman who wants to *know* you or *get* you, what you are." *Studies in Classic American Literature* (1924; reprint ed., Harmondsworth, Middlesex: Penguin Books, 1971), pp. 75–76.

15. F. R. Leavis, *D. H. Lawrence: Novelist*, p. 165.

16. Eliseo Vivas objects to Lawrencian scenes exhibiting this degree of emotional power. He charges such descriptions with "obscenity because of excessive immediacy," claiming that they deprive the reader of the "proper intransitivity of attention." *Failure and Triumph of Art*, pp. 194, 227. Readers less fastidious than Vivas will recognize that the nearly-shocking force of some of Lawrence's writing is often thematically and symbolically justified, and serves the ultimate purpose of exposing hidden being.

17. For David Cavitch the urge toward unconsciousness, with its suggestion of a death-wish, is what basically motivates Gerald towards Gudrun: "in loving Gudrun he seeks only the final obliteration of consciousness." *D.H. Lawrence and the New World* (London: Oxford University Press, 1969), p. 72.

18. *Lady Chatterley's Lover* is the notable exception. See the last page of my introduction.

19. For a notable example of the view that Gerald and Gudrun are equivalently involved in the process, see Spilka, *The Love Ethic of D.H. Lawrence*, pp. 140–42.

20. Gerald's pained humanity earns him a certain sympathy. But critics who defend this character have exaggerated his positive qualities. T.B. Tomlinson, for example, is entirely seduced by Gerald's masculine power, although Lawrence shows it to be ultimately hollow: "The criticisms of [Gerald's] force of 'will' are instantly felt and made by Gudrun, as they are

by Birkin. But the force of even their criticisms spends itself before it has completely comprehended—let alone annulled—the 'perfect line of force' that Gerald can be." "Lawrence and Modern Life: *Sons and Lovers, Women in Love,*" *The Critical Review* 8 (1965), reprinted in W.T. Andrews, ed., *Critics on D.H. Lawrence* (London: Allen and Unwin, 1971), pp. 64–65.

21. The idea is stated vividly in "The Crown": "within the glassy, null envelope of the enclosure, no union is sought, no union is possible; after a certain point, only reduction. Ego reacts upon ego only in friction." *Phoenix II*, p. 394.

22. Though the moon plays a prominent part in the scene of Gerald's dying, the image has received very little critical attention. A related image, the crucifix that also unnerves Gerald as he stumbles in the snow, has elicited comment: "this is . . . the Christ who presides over the whole world of Northern ice-destructiveness, and who symbolizes, like the bright transfixing moonlight, that form of mental-spiritual consciousness which exploits and corrupts the source of life." Spilka, *The Love Ethic of D.H. Lawrence*, p. 142. If Spilka interprets the significance of the moon too narrowly, his belief that this Christ is one who helped establish the mode of mind-centered egoism seems justified. Baruch Hochman takes a similar view of the crucifix: "Jesus . . . has, in Lawrence's judgment, been instrumental in evolving the icy mode of damning intellect." *Another Ego: The Changing View of Self and Society in the Work of D.H. Lawrence* (Columbia, S.C.: University of South Carolina Press, 1970), p. 144.

23. Critics who take this traditional view include: Harry T. Moore, *The Life and Works of D.H. Lawrence* (New York: Twayne, 1951), p. 160; Spilka, *The Love Ethic of D.H. Lawrence* pp. 125–27; Leavis, *D.H. Lawrence: Novelist*, pp. 174–76. Daleski, though he has, like Vivas and Robson, serious qualifications about the portrayal of Ursula and Birkin, nevertheless believes that the two characters are waging a creative struggle against the novel's forces of destruction, *The Forked Flame*, p. 132; George H. Ford, while endeavoring to avoid a bald acceptance of the moral dichotomy, does, finally, confirm it: "To say that the basic pattern of the novel features one pair of lovers representing a dance of life and the other pair a dance of death is, of course, a crude simplification which must be constantly corrected in what follows, yet it can stand as a point of departure." *Double Measure: A Study of the Novels and Stories of D.H. Lawrence* (New York: W. W. Norton & Co., 1965), p. 209.

24. A full-dress case for the centrality of corruption in Lawrence's work (complete with pejorative tone toward the older view), is made by Colin Clarke, in *River of Dissolution: D.H. Lawrence and English Romanticism* (London: Routledge and Kegan Paul, 1969). Clarke's study is a model of critical ambiguity; he magnifies the importance of corruption in Lawrence's fiction, but claims, at the same time, to be interested in seeing that both integration and corruption receive their due. To witness the complex strategy it is necessary to read Clarke's book in its entirety. Frank Kermode, though less obsessive, agrees with many of Clarke's premises; see his "D.H. Lawrence and the Apocalyptic Types," in Frank Kermode, *Modern Essays* (Fontana/Collins, 1971), pp. 153–58, and, as well, the book that seems to have grown out of that essay, *Lawrence* (Fontana/Collins, 1973). But the idea that corruption is a positive, essential value, in *Women in Love*, has been argued most convincingly by R.E. Pritchard: "Birkin-Lawrence asserts that decay and death are part of the human condition, and need to be accepted for full existence. . . . Birkin demands the acceptance of the entire bodily process, particularly perhaps the excremental, wherein lies 'the real reality'." *D.H. Lawrence: Body of Darkness*, p. 95. The problem is that Birkin does not merely *accept* corruption, he *glorifies* it. And this glorification should signal us that

corruption has some covert importance, that we are not dealing here with a philosophical question of whether the process has been sufficiently acknowledged in our view of man's nature.

25. Clarke, *River of Dissolution*, p. 100.

26. The views are juxtaposed, with revealing results, in a pair of articles that were printed consecutively some years ago: Mark Spilka, "Lawrence Up-Tight, or the Anal Phase Once Over," *Novel*, no. 4 (1971), pp. 252–67; George Ford, Frank Kermode, Colin Clarke, and Mark Spilka, "On 'Lawrence Up-Tight': Four Tail-Pieces," *Novel*, no. 5 (1971), pp. 54–70. Spilka gets the better of the confrontation, I believe, indicating that, after all, we cannot deny that there is any difference between health and sickness in *Women in Love*. Yet, Spilka's view that the scene at the inn, in "Excurse," marks Birkin's purgation of corruptive "anality," so that he may move forward to creative genitality, seems too bland and neat. In order to maintain his hopeful and, as he puts it, "oral-moral," approach, Spilka is forced to minimize the strong approbation of anal corruption that does exist in the novel.

27. Vivas is one commentator who recognizes that Birkin's involvement with sensual dissolution is not just objective and aesthetic: "in spite of his resolution to abandon 'the African way,' Birkin does not seem to have abandoned it." *Failure and Triumph of Art*, p. 267.

28. The two consciousnesses, so important to Lawrence's values, are discussed at complex length in "Psychology of the Unconscious" and "Fantasia of the Unconscious." See, for examples, pp. 48, 202.

29. The horse, in Lawrence's work, that most thoroughly demonstrates this equation is St. Mawr. Leavis' comments on this stallion are apposite here: "By 'body,' then, Lawrence means all that deep spontaneous life which is not at the beck and call of the conscious and willing mind, and so in that sense cannot be controlled by it, though it can be thwarted and defeated. St. Mawr, the stallion, *is* that life." *D.H. Lawrence: Novelist*, p. 231.

30. The contradiction in Loerke's aesthetics is observed by Daleski, *The Forked Flame*, p. 151.

31. Keith Sagar notes that the butterflies embody Ursula's "distinctiveness and self-hood." *The Art of D.H. Lawrence* (Cambridge: Cambridge University Press), p. 83.

32. Bertocci comments vaguely on Ursula's "golden light," defining the image only in relation to what it opposes: "The alternative [to deathly 'whiteness'] was the 'lovely golden light of spring,' tranfused through Ursula's eyes." But his footnote regarding the matter is more interesting: "Lawrence insists in many passages on the 'strange golden light' radiating from Ursula. Like Novalis' 'beloved object,' who also can be reached only through an 'accord' *(Stimmung)*, she seems to be the 'center of a paradise.' But at times the same quality of luminousness can ring her round in 'supreme repudiation' and 'perfect hostility.'" *D.H. Lawrence Miscellany*, pp. 95, 102.

33. See chap. 1, note 7.

34. In her appreciation of the separate being, the *isness*, of an animal, Ursula expresses a value that Lawrence himself frequently upholds. Many of the poems in "Birds, Beasts and Flowers," for example, are based on an awareness of the specific essences, the souls of various creatures. *The Complete Poems of D.H. Lawrence*, ed. Vivian de Sola Pinto and F. Warren Roberts (New York: Viking Press, 1971), pp. 331–405.

35. In a cogent point, Mark Schorer finds the meaning of *Women in Love* in the antagonism between these two forces: "Lawrence's theme . . . is dramatized in terms of a struggle between what he calls Will (which may be either sensual or 'spiritual,' a death

impulse in either case) and Being, that integration of the total self which is life. Will is the integration of the drive of ego toward power, toward domination; it has its inverse in the desire to be overpowered, to be dominated, to yield everything to dissolution. . . . Being is the integration of life forces in total and complete self-responsibility." "*Women in Love,*" in *The World We Imagine: Selected Essays by Mark Schorer* (New York: Farrar, Straus and Giroux, 1968), p. 117.

36. The self-contradicting nature of Birkin's theories has been shrewdly observed by Charles Rossman: "Birkin's 'star-equilibrium' holds out, theoretically, the possibility of a love-relationship which maintains a delicate balance between individual integrity and fusion, but in practice it assumes that both 'stars' orbit in a path that the male selects." "D. H. Lawrence and Women," *The D. H. Lawrence Review* 8, no. 3 (Fall 1975): 281. Barbara Hardy is one of the few critics to defend the statements Birkin makes in this chapter: "Birkin . . . is actually not talking about male superiority but about stability, strays and wildness. . . . [The scene] suggests the need for permanence, not the need to be knocked into shape by the male." "Women in D. H. Lawrence's Works," in Stephen Spender, ed., *D. H. Lawrence: Novelist, Poet, Prophet* (London: Weidenfeld and Nicolson, 1973), p. 97. This argument begs the question: forcing the female to accept a value determined by the male remains bullying.

37. Lawrence's stating of both sides of the matter has earned him strong praise from one critic: "It is the courageous truthfulness of Lawrence which is remarkable here, writing the two sides of the case, himself really seeking and wondering who is right." Anais Nin, *D. H. Lawrence: An Unprofessional Study* (Denver, Colo.: Swallow Press, 1964), p. 80. David J. Gordon suggests, contrarily, that Lawrence uses the technique to reinforce the finality of Birkin's arguments: "it is indicative of Lawrence's effort to be honest with himself that Birkin and his ideas are frequently subjected to criticism by the other characters. But the effort is sometimes crude. Mockery of Birkin is likely to be itself canceled by mockery. . . . The long haggle between Birkin and Ursula over the meaning of love is apparently supposed to result in some sort of compromise, but it is difficult to see that their final understanding is anything but a capitulation on Ursula's part. "*Women in Love* and the Lawrencean Aesthetic," in Stephen J. Miko, ed. *Twentieth Century Interpretations of "Women in Love"* (Englewood Cliffs, N.J.: Spectrum Books, 1969), p. 54.

38. Robert Graves, *The Greek Myths* (Harmondsworth, Middlesex: Penguin Books, 1955), 1: 71.

39. Graham Hough, for example, maintains that "the moon is the white goddess, the primal woman image, *das ewig weibliche,* by whom [Birkin] is obviously haunted." *The Dark Sun: A Study of D. H. Lawrence* (1956; reprint ed., London: Duckworth, 1970), p. 79. Colin Clarke has provided an original interpretation of the moon-stoning scene; he sees the shattering of the reflection as a therapeutic action, a necessary breaking down of the hard, isolate ego: "Birkin's stone-throwing . . . is an attack on that deathly supremacy of the ego that makes for mere separateness and indifference. . . . His violence renews the flow of life, which is at the same time a flowing in of darkness. The pure supremacy of light—the supremacy of the ego—gives way to a proper tension between light and dark. . . . The individuality of the ego gives way to a true individuality, though a precarious one." *River of Dissolution*, pp. 101–2. The problem with this approach to the scene is that, on the literal level, the darkness impinges on the light only temporarily, the moon inevitably re-forms (and so does its symbolic referent—in this Clarke is right—the female ego); thus Birkin has not

substantively changed anything. Also, the later passage where Birkin asserts his own "will" contraverts the belief that Birkin's aim is to generally transcend the limiting ego, since will and ego are linked.

40. For Pritchard, the going beyond the conscious ego is one of the major injunctions of the novel: "Lawrence depends on the paradox that he who would save his life must lose it. . . . Those who hold on to egoistic selfconsciousness, contained in a hard shell of separateness, are caught . . . in the 'flux of corruption.'" *Body of Darkness*, p. 81.

41. John E. Stoll refers to this problem when he describes the "accusation that Birkin's fear of fusion is Ursula's fault," as "self-justifying and untrue." *The Novels of D. H. Lawrence: A Search for Integration* (Columbia, Mo.: University of Missouri Press, 1971), p. 187.

42. George H. Ford notices the contradiction that has eluded most critics: "if the 'dreadful mysteries, far beyond the phallic cult' associated with the beetle-faced statue are represented in one scene as degenerate and in another scene (with only a slight shift in terminology) as redemptive—when Ursula is transfigured by her discovery of a 'source deeper than the phallic source'—how is a reader supposed to respond to what seems like a total contradiction?" *Double Measure: A Study of the Novels and Stories of D. H. Lawrence* (New York: W. W. Norton & Co., 1965), p. 205. Having raised the essential problem, Ford presents a weak solution: "We are being expected to discriminate between sensual experiences enjoyed by a pair of loving men and women (which are regarded by the novelist as innocently enjoyed) on the one hand, and degenerate indulgences of a society which has cut all connections with spiritual values on the other." Ibid. The problem with this is that it makes an absolute distinction between Birkin and his surrounding society that is not justified by the text. Astonishingly, Ford then cites a passage from *Pornography and Obscenity* that undercuts, rather than strengthens, his argument: "The sex functions and the excrementory functions in the human body work so close together, yet they are, so to speak, utterly different in direction. Sex is a creative flow, the excrementory flow is towards dissolution, decreation, if we may use such a word. In the really healthy human being the distinction between the two is instant, our profoundest instincts are perhaps our instincts of opposition between the two flows. But in the degraded human being the deep instincts have gone dead, and then the two flows become identical. . . . It happens when the psyche deteriorates, and the profound controlling instincts collapse." *Phoenix*, p. 176. Apparently, Ford believes that the passage decisively demonstrates the difference between the "sensual" experience of Ursula and Birkin, and the "degenerate" experiences of the novel's other characters. But, quite to the contrary, in light of the quotation it seems clear that Birkin and Ursula have failed to distinguish between the two "flows," and are attributing sexual properties to the excremental flow, thus showing themselves to be "degraded"; despite Ford the citation from Lawrence's essay makes the scene in "Excurse" more problematical, not less so.

43. The prose style of "Excurse" has often been negatively criticized. Hough, for example, says of Birkin and Ursula's experience at the inn: "The scene is possible enough, but when described it borders on the ridiculous. And it is only by a charitable effort of the imagination that one realises what is supposed to be happening." *The Dark Sun*, p. 82. Even Leavis disparages the writing in the Egyptian Pharoah passage: "Lawrence betrays by an insistent and over-emphatic explicitness, running at times to something one can only call jargon, that he is uncertain—uncertain of the value of what he offers; uncertain whether he

really holds it." *D. H. Lawrence: Novelist*, p. 148. And Robson asserts that, in the chapter, Lawrence fails to "express[es] the ineffable . . . by his obscure, repetitious, periphrastic style." *Pelican Guide*, 7: 299.

44. Daleski takes note of the inequality, and revealingly connects Birkin and Ursula to Mino and the female cat: "The scene, as Ursula kneels before Birkin, is a little too reminiscent of the wild cat and the Mino to be quite comfortable." *The Forked Flame*, p. 180.

45. Spilka determinedly fastens on a positive reading of the scene: "The key word here is pride. In the anal stage, says Erik Erikson, autonomy and pride emanate from the sense of inner goodness; doubt and shame, from the sense of badness. By this view, Birkin has just received his missing anal heritage. Ursula's exposure of his shame has broken the tight control of will and intellect over inner 'badness'; her floral affirmation of selfhood has eased self-doubt; her acceptance of him 'at the quick of death' has affirmed 'inner goodness,' and the floods of 'ineffable riches' which follow are—in effect—emanations of autonomy and pride." "Lawrence Up-Tight, or the Anal Phase Once Over," p. 259. Spilka's invoking of Erikson is of dubious relevance. There is little evidence, in *Women in Love*, that Lawrence shares Erikson's belief that the healthy human being is one who, having successfully passed through the oral and anal stages of childhood, retains no harmful hold-overs from those preliminary periods, and moves on to "genitality" and "mutality." For Erikson's schema of human development see *Childhood and Society* (New York: W. W. Norton & Co., 1950), pp. 72–108. Moreover, there is no question during the encounter of Ursula freeing Birkin from shame; instead, it is Ursula who is delivered by her contact with a quantity that, rather than needing to be redeemed by acceptance, is made to have redemptive properties in itself.

46. Calling a passage ineffective while extracting an intention from it would be one form of "the intentional fallacy." The authors of the famous article by that name do not believe that unsuccessful art can give genuine evidence of a preconceived design or plan: "One must ask how a critic expects to get an answer to the question about intention. How is he to find out what the poet tried to do? If the poet succeeded in doing it, then the poem itself shows what he was trying to do. And if the poet did not succeed, then the poem is not adequate evidence, and the critic must go outside the poem—for evidence of an intention that did not become effective in the poem." W. K. Wimsatt and Monroe C. Beardsley, "The Intentional Fallacy," in W. K. Wimsatt, *The Verbal Icon* (Lexington, Ky.: University of Kentucky Press, 1967), p. 4. But Lawrence's theory about the division between tale and teller is in essential disagreement with the concept of "the intentional fallacy." If we believe that we can distinguish between the tale and the teller, then we also believe that we can distinguish, within the work of art, between the intention and the performance. For Lawrence's theory focuses on an aesthetic halfway point; he is concerned with a level of partial literary success, wherein the artist is able to reveal his design, but not to achieve it.

Bibliography

Adamowski, T. H. "*The Rainbow* and 'Otherness.' " *The D. H. Lawrence Review* 7, no. 1 (Spring 1974): 58–77.

Aldington, Richard. *D. H. Lawrence: Portrait of a Genius But.* . . . 1950. Reprint. New York: Collier Books, 1961.

Alldritt, Keith. *The Visual Imagination of D. H. Lawrence*. London: Edward Arnold, 1971.

Allen, Walter. *The English Novel: A Short Critical History*. New York: E. P. Dutton, and Co., 1954.

Andrews, W. T., ed. *Critics on D. H. Lawrence*. London: Allen and Unwin, 1971.

Barber, David. "Community in *Women in Love*." *Novel* 5 (Fall 1971), 32–41.

Beal, Anthony. *D. H. Lawrence*. Edinburgh: Oliver and Boyd, 1961.

Boehme, Jacob. *The Signature of All Things and Other Discourses*. London and New York: Everyman's Library, 1912.

Booth, Wayne. *The Rhetoric of Fiction*. Chicago: University of Chicago Press, 1961.

Bowra, C. M. *The Romantic Imagination*. 1950. Reprint. London: Oxford University Press, 1961.

Bradbury, Malcolm. *The Social Context of Modern English Literature*. Oxford: Blackwell, 1971.

Bramley, J. A. "D. H. Lawrence's Sternest Critic." *Hibbert Journal* 63 (1964–65): 109–11.

Burke, Kenneth. *Language as Symbolic Action: Essays on Life, Literature and Method*. Berkeley, Cal.: University of California Press, 1966.

Burns, Robert. "The Novel as Metaphysical Statement: D. H. Lawrence's *The Rainbow*." *Southern Review* (Australia) 4 (1970): 139–60.

Cavitch, David. *D. H. Lawrence and the New World*. 1969. Reprint. London: Oxford University Press, 1971.

Chamberlain, Robert L. "Pussum, Minette, and the Africo-Nordic Symbol in Lawrence's *Women in Love*." *PMLA* 78 (1963): 407–16.

Chambers, D. C. "Memories of D. H. Lawrence." *Renaissance and Modern Studies* 16 (1972): 5–17.

Chambers, Jessie (E. T.). *D. H. Lawrence: A Personal Record*. 2nd ed. London: Frank Cass & Co., 1965.

Clarke, Colin. *River of Dissolution: D. H. Lawrence and English Romanticism*. London: Routledge & Kegan Paul, 1969.

Coleridge, S. T. *Selected Poetry and Prose*. Edited by Elisabeth Schneider. New York: Holt, Rinehart and Winston, 1951.

Corke, Helen. *In Our Infancy: An Autobiography*. Cambridge: Cambridge University Press, 1975.

Daiches, David. *The Novel and the Modern World*. Rev. ed. Chicago: University of Chicago Press, 1971.

Daleski, H. M. *The Forked Flame: A Study of D. H. Lawrence*. Evanston, Ill.: Northwestern University Press, 1965.

Delaney, Paul. "Lawrence and E. M. Forster: Two Rainbows." *The D. H. Lawrence Review* 8, no. 1 (Spring 1975): 54–61.

Engleberg, Edward. "Escape From the Circles of Experience: D. H. Lawrence's *The Rainbow* as a Modern *Bildungsroman*." *PMLA* 78, no. 1 (March 1963): 103–13.

Erikson, Erik. *Childhood and Society*. New York: W. W. Norton & Co., 1950.

Fairchild, Hoxie Neale. *The Romantic Quest*. 1931. Reprint. New York: Russell and Russell, 1965.

Farr, Judith, ed. *Twentieth Century Interpretations of Sons and Lovers: A Collection of Critical Essays*. Englewood Cliffs, N.J.: Prentice-Hall, 1970.

Fiedler, Leslie. *Love and Death in the American Novel*. New York: Stein and Day, 1966.

Ford, Boris, ed. *The Pelican Guide to English Literature*. Vol. 7. Harmondsworth, Middlesex: Penguin Books, 1961.

Ford, George H. *Double Measure: A Study of the Novels and Stories of D. H. Lawrence*. 1965. Reprint. New York: W. W. Norton & Co., 1969.

Freeman, Mary. *D. H. Lawrence: A Basic Study of His Ideas*. Gainesville, Fla.: University of Florida Press, 1955.

Freud, Sigmund. *The Collected Papers of Sigmund Freud*. Translated by Joan Riviere. Vol. 4. London: Hogarth Press, 1953.

―――. *The Complete Introductory Lectures on Psychoanalysis*. Translated and edited by James Strachey. 1933. Reprint. New York: W. W. Norton & Co., 1966.

―――. *The Interpretation of Dreams*. Translated and edited by James Strachey. New York: Avon, 1965.

―――. *The Standard Edition of the Complete Psychological Works of Sigmund Freud*. Translated and Edited by James Strachey. Vol. 12. London: Hogarth Press, 1958.

Friedman, Alan. "The Other Lawrence." *Partisan Review* 37, no. 2 (Summer 1970): 239–53.

Garrett, Peter K. *Scene and Symbol from George Eliot to James Joyce: Studies in Changing Fictional Mode*. New Haven, Conn.: Yale University Press, 1969.

Gerber, Stephen. "Character, Language and Experience in 'Water Party.' " *Paunch*, 36, no. 7 (April 1973): 3–29.

Gifford, Henry. "Anna, Lawrence and 'The Law.' " *The Critical Quarterly* 1, no. 3 (Autumn 1959): 203–6.

Gleckner, Robert F., and Enscoe, Gerald E., eds. *Romanticism: Points of View*. 2nd ed. Englewood Cliffs, N.J.: Prentice-Hall, 1970.

Goldberg, S. L. *Joyce*. Edinburgh: Oliver and Boyd, 1962.

―――. "*The Rainbow:* Fiddle-Bow and Sand." *Essays in Criticism* 11, no. 4 (October 1961): 418–34.

Goodheart, Eugene. *The Utopian Vision of D. H. Lawrence*. Chicago: University of Chicago Press, 1964.

Graves, Robert. *The Greek Myths*. 2 vols. Harmondsworth, Middlesex: Penguin Books, 1955.

Gregory, Horace. *Pilgrim of the Apocalypse: A Critical Study of D. H. Lawrence*. New York: Viking Press 1933.

Grout, Donald Jay. *A History of Western Music*. Shorter ed. New York: W. W. Norton & Co., 1960.

Gurko, Leo. "*The Trespasser:* D. H. Lawrence's Neglected Novel." *College English* 24 (1962): 29–34.

Hamalian, Leo, ed. *D. H. Lawrence: A Collection of Criticism*. New York: McGraw-Hill Book Co., 1973.

Hartman, Geoffrey H. *The Unmediated Vision: An Interpretation of Wordsworth, Hopkins, Rilke and Valéry*. 1954; Reprint. ed., New York: Harcourt, Brace and World, 1966.

Heilman, Robert. "Nomads, Monads, and the Mystique of the Soma." *The Sewanee Review* 68 (1960): 635–59.

Hochman, Baruch. *Another Ego: The Changing View of Self and Society in the Work of D. H. Lawrence*. Columbia, S.C.: University of South Carolina Press, 1970.

Hoffman, Frederick J. *Freudianism and the Literary Mind*. 1945. Reprint. New York: Grove Press, 1959.

Hough, Graham. *The Dark Sun: A Study of D. H. Lawrence*. 1956. Reprint. London: Duckworth, 1970.

Howarth, Herbert. "D. H. Lawrence from Island to Glacier." *University of Toronto Quarterly* 37, no. 3 (April 1968): 215–29.

Howe, Marguerite Beede. *The Art of the Self in D. H. Lawrence*. Athens, Ohio: Ohio University Press, 1977.

Jarrett-Kerr, William Robert (Father William Tiverton). *D. H. Lawrence and Human Existence*. New York: Philosophical Library, 1951.

Joyce, James. *Dubliners*. 1916. Reprint. New York: Viking Press, Compass Books, 1958.

Jung, Carl G. *The Integration of the Personality*. Translated by Stanley M. Dell. New York: Farrar & Rinehart, 1939.

———. *The Spirit in Man, Art and Literature*. Translated by R. F. C. Hull. London: Routledge & Kegan Paul, 1966.

Karl, Frederick, and Magalaner, Marvin. *A Reader's Guide to Great Twentieth Century Novels*. New York: Noonday Press, 1959.

Keith, W. J. "D. H. Lawrence's *The White Peacock:* An Essay In Criticism." *University of Toronto Quarterly*, 37 (1968): 230–45.

Kermode, Frank. *Lawrence*. Fontana/Collins, 1973.

———. *Modern Essays*. Fontana/Collins, 1971.

Kettle, Arnold. *An Introduction to the English Novel*. 1951; reprint ed. New York: Harper & Row, 1968.

Kleinbard, David J. "D. H. Lawrence and Ontological Insecurity." *PMLA* 89, no. 1 (January 1974): 154–63.

———. "Laing, Lawrence and the Maternal Cannibal." *The Psychoanalytic Review* 58, no. 1 (Spring 1971): 5–13.

Knight, G. Wilson. "Lawrence, Joyce and Powys." *Essays in Criticism* 11, no. 4 (October 1961): 403–17.

Laing, R. D. *The Divided Self: An Existential Study in Sanity and Madness*. Harmondsworth, Middlesex: Penguin Books, 1965.

Lainoff, Seymour. "*The Rainbow:* The Shaping of Modern Man." *Modern Fiction Studies* 1, no. 4 (November 1955): 23–27.

Langbaum, Robert. *The Mysteries of Identity*. New York: Oxford University Press, 1977.

Langer, Susanne K. *Philosophy in a New Key: A Study in the Symbolism of Reason, Rite, and Art*. New York: Mentor, 1951.

Lawrence, D. H. *Aaron's Rod*. 1922. Reprint. Harmondsworth, Middlesex: Penguin Books, 1950.

————. *Apocalypse*. Introduction by Richard Aldington. 1931. Reprint. New York: Viking Press, Compass Books, 1966.

————. *The Collected Letters of D. H. Lawrence*. 2 vols. Edited by Harry T. Moore. London: William Heinemann, 1962.

————. *The Complete Poems of D. H. Lawrence*. Edited by Vivian de Sola Pinto and F. Warren Roberts. New York: Viking Press, 1964.

————. *The Complete Short Stories of D. H. Lawrence*. 3 vols. New York: Viking Press, Compass Books, 1961.

————. *Etruscan Places*. 1932. Reprint. New York: Viking Press, Compass Books, 1957.

————. *The First Lady Chatterley*. 1944. Reprint. Harmondsworth, Middlesex: Penguin Books, 1969.

————. *Kangaroo*. 1923. Reprint. Harmondsworth, Middlesex: Penguin Books, 1950.

————. *Lady Chatterley's Lover*. 1928. Reprint. Harmondsworth, Middlesex: Penguin Books, 1960.

————. *The Letters of D. H. Lawrence*. Edited by Aldous Huxley. New York: Viking Press, 1932.

————. *The Lost Girl*. 1920. Reprint. Harmondsworth, Middlesex: Penguin Books, 1950.

————. *Mornings in Mexico/Etruscan Places*. 1927/1932. Reprint. Harmondsworth, Middlesex: Penguin Books, 1960.

————. *Phoenix: The Posthumous Papers of D. H. Lawrence*. Ed. Edward D. McDonald. 1936. Reprint. New York: Viking Press, 1968.

————. *Phoenix II: Uncollected, Unpublished and Other Prose Works by D. H. Lawrence*. Edited by Warren Roberts and Harry T. Moore. London: William Heinemann, 1968.

————. *The Plumed Serpent*. 1926. Reprint. Harmondsworth, Middlesex: Penguin Books, 1950.

————. *"Psychoanalysis and the Unconscious"* and *"Fantasia of the Unconscious."* Introduction by Philip Rieff. 1921. Reprint. New York: Viking Press, 1960.

————. *The Rainbow.* 1915. Reprint. Harmondsworth, Middlesex: Penguin Books, 1949.

————. *Sea and Sardinia.* 1923. Reprint. Harmondsworth, Middlesex: Penguin Books, 1944.

————. *Sons and Lovers.* 1913. Reprint. Harmondsworth, Middlesex: Penguin Books, 1948.

————. *Studies in Classic American Literature.* 1924. Reprint. Harmondsworth, Middlesex: Penguin Books, 1971.

————. *The Symbolic Meaning: The Uncollected Versions of "Studies in Classic American Literature."* Edited by Armin Arnold. New York: Viking Press, 1961.

————. *Three Plays.* Introduction by Raymond Williams. Harmondsworth, Middlesex: Penguin Books, 1969.

————. *The Trespasser.* 1912. Reprint. Harmondsworth, Middlesex: Penguin Books, 1961.

————. *Twilight in Italy.* 1916. Reprint. Harmondsworth, Middlesex: Penguin Books, 1960.

————. *The White Peacock.* 1911. Reprint. Harmondsworth, Middlesex: Penguin Books, 1950.

————. *Women in Love.* 1912. Reprint. Harmondsworth, Middlesex: Penguin Books, 1960.

Lawrence, Frieda. *The Memoirs and Correspondence.* Edited by E. W. Tedlock, Jr. London: William Heinemann, 1961.

————. *Not I, But the Wind.* . . . New York: Viking Press, 1934.

Leavis, F. R. *D. H. Lawrence: Novelist.* New York: Clarion, 1955.

Legman, G. Introduction to *My Secret Life.* New York: Grove Press, 1966.

Lesser, Simon O. *Fiction and the Unconscious.* New York: Vantage Books, 1957.

Lodge, David, ed. *Twentieth Century Literary Criticism: A Reader.* London: Longman, 1972.

Lucas, F. L. *The Decline and Fall of the Romantic Ideal.* 1936. Reprint. Cambridge: Cambridge University Press, Paperback Edition, 1963.

Mailer, Norman. "The Prisoner of Sex." *Harper's,* March 1971, pp. 41–92.

Miko, Stephen J. *Toward "Women in Love": The Emergence of a Lawren-cian Aesthetic.* New Haven, Conn.: Yale University Press, 1971.

———, ed. *Twentieth Century Interpretations of "Women in Love."* Englewood Cliffs, N.J.: Spectrum, 1969.

Moore, Harry T., ed. *A D. H. Lawrence Miscellany.* Carbondale, Ill.: Southern Illinois University Press, 1959.

———. *The Intelligent Heart: The Story of D. H. Lawrence.* New York: Farrar, Straus and Young, 1954.

———. *The Life and Works of D. H. Lawrence.* New York: Twayne, 1951.

Mori, Haruhide. "Lawrence's Imagistic Development in *The Rainbow* and *Women in Love.*" ELH 31, no. 4 (December 1964): 460–84.

Mortland, Donald E. "The Conclusion of *Sons and Lovers:* A Recon-sideration." *Studies in the Novel* 3, no. 3 (Fall 1971): 305–15.

Moynahan, Julian. *The Deed of Life: The Novels and Tales of D. H. Lawrence.* Princeton, N.J.: Princeton University Press, 1963.

Mudrick, Marvin. "The Originality of *The Rainbow.*" *A D. H. Lawrence Miscellany.* Edited by Harry T. Moore. Carbondale, Ill.: Southern Illinois University Press, 1959.

Murry, J. M. *D. H. Lawrence: Son of Woman.* 1931. Reprint. London: Jonathan Cape, 1954.

Nehls, Edward. *D. H. Lawrence: A Composite Biography.* 3 vols. Madi-son, Wis.: University of Wisconsin Press, 1957–59.

Neumann, Erich. *The Great Mother: An Analysis of an Archetype.* London: Rutledge and Kegan Paul, 1955.

Nicholes, E. L. "The 'Simile of the Sparrow' in *The Rainbow* by D. H. Lawrence." *Modern Language Notes* 64, no. 3 (March 1949): 171–74.

Nin, Anais. *D. H. Lawrence: An Unprofessional Study.* Denver, Colo.: Swallow Press, 1946.

Ort, Daniel. "Lawrence's *Women in Love.*" *Explicator* 27, no. 5 (January 1969): item 38.

Osgerby, J. R. "D. H. Lawrence's *The White Peacock.*" *The Use of English* no. 4 (Summer 1962): 256–61.

Pepper, Stephen Coburn. *The Basis of Criticism in the Arts.* Cambridge, Mass.: Harvard University Press, 1945.

Pritchard, R. E. *D. H. Lawrence: Body of Darkness.* London: Hutchinson University Library, 1971.

Rieff, Philip. *The Triumph of the Therapeutic: Uses of Faith After Freud*. New York: Harper & Brothers, 1968.

Ross, Charles L. "The Composition of *Women in Love:* A History, 1913–1919." *D. H. Lawrence Review* 8, no. 2 (Summer 1975): 198–212.

Rossman, Charles. " 'You are the call and I am the answer': D. H. Lawrence and Women." *D. H. Lawrence Review* 8, no. 3 (Fall 1975): 255–324.

Rothgeb, Carrie Lee, ed. *Abstracts of The Standard Edition of the Complete Psychological Works of Sigmund Freud*. New York: International Universities Press, 1973.

Rubin, Louis D., Jr. *The Teller in the Tale*. Seattle, Wash.: University of Washington Press, 1967.

Sagar, Keith. *The Art of D. H. Lawrence*. Cambridge: Cambridge University Press, 1965.

————. "The Best I Have Known: D. H. Lawrence's 'A Modern Lover' and 'The Shades of Spring.' " *Studies in Short Fiction* 4:143–51.

Sale, Roger. "D. H. Lawrence 1912–1916." *The Massachusetts Review* (Spring-Summer 1965): 467–80.

————. "The Narrative Technique of *The Rainbow*." *Modern Fiction Studies* 5, no. 1 (Spring 1959): 29–38.

Salgado, Gamini, ed. *A Casebook on "Sons and Lovers."* London: Macmillan & Co., 1969.

Sanders, Scott. *D. H. Lawrence: The World of the Five Major Novels*. New York: Viking Press, 1973.

Scholes, Robert, and Kellogg, Robert. *The Nature of Narrative*. Oxford: Oxford University Press, 1966.

Schorer, Mark. *The World We Imagine: Selected Essays by Mark Schorer*. New York: Farrar, Straus and Giroux, 1968.

Sharpe, Michael C. "The Genesis of D. H. Lawrence's *The Trespasser*." *Essays in Criticism* 11, no. 1 (January 1961): 34–39.

Spender, Stephen, ed. *D. H. Lawrence: Novelist, Poet, Prophet*. London: Weidenfeld and Nicolson, 1973.

Spilka, Mark. "Lawrence's Quarrel With Tenderness." *The Critical Quarterly* 9, no. 4 (Winter 1967): 363–76.

————. "Lawrence Up-Tight, or the Anal Phase Once Over." *Novel*, no. 4 (Spring 1971), pp. 252–67.

―――. *The Love Ethic of D. H. Lawrence*. Bloomington, Ind.: Indiana University Press, 1955.

――― et al. "On 'Lawrence Up-Tight': Four Tail-Pieces." *Novel*, no. 5 (Fall 1971), pp. 54–70.

Squires, Michael. "Lawrence's *The White Peacock:* A Mutation of Pastoral." *Texas Studies in Literature and Language* 12, no. 2 (Summer 1970): 263–83.

Stanford, Raney. "Thomas Hardy and Lawrence's *The White Peacock*." *Modern Fiction Studies* 5, no. 1 (Spring 1959): 19–28.

Stoll, John E. *The Novels of D. H. Lawrence: A Search for Integration*. Columbia, Mo.: University of Missouri Press, 1971.

Sypher, Wylie. *Loss of Self in Modern Literature and Art*. New York: Random House, 1962.

Tedlock, E. W., Jr. *D. H. Lawrence, Artist and Rebel: A Study of Lawrence's Fiction*. Albuquerque, N.M.: University of New Mexico Press, 1963.

―――, ed. *D. H. Lawrence and "Sons and Lovers": Sources and Criticism*. New York: New York University Press, 1965.

Tindall, William York. *D. H. Lawrence and Susan His Cow*. New York: Columbia University Press, 1939.

―――. *The Literary Symbol*. Bloomington, Ind.: Indiana University Press, 1955.

Van Ghent, Dorothy. *The English Novel: Form and Function*. 1953. Reprint. New York: Harper & Brothers, 1961.

Vivas, Eliseo. *D. H. Lawrence: The Failure and the Triumph of Art*. 1960. Reprint. Bloomington, Ind.: University of Indiana Press, 1964.

Watt, Ian. *The Rise of the Novel: Studies in DeFoe, Richardson and Fielding*. Harmondsworth, Middlesex: Penguin Books, 1963.

Weiss, Daniel A. *Oedipus in Nottingham: D. H. Lawrence*. Seattle, Wash.: University of Washington Press, 1962.

Werblowsky, R. J. Zwi. *Lucifer and Prometheus: A Study of Milton's Satan*. London: Routledge and Kegan Paul, 1952.

West, Anthony. *D. H. Lawrence*. Denver, Colo.: Swallow Press, 1950.

Williams, Raymond. "Lawrence and Tolstoy." *The Critical Quarterly* 2 (1960): 33–39.

Wilson, Edmund. *The Wound and the Bow: Seven Studies in Literature*. New York: Oxford University Press, 1965.

Wimsatt, W. K. *The Verbal Icon: Studies in the Meaning of Poetry*. Lexington, Ky.: University of Kentucky Press, 1967.

Wollheim, Richard. *Freud*. Fontana/Collins, 1971.

Yeats, W. B. *The Collected Poems of W. B. Yeats*. Definitive ed. New York: Macmillan Co., 1956.

Yudishtar. *Conflict in the Novels of D. H. Lawrence*. Edinburgh: Oliver & Boyd, 1969.

Zyratuk, George J. "The Chambers Memoirs of D. H. Lawrence. Which Chambers?" *Renaissance and Modern Studies* 17 (1973):5-37.

Index